Women and
Social Change
in America

ALSO BY GERHARD FALK
AND FROM McFARLAND

The Jew in Christian Theology (1992)
*Murder: An Analysis of Its Forms,
Conditions and Causes* (1990)

Women and Social Change in America

A Survey of a Century of Progress

GERHARD FALK

McFarland & Company, Inc., Publishers
Jefferson, North Carolina, and London

I thank my wife, Dr. Ursula Falk, for proofreading the entire manuscript and my son, Clifford, for proofreading and dealing with the vagaries of the computer. Without them I could not have produced this book.

LIBRARY OF CONGRESS CATALOGUING-IN-PUBLICATION DATA

Falk, Gerhard, 1924–
    Women and social change in America : a survey of a century of progress / Gerhard Falk.
       p.   cm.
    Includes bibliographical references and index.

    ISBN 978-0-7864-4035-1
    softcover : 50# alkaline paper ∞

    1. Women — United States — Social conditions.   2. Social change — United States.   I. Title.
HQ1421.F35   2009
305.40973'09045 — dc22   2009014653

British Library cataloguing data are available

©2009 Gerhard Falk. All rights reserved

No part of this book may be reproduced or transmitted in any form or by any means, electronic or mechanical, including photocopying or recording, or by any information storage and retrieval system, without permission in writing from the publisher.

Cover images ©2009 Shutterstock

Manufactured in the United States of America

McFarland & Company, Inc., Publishers
  Box 611, Jefferson, North Carolina 28640
    www.mcfarlandpub.com

Table of Contents

Preface	1
1. The Ascendancy of Women in American Life	3
2. Women and Change in the 20th Century — Education, Emancipation, Work and the Law	25
3. The Families of Women Achievers	47
4. Women in the Military and the Police — Storming the Last Bastion	67
5. Women in American Religion — The Patriarchy Trembles	86
6. Women in Science	105
7. Women in Government and Politics	125
8. From Walter Cronkite to Katie Couric	144
9. The Sexual Revolution	164
10. The Sociology of Social Change	184
Chapter Notes	203
Bibliography	219
Index	235

Preface

Over the many years that I have been teaching at the State University College at Buffalo I have noticed a steady increase in the proportion of women in my classes. Each year, the student body includes fewer and fewer men.

Colleagues across the country tell me the gender ratio has shifted on their campuses, too. The shift began in a small way about 1980 and became dramatically obvious by the 1990s. National statistics from government and educational institutions back up these assertions. Higher education has undergone a revolution: Women dominate the ranks of the educated, and men have fallen behind.

As more women graduate from universities and professional schools, the trend has become obvious in society, with more female pharmacists, physicians, pilots, lawyers, and so on. When my daughter graduated from law school and my granddaughter from medical school I decided that it was time to explain this great change in sociological terms. That is the purpose of this book.

I began my research by talking to colleagues teaching courses in gender studies. Such courses are now found in the curricula of almost all American colleges and universities. In fact, some schools give degrees in gender studies, and a number of journals are devoted to that topic.

I went on to explore the topic in government statistics and a broad range of scholarly and popular publications. I also interviewed a number of highly successful women who are the role models for others now following them.

Beginning in the mid–20th century, technological inventions and birth control changed women's daily lives in ways that made it possible for them to seek new opportunities outside the home. Higher education for women became more normative, and women began to enter the military, police work, science, religion, government, communications, and many other fields. This change has taken place across every ethnic group in America.

In the 1960s several major upheavals in American culture occurred simultaneously. Included was the so-called sexual revolution, which had permanent effects on gender relations in society. The sexual revolution may be regarded as a thing of the past, but gender revolution is here to stay.

The so-called sexual revolution of the 1960s and 1970s has led to permanent change in the relationship between the genders in the United States. This transformation of gender roles is to the advantage of both men and women in 21st-century America.

This book explains why and how this revolution came about and how women and men are benefiting from these great changes in the lives of Americans.

CHAPTER 1

The Ascendancy of Women in American Life

The Education of American Women in the 21st Century

In May of 2007, the population of the United States reached about 302 million. At the end of 2005 the American population consisted of 141,274,964 males and 147,103,173 females for a total population of 288,378,137. From birth until age 40, the number of males in the American population exceeded the number of females by a few percentage points in each age group. Thereafter, the reverse was true as the female population exceeded the male population more and more until at age 70 the excess of women over men led to an overall sex ratio of 96 men for every 100 women. This uneven sex ratio became visible in 1950. Prior to that year, the male population exceeded the female population of the U.S. for the century beginning with 1850.[1]

It has been estimated that there were approximately 82.5 million mothers in this country in 2006 with an average of 1.9 children per woman. Thirty years earlier, in 1976, the birth rate was 3.1 per woman aged 15 to 40, thus constituting a 40 percent decline.

In 1900 women accounted for 18 percent of the American labor force. In 2006, women were 46.3 percent of the American labor force. It is now projected that by 2014 there will be 76 million working women or 46.8 percent of the labor force so that men's share of the labor force will decline to 53.2 percent. In 1900 only 20 percent of women worked; in 2006 that had risen to 60 percent. The influence of working women on the American economy and polity will become greater and greater because the majority of women, 57 percent, are entering professional occupations, a number which will increase more than 20 percent before 2014. Seventy-two percent of all working women work in white collar jobs.

The number of women who owned businesses increased by 20 percent between 1997 and 2002 to 6.5 million so that 7.1 million Americans were employed by a female-owned firm in 2002. Over 117, 000 women owned firms earned more than $1 million in 2002. The median annual earnings of women in 2004 was $31,223. Among women working in computer or other mathematical employment the median income in 2004 was $56,585, which meant that women in those occupations were earning about 90 percent of men's income. The military employed 212,000 women on active duty that year so that 15 percent of the members of the armed forces that year were women.

Almost 66 percent of women voted in the 2004 presidential election as compared to 62 percent of men. Fifty-nine percent of women participated in the labor force in 2004 compared to 73 percent of men. In 2004 there were 63 million married women in the U.S. This included those who were separated but not legally divorced. There were then 54 million unmarried women in the U.S.[2]

Educational Attainment

Anyone who asked for a doctor or a lawyer in 1957 expected to meet a man. Fifty years later that is by no means the case. In 1957 pharmacists were men as were the presidents of colleges and all of the military.

Now women have entered all of these professions in such large numbers that only older Americans find it in any manner surprising to meet a female professional.

The evidence for this major social change in American culture may be found in the educational attainment of American women over the years. For example, in 2004, 48.5 percent of female high school graduates enrolled in a four year college by the October following their graduation. Only 39.6 percent of male high school graduates did so. Including two year colleges, the total difference for all college enrollment of recent high school graduates as of 2004 was 61.4 percent for males and 71.5 percent for females.

This dramatic shift in college enrollment in favor of women is best understood if we compare college enrollment by sex over the past 40 decades. Thus, in 1977 52.1 percent of male high school graduates enrolled in college but only 49.3 percent of female graduates did so. In 1987 the difference favored men 58.3 percent to 55.3 percent. Excluding two-year colleges 41 percent of male high school graduates enrolled in a four year college in 1987 but only 35 percent of women did so that year. By 1997 the reversal of college enrollment by gender had become plainly visible. In that year only 38 percent of male high school graduates enrolled in a four year college and only 62.4 percent enrolled in all colleges including two-year schools. In that same year 70.3 percent of female highschool graduates had enrolled in a college including both two-year and four-year institutions.[3]

Enrollment in college by African American women is 11 percent less than among European American women and the enrollment of women of Hispanic origin is 7 percent lower than that of European American women.[4]

Therefore, while in 1960 65 percent of bachelor's degrees were earned by men and 35 percent by women, in 2004 58 percent of bachelor's degrees were earned by women and only 42 percent by men. This trend continued into 2006 when women earned 59 percent of the bachelor's degrees and 60 percent of the master's degrees at American colleges and universities.[5]

There was a time when American women were almost entirely excluded from colleges and universities. That began to change when in the 1970s some all-male colleges started to accept women. In 1972 the United States Department of Education announced that thereafter "no person in the United States shall, on the basis of sex be excluded from the participation in, or denied the benefits of, or be subjected to discrimination under any program or activity receiving Federal aid. (Title IX of Public Law U.S.C. 1681–1688).[6]

The Title IX amendment was certainly not the only reason for this development. In fact, it was undoubtedly a reflection of the stratification reversal now in progress in the United States which will soon present a reversal also in the gender gap concerning wages, labor force participation, marriage and parenting.

Research has shown that the value of college completion "in terms of its combined impact on labor market earnings, marriage, household standard of living, and insurance against income deprivation has risen faster for women than for men."[7]

No doubt the most telling reason for the dramatic increase of women's participation in higher education has been the application of family resources to the education of girls. While these resources were erstwhile spent only on boys on the grounds that a college education for girls was a waste, the increasing opportunities for female employment in college-level occupations has reversed this trend. No longer can it be said that a female college graduate cannot succeed in the economy and earn as much as, if not more than, some men. Therefore it is reasonable and productive for families to invest in the education of their daughters as well as the education of their sons This is so despite the fact that female income even at the college level still lags considerably behind the income of men.

If the application of family resources were the only reason for entrance into college then the gender discrepancy in favor of women would not exist. However, over many years, girls have outperformed boys in academic achievement. This was not giving girls much advantage in the past because women were not encouraged to enter higher education. In the 21st century, the better academic averages attained by girls and women do make a difference in the opportunity to enter college as the erstwhile discriminatory practices are no longer in evidence. Moreover, there is a gender difference in college completion rates. Men have a higher college drop-out rate than women.[8]

Because socialization into gender roles depends on the model delivered by the parent of the same sex, it is reasonable to expect that girls will look to their mothers and boys to their fathers as they attain adult status. Therefore, the daughters of educated mothers will emulate such a female status-role even as their brothers will emulate their father. It is therefore evident that absentee fathers deliver a serious disadvantage to boys as they enter adolescence without knowing their father or seeing him only on occasion.

In 2006 24 percent of American children were living in fatherless homes. Among African Americans 48 percent lived in fatherless homes.[9] The consequences of this high rate of absenteeism are not the same for both sexes. While the female children of absentee fathers are more likely to become pregnant in adolescence than is true of those whose families are intact, the deviant conduct of boys is such that boys are more often adjudicated delinquents. Boys who live in a fatherless family are more likely to engage in gang banging, including auto theft, robbery, burglary, assault and even murder, than is true of boys from intact families.[10]

Therefore, the absence of fathers from the family is far more likely to affect the failure of boys to enter higher education than is true for girls, despite the pain such absence inflicts on both genders.

Fathers make a number of contributions to the well being of their children which cannot be replaced by mothers. Among these are that fathers encourage independence, are less protective of children than are mothers and are more assertive than mothers. All these characteristics are needed by sons in order to become men, not merely males. Fathers also introduce children, especially sons, to new experiences including their jobs. Fathers also reduce stress in mothers because they can be supportive of mothers and take over so as to give mothers a break from their responsibilities. Fathers are better disciplinarians who demand more of their children than is true of mothers. All these qualities militate in favor of boys attending higher education. Consequently, the absence of fathers defeats boys' aspirations and reduces their chances of attaining a college education.[11]

Buchman and DiPrete in their recent study of the role of family background and academic achievement have shown that during the forty years ending in 2007, a gradual reduction of male advantages in math and science with no reduction in female advantage in verbal skills has also contributed to the female advantage in higher education. High school girls are also more attentive and are better organized than boys thereby increasing their chances of entering college. Teachers have consistently rated girls as less disruptive than boys in school and have also found girls to be more attentive than boys.[12]

Declining discrimination against female participation in the economy therefore enhances the chances of women becoming ascendant in earning power, occupational prestige, independence from male domination and political influence.

In 1975, median earnings for female four year college graduates were 37 percent higher than median earnings for female high school graduates. That gap grew to 47 percent in 1935 and reached 70 percent in 2005. Even the median earnings of women with only some college education but no degree exceeded high school graduates without college by 41 percent in 2005.[13]

The U.S. Census Bureau has published the educational attainment statistics for the years 1960 to 2005. These plainly show the great strides women have made in gaining a higher education during those forty-five years. In 1960 only 5.8 percent of women of college age graduated from college. In 1970 this had risen to 8.1 percent and continued to rise steadily to 12.8 percent in 1980, 18.4 percent in 1990, 20.2 percent in 1995 and to 26.5 percent in 2005.[14]

Of particular interest is the increase of women earning bachelor's degrees in science and engineering. Beginning in 2000 women have earned more science and engineering degrees than men. The bachelor's degrees awarded to women in science and engineering has increased since 1966, reaching 227,813 in 2004 at a time when men earned only 224,525 such degrees.

The Female Labor Force

The number of working women in 1900 was 5.1 million or 18 percent of the labor force. In that year 20.4 percent of all women worked. In 1950, 18.4 million women worked and in 2006 that had risen to 66.9 million female workers or 60 percent of all American women. Working women, in 2006 constituted 46.3 percent of the labor force.

Because the United States has entered the post-industrial age, muscle work has declined rapidly in favor of white collar and professional jobs. Therefore, women are employed in ever greater numbers so that women are the majority, namely 57 percent of workers in those occupations which are expected to grow most rapidly.

Labor force participation has grown most rapidly among married women as marriage has proved to be an uncertain state and the education of women has increased. In fact, as of 2006 most mothers, even with young children, participated in the labor force.

Earnings of American Women

In 2004 women earned 80.4 percent of men's earnings in a labor force of 101,224,000 of which women constituted 44,223,000. In management and related occupations women earned only 71 percent of men's income although female lodging managers or hotel managers earned 85 percent of what men earned that year.

Among women employed in business or financial operations, human resources and labor relations specialists earned 79.3 percent of men's income while the overall ratio of women's earnings to men's earnings was 74.1 percent.[15]

Professional women earned 73.1 percent of men's income in 2004. Female computer support specialists earned 95.6 percent of men's income or $813 per week that year while men earned $850 per week in that occupation. The closest women came to earning as much as men was in social work. In that occupation women earned 96 percent of men's income which represented $689 per week as compared to $720 for men. The average income of social workers was therefore $698 per week or $36,296 annually.

Of the 621,000 American lawyers, 208,000 were women in 2004. Their earnings were 73.4 percent of men's earnings for an average weekly income of $1,255 for women and $1,710 for men or $1,561 weekly income for both genders or $81,172 annually.

In education, a profession in which women predominate with 4,273,000 women to 1,668,000 men women earned 76.8 percent of male income in 2004, the average teacher earning $781 per week or $40,612 annually.

Women physicians constituted 32 percent of all physicians in 2006. Since 49 percent of all medical students in 2006 and 2007 were women, this proportion in favor of women will change in the next few years. Nevertheless, female physicians earned 38 percent less than male physicians in 2006 when the median income for physicians was $183,840 for internists. Specialists earned a good deal more, depending on the specialty. Thus, dermatologists earned a median income of $306,935 and oncologists earned $263,284.[16]

Nursing is indeed a female dominated profession. Of the 1,800,000 registered nurses employed in 2004, 1,651,000 were women. The median weekly earnings of nurses as reported by the Bureau of Labor Statistics that year were $904 per week or $47,008 per year. The 148,000 male registered nurses earned $1,031 or $53,612 or 13 percent more than female nurses.

In the nearly all male occupation of police patrol officer, women earned 99.5 percent of men's earnings. Of the 844,000 officers employed in 2004 only 83,000 were women who earned $841 per week as compared to $845 earned by men ($43,940 annually).

The ten occupations with the highest median weekly earnings among women who were full-time wage earners in 2006 were pharmacists, $1,564; chief executives, $1,422; lawyers, $1,353; physicians, $1,329, including interns; computer and information systems managers, $1,300; computer software engineers, $1,227; physical therapists, $1,036; management analysts, $1,069; health service managers, $1,064; and computer scientists, $1,039.[17]

Because the U.S. Department of Labor provides statistics including the whole country, these salaries may seem incongruous in various locations.

Male Dominated Occupations

There are some professions which carry so much prestige that they serve as an indicator of the status role women have achieved in the early 21st century. We define a status as the sum of rights and privileges and a role as the sum of obligations pertaining to an occupation or any other position in any human arrangement.

Accordingly, the status role of college or university president reflects high achievement although these positions are largely attained by political acumen.

In February of 2007, *The Chronicle of Higher Education* published a presidential survey. This survey, conducted by the American Council on Education, revealed that at the end of 2006 77 percent of college presidents in the U.S. were male and 33 percent female. In 1986, when such a study was first conducted, 92 percent of college presidents were male. This increase in female participation in the college presidency may seem slow. Nevertheless, the study, which surveyed 2,148 college presidents, reveals a better than four-fold increase in the ascendancy of women to the lead in higher education.[18]

This increase in the number of women occupying college presidencies is related to the increase in the proportion of female faculty to 41 percent in 2006 from 38 percent in 1999. In view of the ever increasing number of women who achieve the doctorate, that number will increase rapidly in the next few years.[19]

An example of the manner in which women have risen to prominence in higher education was the recent election of Drew Faust to the presidency of Harvard University. Faust is the first woman president of Harvard University, a college founded in 1632. Faust is a historian with a major interest in the history of the Civil War. She has published six books on that subject including *Mothers of Invention*, which was awarded the prize for the best non-fiction book by the Society of American Historians.

Faust is a Bryn Mawr graduate. She earned her master's and doctor's degrees from the University of Pennsylvania and went on to spend 25 years on the faculty of that school. There she collected innumerable honors for her research, teaching and committee work. She then came to Harvard and entered upon another career of awards, honors and recognitions for her work as dean of the Radcliffe Institute. She is married to Professor Charles Rosenberg, also of the Harvard history department and also the recipient of numerous academic honors.[20]

Four of the eight Ivy League universities now have female presidents. In addition to Faust at Harvard, Amy Gutman is president of the University of Pennsylvania, Ruth Simmons is president of Brown University and Shirley Tighman heads Princeton.

Numerous other colleges and universities have appointed women as presidents in 2007. There can be little doubt that the appointment of women to these positions is popular among boards of trustees and will shortly result in eliminating the gender gap in that profession.

There are also numerous women scholars and scientists included in the faculties of American universities. One example of a major academic female achiever is Susan L. Graham, a distinguished professor of electrical engineering at the University of California at Berkeley. Her academic credentials are outstanding as is her research record, which includes building the Pascal system. She is the founding editor of a journal in programming and has received numerous awards from professional associations in the area of mathematics and computer sciences. Her distinguished career led to her selection as chair of her alma mater's college, the Harvard Board of Overseers.[21]

Linda L. Buck is another high achiever within the scientific community. Buck received the Nobel Prize for physiology or medicine in 2004. She was at that time associated with the Fred Hutchinson Cancer Research Center in Seattle, Washington, having previously been associated with the University of Texas, Columbia University and Harvard University.[22]

The most outstanding achievement by any woman scientist in the twentieth century belongs to Rosalind Franklin, the discoverer of the double helix and therefore also responsible for the discovery of deoxyribonucleic acid, commonly known as DNA.

Franklin achieved this most important result after working at the King's College laboratories in London, England, for several years in the 1950s. Unaware of the deceit of her colleague, Maurice Wilkins, she died of an overdose of radiation in 1958 at the age of 37. Wilkins had given the results of her work to his friends James Watson and Francis Crick who were working on the DNA problem at Cambridge University. Upon her death, Watkins published a book, *The Double Helix*, in which he claimed to have discovered the structure of DNA. He gave no credit to Franklin and was subsequently awarded the Nobel Prize for a discovery he did not make.

There are now several books and journal articles available which describe how Franklin achieved this remarkable result. Nevertheless, almost all encyclopedias and Internet sources falsely credit Watson and his associate Crick with this discovery.[23]

Scientists and academics are of course not the only examples of female achievement. There are also a number of women who have become the chief executive officers of large Fortune 500 corporations. Among these is Catherine E. Hughes. She is the first African American woman to head a firm publicly traded on a United States stock exchange. Her company is TV One, a cable channel aimed at the black community. Hughes built this business herself by starting in a small radio station in Washington, D.C., and then progressing by purchasing stations in other cities. Today, her company is the nation's largest black owned radio chain.

In 1967, Muriel Siebert became the first woman to purchase a seat on the New York Stock Exchange. For ten years thereafter she was the only woman among 1,366 members. She achieved this after first working as a trainee researcher for the Wall Street firm of Bache and Co. From that minimal beginning she continued her business career by working for a number of firms until she founded her own company, Siebert Financial Corp. In 2002 she published her autobiography, entitled *Changing the Rules: Adventures of a Wall Street Maverick*.

Patricia Russo is yet another female CEO. She heads the Lucent Technologies Division of Bell Laboratories. Russo began her business career by working for IBM for eight years until she joined AT&T in 1981. There she founded a new company, Avaya, by reorganizing AT&T's business communications systems division. From there she became president and CEO of Eastman Kodak and then took on Lucent in 2002. In 2005 Russo was paid a $1.2 million salary, a $1.9 million bonus and stock options amounting to $8.7 million.[24]

One of the most closed male bastions in the world has been the profession of symphony conductor. The very manner in which conductors lead orchestras has traditionally been identified with a high testosterone personality. Yet, here too, women are gradually making inroads into this profession. The image of a male conductor was developed over several hundred years ever since conductors were first employed in European orchestras.[25]

This total male domination was interrupted briefly when in the 1930s Nadia Boulanger briefly conducted the Boston and New York symphonies and when in 1976 Sarah Caldwell became the first female conductor at the Metropolitan Opera in New York. Since then about 35 women have been appointed to lead American orchestras. Among them is Joanne Faletta, who has been the conductor of the Buffalo Philharmonic Orchestra since 1999. She is also the conductor of the Virginia Symphony Orchestra. She holds a doctorate from the Juilliard School of Music and has been exceptionally successful in both positions. She is joined by Marin Alsop, who was appointed conductor of the Baltimore Symphony Orchestra in 2005, Karen Keltner of the Baltimore Opera, Anne Marson of the Kansas City Symphony Orchestra and a number of other women both in the United States and in Europe and Asia.[26]

In 1981 President Reagan nominated Sandra Day O'Connor to became the first woman to join the Supreme Court of the United States. She served as an associate justice until her retirement in 2005. Her rise to the most prestigious position a lawyer can attain in the United States reflects the long road women have traveled in their effort to gain gender equality in this country. Born in 1930 in Texas, she graduated from the Stanford University School of Law in only two years and was third in a class of 102. Nevertheless, no law firm in California was willing to hire her or any woman. She therefore entered public service as assistant attorney general of Arizona and thereafter was elected to a number of offices in that state before coming to the attention of President Reagan, who appointed her to the Supreme Court. She participated in the case of *Bush v. Gore* which on December 12, 2000, gave the presidency of the United States to George W. Bush.[27]

The second woman to reach membership in the Supreme Court of the United States is Ruth Bader Ginsburg. She was nominated by President Clinton in 1993 and continues to serve on the court (2007). Ginsburg was so outstanding a student at the Harvard Law School that the dean of that school proposed to Justice Felix Frankfurter in 1960 that she become his law clerk. Frankfurter refused on the grounds that he could not appoint a woman.

Ginsburg, during her career as an attorney, became known for her advocacy of women's rights. She won five of six such cases before the Supreme Court including the *Frontiero* case, which dealt with gender discrimination in the Air Force.[28]

Obviously, there are male dominated occupations which do not include such high status work as college president or symphony conductor and supreme court justice. The most common of these is law enforcement or police officer.

The Bureau of Labor Statistics reports that there were about 844,000 police in the United States in 2004. Of these, 83,000 or about 13 percent were women. Both men and women employed in that occupation earn approximately $43,940 a year.

The appointment of women to high ranks in police departments is now commonplace, and a number of large cities and many smaller ones have appointed women to chief. Among these are Heather Fong in San Francisco, Cathy L. Lanier of the District of Columbia, Ella M. B. Cummings of Detroit, Nanette Hegerty in Milwaukee and Kathleen O'Toole in Boston. Hegerty resigned three years after her appointment.

In addition to these female chiefs in large cities, there are a number of female police C.E.O.s such as Terri Wilfong of Greenville, South Carolina, which has 21 women officers among a total force of 192. In December 2006 Kimberly S. Lettner was appointed chief of the Virginia Capitol Police, the oldest police department in the United States. There are now about 200 female police chiefs in the country.[29]

Another occupation traditionally associated with men is aviation. This despite Amelia Earhart (1897–1937) and other flying heroines. In 2007, women made up only 5.5 percent of all aviation workers. For example, there are 30 women working in the shop floor of Kelly Aviation Center in San Antonio, Texas, among 400 men. Boeing Aviation, which has 1,500 employees working on equipment maintaining military aircraft, employs only 11 women in that capacity. Nevertheless, Marilyn Hawson was in charge of the Kelly Aviation Center and now runs a Lockheed division in Fort Worth, Texas. Colleen Barrett is president of Southwest Airlines and Marion C. Blakely was appointed by President George W. Bush to be administrator of the Federal Aviation Administration. All told, more than 120,000 women are involved in non-pilot roles in American aviation including 100,000 flight attendants. Meanwhile, the number of women working as mechanics has grown 18 percent since 2000.[30]

Female Dominated Occupations

The Nursing Profession

Although the entrance of women into such erstwhile all male professions as college president and symphony conductor indicate the gradual ascent of women into the upper reaches of occupational prestige and income, the incumbents in these positions are so few that they cannot represent the vast majority of American women.

It is therefore of interest to take a look at the nursing profession whose practitioners are mainly women and whose profession has historically been exclusively female.

In 2006, the U.S. Bureau of Labor Statistics reported that there were then 2.7 million licensed registered nurses in the country. Of these, 2.2 million were employed as registered nurses. In addition, there were then also 700,000 licensed practical nurses and 600,000 home health aides working in the health care occupation. No more than 6 percent of these nurses were men. Therefore, this almost all female profession allows us to see how women have advanced financially as a greater number of nurses earned both undergraduate and graduate degrees in the 21st century than ever before.

In 1980 only 19 percent of nurses held an associate's degree. In 2004 this had risen to 42.2 percent, a more than 100 percent increase. In 1980, only 17 percent of nurses held a bachelor's degree; but in 2004, 30.5 percent of nurses had a bachelor's degree while 13 percent had earned a master's or doctor's degree.

The consequences of this increase in education are quite visible. In 2004, registered nurses earned an average annual salary, nationwide, of $57,784. In 2000 the average annual earnings of nurses was $46,782.

As the education of nurses progressed, a number of nurses promoted the profession to the level of advanced practice registered nurse (APRN). This designation includes clinical nurse specialists, nurse anesthetists, nurse midwives and nurse practitioners. Nurse practitioners claim to do everything also done by physicians, leading to the presumption that medical schools will become obsolete.

According to the journal *Advance for Nurse Practitioners,* the average salary for nurse practitioners is more than $69,000 annually. Nurse practitioners who own their own practice earn more than $94,000 annually. This compares to family physicians who earn about $150,000 a year. The evidence is, therefore, that this nearly all female profession has increased the earnings and the independence of women immensely during the thirty years ending in 2007.[31]

Traditionally, nurses were viewed by physicians and patients as handmaids to male doctors. It is well known that the nursing profession originated during the Crimean War (1853–1856) in which the Ottoman Empire and its allies, Britain, France and Sardinia fought Russia. During that conflict, Florence Nightingale (1820–1910) introduced 38 women into the battlefield to help the wounded.[32]

At the beginning of the 20th century, American medicine had become a profession. This was not true of nursing, which depended entirely on the approval of the medical profession, particularly because nursing education was run entirely by hospitals with doctors in charge. Nurses were taught to be passive and subservient to physicians, while medical students were taught to be assertive and independent. This control by physicians was possible because physicians had specialized knowledge not open to anyone else and because the medical profession controlled itself and was not supervised by outsiders.[33]

The subservient relationship of nursing to medicine continued throughout the principal part of the 20th century but has changed dramatically during the twenty-five years ending in 2007. This increase in the autonomy of the nursing profession came about because nursing education became more and more controlled by nurses themselves as nurse professors with advanced degrees designed and administered the curriculum. This in turn has led to the development of nurse specialists and the right of nurses to administer drugs based on the nurses' own knowledge and expertise. All this led to more assertiveness among nurses resulting in a gradual but steady independence from the medical profession.[34]

There are approximately 45 million Americans who have no health insurance and cannot therefore access the services of a physician. As a consequence nurses with advanced degrees have become the only health professionals in many rural areas lacking a doctor. In addition, in-store health clinics are rapidly opening in pharmacies and department stores like Wal-Mart. These clinics are staffed by registered nurses who charge between $25 and $60 for a visit. No appointments are needed so that patients do not have to wait for hours in doctors' waiting rooms. While these clinics are undoubtedly a considerable advantage for patients with minor complaints, the medical profession fears that simple symptoms can hide serious problems which nurses cannot recognize.[35]

The Social Work Profession

In 2004 the Bureau of Labor Statistics reported that 78 percent of all social workers were women. At that time the mean annual income of social workers was $44,950, including those with the MSW or master's degree.

This profession has undergone two major changes during the past thirty years. First was the introduction of the bachelor's degree in the 1960s and second was the development of private practice. Prior to the introduction of the B.A. degree in social work, only those holding the MSW were afforded membership in the National Association of Social Workers. This did not prevent numerous employers from hiring people into social work positions who had no training in social work at all. Therefore, the profession has had to compete with people who were and are willing to accept wages below the average paid to professional social workers. In May 2006 the Bureau of Labor Statistics reported the average income for social workers at $44,950 annually.[36]

Salaries of social workers are the lowest among all professionals as they earn about 11 percent less than people working in all other occupations, taken together.[37]

That is why this female dominated profession has given a minority of social workers an opportunity to establish themselves as independent practitioners although the income of independent social workers is not necessarily better than that of those employed by social work agencies.

The main advantage for social workers with master's degrees qualifying them for private practice is the opportunity to work outside the constrictions of so-called agencies which are so top heavy with administrators that independent decision making is almost impossible amidst the bureaucracies dominating these agencies. It is nevertheless the burden of social workers who are on their own to deal with an enormous amount of paperwork before and after seeing a patient because the income of social workers depends almost entirely on insurance payments. Insurance companies, utterly disinterested in the needs of patients, force social workers (and others) to employ only a limited number of diagnoses in order to be paid for their services. These prescribed diagnoses may be unrelated to the facts concerning any patient but must nevertheless be used because insurance companies refuse to recognize any other conditions pertaining to a patient. Insurance companies also severely limit the number of sessions for which they are willing to pay. Therefore, many patients who need help can hardly expect much in one to three sessions with a social work therapist.[38]

Elementary Education

Another female dominated profession is elementary and middle school teacher. The Bureau of Labor Statistics listed 1,772,000 such teachers in 2004. Of these, only 435,000 or 2.5 percent were men. Women in this profession earned $40,352 or 85 percent of men's earnings which were $47,684 in 2004. It is evident that this almost all female occupation is vastly underpaid and hardly appreciated by the American public despite its immense importance as the bedrock of all education in this country. It is most likely that this failure to support elementary education is rooted in the view that work done mostly by women is not worth as much as work done mostly by men.[39]

Teachers at all levels, including post-secondary education, are mainly women; 5,491,000 teachers are employed in our educational institutions. Of these 4,273,000 are females earning about 76.3 percent of men's earnings.

The Gender Ratio of Earning Power

It is evident from the foregoing that although women are making major inroads into occupations once totally dominated by men, the average earning power of women as compared to men is still only about 77 percent to 80 percent of men's wages. This overall difference may be partially explained by the difference in work patterns between the sexes. This includes that women have fewer years of work experience than men; that women work fewer hours per year, that they are less likely than men to work full time and that they leave the labor force for extended periods of time, including for maternity leave.[40]

The financial gender gap cannot be understood only in present day terms. A better understanding of the difference between the earnings of women and men is derived from looking at the past so that the rise in women's income over the decades can be appreciated.

Such a review demonstrates that in 1979 the annual earnings of women were only 59.2 percent of men's earnings. By 1989, this had risen to 68.7 percent and in 1992 a further increase to 70.6 percent could be recorded.

In 2005 women working full time, year around, earned between 77 percent and 80 percent of men's earnings. The difference in earnings by age is therefore significant. Thus, women between the ages of 20 and 24 earned 94 percent of men's income, those 34 to 44 years old earned 75.6 percent of men's income and women aged 55 to 64 earned 74.7 percent of men's earnings. No doubt the higher earnings of younger women reflect the higher level of education attained by younger women in the past several years. Thus, the earnings of women with bachelor's degrees increased by 34.2 percent since 1979 while male college graduates earned only 18.2 percent more than they earned in 1979.[41]

There can be no doubt that education makes a difference at every level of achievement. In 2005 those who did not graduate from high school earned $409 a week or $21,268 a year. High school graduates earned $583 per week or $30,316 per year; college graduates earned an average of $937 or $48,724; those holding a master's degree earned $1,129 or $58,708 and doctors, whether academic or professional, earned a median of $1,395 or $72,540. The median income here described is of course the midpoint between the highest and lowest in the educational group. Undoubtedly physicians earn more than any other doctors.[42]

Consider that the earnings of college graduates are a good deal higher than the earnings of those without such an education.

In money terms these statistics mean that in 2005 men who were employed full time for a year earned a median annual income of $41,386 and women earned $31,858. It is also remarkable that in 2005, one-quarter of married women earned more than their husbands. This was only true of 18 percent of working wives in 1987.[43]

In 2004 women held half of all positions in management, professional and related occupations. That year, 60 percent of women who worked did so full time all year. While only 26 percent of all Americans have a college degree, 33 percent of working women age 25 to 64 are college graduates. In 2004, 72 percent of female high school graduates enrolled in either a junior or senior college while only 61 percent of men did so.

Looking back to 1970 we see that then only 41 percent of women worked full time all year and only 11 percent of women aged 25 to 64 had a college degree.[44]

Per hour worked, women's earnings were about 80 percent of men's earnings as of 2007. Claudia Goldin reports that in 1820, the ratio of female to male earnings was only 0.3 in an almost all farm economy. By 1859 manufacturing was beginning in this country so that the ratio of female to male earnings rose to 0.5. Then, during the first three decades of the twentieth century clerical and sales jobs became available to women and the ratio rose to 0.56. In 1940 only 7 percent of married women with children worked full time; in 2000 it was 46 percent Then, from 1950 to 1980 the ratio of income for full time employed women who worked all year to men with similar work histories rose to 0.60 and remained there until in 1991 it had risen to 0.74. Furthermore, in 1890 only 2.5 percent of married women worked outside the home. By 2000, 66 percent of married women were in the labor force, 47 percent full time. In 1940, the labor force participation of women was 15 percent; in 1950 it was 20 percent and reached 65 percent in 1990.[45]

In view of the evidence that more women have a college education than is true of men, the persistence of the gender gap in earnings cannot be attributed to educational attainment. The reasons for the difference must be sought elsewhere. Melissa S. Kearny has explained this discrepancy by listing several reasons other than education for this condition. First, she shows that women "have historically worked fewer years ... than men and have been more likely to work part time."[46]

According to Kearney, women are much more likely than men to leave work to take care of children. This leads to career interruption and a consequent wage drop. In addition, women are more often employed in support positions which pay less than executive jobs. This means that the gender gap in income is explained far better by looking at the kind of work women do and not at education. It may well be that women will work in occupations of their choice which pay less than is paid men, and that occupational differences are not only and always the product of discrimination. Furthermore, there are some women who cease full time work at marriage which is seldom true of men.[47]

One reason for the increase in labor force participation by women has been the decrease in marriage rates. In 1960, 73 percent of women age 18 to 34 were married. In 1980 this had declined to 54 percent and then fell further to 44 percent in 2000. The share of women's earnings to total family income was 26.6 percent in 1980, 30.7 percent in 1990 and rose to 35.5 percent in 2003. In that year also, 25 percent of women earned more than their husbands.[48]

Male Reaction to the Ascendancy of Women

One reaction of men to the ascendancy of women is retreat. This is best seen by comparing the educational achievements of men and women during the twenty years ending in 2007. Evidently, men are falling behind women in finishing high school or entering college.

Another reaction to the ascendancy of women is sexual harassment. While it is commonly assumed that sexual harassment has to do with male efforts at sexual gratification, the evidence is that the real reason for such unreasonable action is the wish to protect men's social status. The evidence for this view is that women who challenge male dominance are more likely to become the target of gender and sexual harassment than women who accept such dominance.

Maass and her colleagues have shown that as male status advantages are increasingly seen as illegitimate, sexual harassment also increases. The threat to men's dominance has been particularly worrisome to men in professions which were at one time entirely male dominated and which have seen the entrance of women with better credentials and more education than many men already entrenched in these occupations.[49]

A second reason for sexual harassment of women at work is, according to Maass, the threat such women pose to the value of the in group, i.e., men. This motive may be seen by the introduction of pornography on the job because the purpose of pornography is to demean women.

Thirdly, there are men who feel their masculinity threatened by women who are high achievers within their occupational or work group and who seek to restore their manhood by demeaning women.

These arguments are summarized as threats to male identity and are therefore less sexual and far more defensive than is commonly believed.[50]

The evidence that sex based harassment is related to the threat less powerful individuals pose for more powerful individuals can be seen in female to female harassment. A woman who believes that her status is threatened by another woman is likely to seek the approval of higher status men. Such maneuvers will include mothering or sexual desirability or beauty and dress makeovers. Such harassment can of course also occur between men as one man feels his social standing threatened by another man.[51]

For all the years of American history before 1970, white men have been the leaders and arbiters of American values and American virtues. White men have been the authorities in almost every realm of America including the family, religion, economics, education and government. Until about 1970 women were prevented from dominating in any of these social institutions.

The exclusion of women from public life was particularly severe. Women voted for the first time in federal elections in 1920 although there were a few women who had voted in some state elections in earlier years. Hardly any women were elected to any office until then and very few were elected before 1990.

A fourth male reaction to the rise of women economically and socially has been the so-called pro-family campaign which was also invoked in past years when women appeared to demand equal rights. This relates to falling marriage rates, high divorce rates, single parenthood and same-sex marriage, all of which are viewed by traditionalists as the consequence of women's efforts to achieve equality with men.[52]

Beginning in the 1960s and increasingly vocal in the 1980s a backlash movement of white, middle class men and women sought to blame all the troubles of the American family on the women's rights movement, also called feminism. As female access to education and erstwhile all male occupations increased, marriage rates and birthrates dropped while divorce rates increased. For example, in 2004, 8.2 of every 1,000 Americans married while 4.19 divorced. The divorce rate actually doubled after 1964 while the marriage rate, i.e., the number of single women per 1,000 aged 15 or more who married in any one year, declined. In 1946 the rate of marriage was 118; by 1970 it had declined to 93, and then fell to 58 per thousand by 1990. Ten years later, in 2000, the American marriage rate had fallen to 44 per thousand single women.[53]

One consequence of the low rate of marriage has been the decrease of legitimate births, the increase of illegitimate births and the increase of co-habitation. Co-habitation in the United States increased tenfold between 1970 and 2002, reaching 4,200,000 couples that year.

Social Change

This brief review of the changing status of American women at the beginning of the 21st century is the product of many social changes which have occurred in the United States since the First World War. This is not to say that social change did not exist prior to 1917. On the contrary. All human civilization has always been in a state of flux. In some eras this has been rapid as during the Renaissance and during the Age of Exploration. At other times social change has been slow so that some have called the years between the fall of Rome and the fall of Constantinople the Dark Ages. Yet, even then, social change, however minute, existed.

To a large extent, social change depends on advances in knowledge brought about slowly and in opposition to established norms. It took centuries for mankind to free itself from beliefs which did not correspond to reality but enslaved men and women in a culture controlled by religion and superstition. From the time that Anaximander (611–547 B.C.E.) began the investigation of the natural universe in ancient Greece until the beginning of the 21st century the western world gradually allowed some men to ascend to a life of reason and scientific inquiry.

This process permitted the growth of science dependent on education and a worldview at least partially freed from tradition. Included in these advances was the slow reduction in the birth rate and an increase in longevity which together allowed women opportunities heretofore unknown.[54]

For example, in 1900 American life expectancy for both sexes was 47.2 years. Women averaged 4 children with many having five and six or more. Men could expect to live 46.3 years and women 48.3 years. By 1950 this had risen to 65.8 for men and 71.1 for women, and by 1980 women born that year could expect to live 77.4 years. Meanwhile the average number of children born to American women in 1950 was 3.69. In 1980 an average of only 1.81 children were born to American women. Evidently then, women who are married at age 22 and have two children before they reach age 26 can look forward to a whole career until retirement. This was surely not true in 1900 when female life expectancy was only 48.3 years and four children had not reached maturity until their mother was more than forty years old with only a few years yet to live. In short, fertility, life expectancy and death determined the disabilities of women *ipso facto*.[55]

The principal reasons, therefore, for the liberation of women from the age old domination by men were scientific discoveries and inventions not only in the area of birth control and longevity but also in the gradual reduction of muscle work and the subsequent employment opportunities requiring intelligence and skill instead of brute force.

Until the 1940s the overwhelming majority of women were employed in factory work and office occupations. Prior to World War I, women were only 18 percent of the American labor force while in 2007 nearly half of all working Americans were women. The census of 2000 indicates that in that year there were 60,639,069 employed women in America. Of these, over seven million worked in management occupations, including banking; nearly 15 million were employed in the professions, including law and medicine; and 22 million worked in sales. This means that only 26 percent of all employed women were engaged in factory or similar work.[56]

The evidence is that women are not only employed in greater numbers than ever before in U.S. history but that they are also entering numerous occupations at one time held exclusively by men.

The Rise of Mass Society

Large scale immigration, technological advances and immense improvements in communications have made the United States a mass society. In such a society, industry and bureaucracy supplant the traditional social ties of families and neighborhoods and friends. Face to face relationships become less frequent as the Internet and the computer, together with television, make human relations frail and exceptional. Government and other secondary organizations are expected in a mass society to take the place of close relatives and lifelong associates so that the traditional role of the mother and wife no longer applies in many American families. This change in the condition of the American family also contributes to the opportunities women have to enter the workplace and carve out a career. Women are not needed at home as they once were when six children were not unusual, when most families lived on farms, when few children attended school past age 12 and when food preparation alone occupied most of the day as there was no frozen dinner, no packaged food and no refrigeration. Everything had to be made by hand. This was also true of keeping house as there were no labor saving devices. In such a society women were designated house slaves, a status supported by religion and public opinion.

Traditional values are also in transition in a changing society. This is dramatically illustrated by the recent finding that the marriages of some women who work outside the home are more stable than is true of women who do not work. This finding directly contradicts the prior paternalistic view, held for centuries, that working women are poor mothers or that the husband of a working wife is thereby diminished.

According to that research, the divorce rate has leveled off because married couples spend less time together, have fewer shared friends and frequently eat alone. These features of marriage would appear to be detrimental to a lifelong relationship. However, family income has increased as more married women work in better jobs, decision making appears to be more egalitarian and conflict and violence have declined. All of this means that marriage is less confining than in the past. In sum, the four authors of this book show that marriage is an adaptable institution which will undoubtedly continue despite the many obstacles that institution has had to face for the past thirty years.[57]

Therefore we can say with certainty that the domination of the American family by men has come to an end at the outset of the 21st century. Looking back we can see that not only the family but public life was entirely controlled by men before the middle of the 20th century so that the recent election of the first woman to become speaker of the House would have appeared bizarre to those voting only twenty-five years earlier.

The election of Nancy Pelosi to that powerful position means that women have recognized that the only means they have to gain power and income in America is by means of the ballot box. The long struggle for women to achieve the right to vote, which finally succeeded in the 1920s, was followed by the election of more and more women to membership in the House and Senate and to the governor's mansion.[58]

All this has become possible at the beginning of the 21st century because American values concerning status have also changed. Status may be defined as the sum of all of our rights and privileges and role as the sum of our obligations. Sociologists recognize two kinds of status, ascribed and achieved. An ascribed status is given us at birth. Our sex, race, ethnicity, family or religion are generally pre-determined by others so that the position of women before the current revolution was fixed by tradition and necessity. Birth control was unknown or so risky that constant pregnancies led to decades of child rearing and kept women from having any other opportunities. Any deviation from the status-role so ascribed was penalized as can best be understood by reading *The Scarlet Letter* by Nathaniel Hawthorne.

An achieved status is evidently one which each person may attain through his own efforts. This would include education, business success, election to office and dominance in the family. For white Protestant men, achievements in these areas have always been a possibility if not a certainty. Not so for minorities or women.

The history of the United States is in fact a history of ever expanding democracy. The Constitution as first ratified did not allow citizens to vote for senators. They were elected by the legislatures of each state. Only property owners could vote before the vote was extended to all white males. Blacks were next to be given the right to vote although it took a century to enforce that right. We have already seen that women did not vote in a federal election until 1920 and that they were also barred from business, education, public affairs and even the management of their own lives.

There was a time when a woman could not divorce her husband although men could divorce their wives. Even the inheritance of a husband's property by his wife was limited as a woman's son was given the right to administer his mother's land and farm.

All this is now mainly history although the achievements of some women as outlined here are so far by no means universal. Depending on ethnic group, income, race or region of the country, there are considerable differences in the opportunities now available to women. All are by no means equal as yet, but a great leap forward has been made during the first decade of the 21st century.

Summary

In the 21st century American women can look back on considerable achievements in education and income. This can be seen by looking at the dramatic increase in female students in American colleges and universities, including graduate schools devoted to medicine, law, pharmacy and education. The opportunities women have had during the second half of the twentieth century are the product of changes in family values as well as admission to erstwhile all-male education and all male occupations. Female educational achievements are outdistancing those of boys and men as the earnings of American women are growing faster than is true of men. This has led to some female dominated occupations such as pharmacy and audiology. Nursing, social work and teaching, traditionally strongholds of female workers, are now being invaded by men. These men are earning more than women who have been there longer. In general, male reaction to women's achievements have been large divorce rates and other indications of failing marriages. In 2007, achieved status meant a great deal. Earlier in American history ascribed status was far more important so that neither women nor minorities had much of a chance to live the American dream.

Chapter 2

Women and Change in the 20th Century — Education, Emancipation, Work and the Law

The Gradual Liberation of American Women

Throughout the centuries, sex has determined life chances. This was true in America just as it was true all over the world, including Europe, the principal contributor to immigration to the U.S. before the 21st century.

It is therefore of interest to review the manner in which sex was viewed by Americans during the nineteenth and twentieth centuries, prior to the gradual liberation of women from Victorian stereotypes.

Although Queen Victoria of England died in 1901, her legacy lived on into the first half of the twentieth century and beyond. Her views and those of her emulators concerning sex and education were based on a number of assumptions which had little to do with reality but confirmed the dictum that "if men define situations as real they are real in their consequences."[1]

According to the Victorian view, men were generally sexual predators and women the victims of men's insatiable sexuality. Women were also viewed as morally pure and passive. Therefore, education for men and women differed to accommodate these presumed, inherited conditions. This meant that girls were taught only that which was needed to shield them from the aggression of men and their corrupt world.[2]

This view became the basis for sex education in the U.S. when, at the outset of the 20th century, it was hoped that sex education would stop the spread of venereal disease by bringing about sexual abstinence. This belief is still viable in the 21st century, as the U.S. government has spent $50 million to teach abstinence only sex education in U.S. schools in 2006–2007.[3]

In the nineteenth century, girls were not taught any subject matter which could be construed as practical. This also meant that women were seldom given access to higher education, as it was believed that girls who attended high school or college would be corrupted by the men they would meet there.[4]

Female sexual expression was particularly discouraged during the Victorian age, even as male sexuality was given wide latitude. The belief that men must be given opportunities to express their sexual needs resulted in the open operation of houses of prostitution in so-called red light districts in American cities. The reasons for maintaining these brothels were that immigrants needed to be given an opportunity to relax from the brutal physical labor they usually endured during long working hours. In addition, brothels were generally located near hotels and dance halls and theaters so that out-of-town visitors could have easy access. Medical regulations were partially enforced in these brothels so that decent people could tell themselves that they would not be infected by the prostitutes or their customers. Furthermore, it was presumed that sexual intercourse was limited to married people and that single women were fallen if they participated. Therefore, prostitution was viewed as necessary, even if not recommended. The most important argument in favor of maintaining bawdy houses was that without prostitutes, decent women would be insulted and seduced. It was believed that without prostitution, crime would increase and frustrated men would assault honorable women. Of course, the poor, immigrants and minorities were viewed as near beasts who needed prostitution to keep them from associating with the decent classes. Finally, prostitution was also used to introduce young men to sexuality in a manner distant from the girls they would court and date and finally marry.[5]

In view of these opinions concerning male sexuality, girls and boys did not attend school together until the beginning of the 19th century, and then in only a few places. It was only the expansion of the public schools in the second half of the nineteenth century which allowed the youngest children to meet those of the opposite gender, as these children were evidently not in danger of knowing much about sex. Therefore, co-education was delayed for high school and college students so as to avoid young women coming in contact with boys and men.[6]

Then there were those who argued before the First World War that it was dangerous to give girls the same education as boys. Schools for girls taught only homemaking skills and social graces as it was deemed that women were too weak to learn mathematics and history and the male curriculum. Therefore single sex schools were popular until it became evident that single sex schools were too expensive. Then, at the beginning of the 20th century, co-ed schools were devised with separate curricula for girls, as even the medical profession claimed that young men would become feminized if they learned so-called female subject matter or sat too long in the same classroom with girls.[7]

It was also argued that the strain of serious study posed a threat to the reproductive systems of adolescent girls, who were believed to be quite frail. This view was widespread among American educators so that girls were not required to take the traditional male course including Latin and Greek as they were the weaker sex who could not possibly carry out the functions assigned to men. Particularly in the South, the segregation of girls from boys and the segregation of the races were held as absolutely essential so as to insure that there be no sexual encounter between black men and white women. Such fears were also linked to the possibility that blacks might gain social equality with whites in all areas of life, including economic advantage.[8]

These beliefs continued throughout the 19th century and receded only gradually in the 20th century. It is commonly assumed that the industrialization of the United States after the First World War suddenly shifted the fortunes of women from being confined housewives to industrial workers. Such a shift did indeed occur. However, it was not sudden but slow and developed during the first half of the twentieth century and beyond. Women working only within their homes were usually excluded from the label of working women, a label reserved for those who earned money outside the home. That belief overlooks the immense amount of work housewives had to do, even as more and more of them also entered the labor market.[9]

The labor market is without doubt the most important means by which Americans support themselves and their families. Therefore, it is evident that the exclusion of women from the labor market has been and continues to be the primary source of income inequality between the genders. Occupation is not only the principal means of attaining an income. It is also the most important means of measuring social prestige in the United States.

An understanding of the position of women in the American work hierarchy may be gained by using the scheme developed by Katz, Stern and Fader. Accordingly, the first question to be answered concerning women's participation in the labor force refers to the number of women who worked at any one time. That number is ambiguous because work may mean several things. According to the Bureau of Labor Statistics, work involves paid employment but not domestic labor. This failure to include domestic work alone guarantees that the extent of inequality to which women have been subjected is not fully visible by recording only paid employment outside the home. Katz et al. show that throughout the twentieth century women have been segregated into a small category of jobs which were usually not available to married women.[10]

Participation

Therefore the increase of married women in the American labor market constitutes the most significant change in women's economic position since the beginning of the twentieth century. This is demonstrated by the percentage of married women in the labor force, which was only 6 percent in 1900. By 1990, 59 percent of married women had entered the labor force. This was still true in 2005 for all women then employed. Among married women born after 1955 the labor force participation rose to 70 percent of all such women.[11]

The Second World War increased the proportion of women in the labor force. After that war, the antiquated prohibition against allowing married women to teach or hold other jobs continued for some years but finally crumbled in the 1960s, when three out of ten married women worked outside the home. By 1980 the proportion had nearly reached a majority and by 1990 the employment of married women had become commonplace. This change came about mainly because women had attained a good deal of education and because muscle work declined rapidly after 1980 while office skills and technological competence became more and more needed. Furthermore, women born after 1960 had the education needed to earn the income which men could no longer provide because male income has stagnated for the past twenty-five years even as female income has increased. In addition, the higher standard of living which educated women demanded could not be met by an increasing number of men. Therefore women went to work not only to gain the additional income their demands required, but also because a second income became mandatory for many a family which could no longer subsist on one man's wages alone. Between 1979 and 2005 men's wages increased only 1.7 percent for middle range earners and increased only 3.3 percent for high earners. For women, these increases were 5.3 percent and 7.1 percent respectively.[12]

Education made it possible for women to earn the extra income their families needed. One example is the health care industry, which is almost entirely dominated by women below the level of physician. Even that distinction may disappear soon, as the proportion of female medical students increases year by year, having reached 50 percent in 2006.

As early as 1910 there were more female high school graduates in the labor force than there were male high school graduates. Women born in 1960 attended college in greater numbers than was true of men, particularly because rising divorce rates, later marriages and an increase in single parenthood gave women reason to recognize the need to support themselves and their children.

Distribution

The kinds of jobs held by women changed considerably during the twentieth century. Early in the century, domestic service and agriculture employed more women than any other work. At the end the century and at the beginning of the 21st century these occupations had become insignificant. Instead, clerical work dominated the employment of women since the First World War (1914–1918). Other than working at home or taking care of children and the sick, clerical work was the only means available to women who wished to enter the labor force. Thus, in 1910, clerical work amounted to 9 percent of women's employment. By 1950 this had risen to 30 percent and to 35 percent in 1970. In 2006 the Bureau of Labor Statistics reported that only 22.6 percent of women worked as clerks.[13]

Early in the 20th century, clerical work consisted of operating a number of new machines invented between 1860 and 1900. Prior to the invention of the typewriter in 1868 clerical work was almost entirely in the hands of men. It was deemed necessary for a clerk to have excellent handwriting, know English and a foreign language very well, and also know some accounting. All this was abandoned when numerous office machines became available. Women were now hired to operate the dictating machines, mimeograph machines, cash registers, and adding machines. These machines made clerical tasks routine, involving repetitious tasks that were assigned to women while men strove for management positions whenever possible.[14]

Four conditions propelled young women into office work early in the 20th century. One was that their education, i.e., high school graduation, was commensurate with work in an office rather than in a factory. In the second place, factory work was unsafe and dirty, while office work was clean and safe. Thirdly, there were numerous office jobs at a time when American business was expanding, and finally, office work is more prestigious than factory work.

Self employment also led to a greater influx of women into the labor market. At one time self employed women were mainly engaged in domestic labor, consisting of child care, cleaning, and cooking services. By the middle of the 20th century such work had almost disappeared and retail store management of all kinds had taken the place of these erstwhile domestics.[15]

In the 1970s women finally entered management positions in greater numbers than ever before. This came about mainly because of legal changes. In 1963, Congress passed the Equal Pay Act. In 1964 the Equal Employment Opportunity Commission was organized as part of the Civil Rights Act of that year. These and other measures resulted in Affirmative Action, whereby women and minorities can sue potential and current employers for acts of discrimination, including unequal pay or unequal opportunities for advancement. One result of this movement was that the share of men in management positions declined from 86 percent in 1950 to 61 percent in 2000. Adding professionals to the female labor force reveals that in 2000 72 percent of women were employed in either clerical-sales or college level occupations.[16]

Women continued to be dominant in traditional female occupations such as nurses, librarians, social workers, and teachers throughout the 20th century. In 1910 women amounted to 81 percent of such workers and in 2000 they accounted for 78 percent of those working in these traditionally female occupations. Nevertheless, women's share in the professions rose from 1 percent in 1910 to 20 percent in 2000.[17]

Women made considerable gains in the world of commerce since 1910. This is most evident in the areas of banking and credit, where women now hold 69 percent of the positions, up from 10 percent in 1970. Likewise women gained considerable additional participation in the insurance business, from 25 percent in 1970 to 65 percent in 2000. These increases came about because women became more attractive to employers and women found white collar employment more attractive than factory work. This does not mean that women took jobs away from men but rather that the fields in which women became the majority were expanding so fast that there were not enough men to fill these vacancies. All this was buttressed by anti-discrimination legislation and the arrival of the computer and other office equipment that could be operated by women willing to take less pay than demanded by men. As more and more women took these jobs and recommended other women to vacancies, the number of women working in these occupations increased until the office jobs and many professional jobs as well became women's work, or at least were seen as gender neutral.[18]

Rewards

Since 1940, large numbers of women have moved into jobs at one time held only by men. The first of these occupations was clerical work. This was soon followed by real estate, insurance, advertising and investments. Comparing the number of women who were employed in these industries 68 years ago to those now engaged in this work shows a dramatic increase in work opportunities for women over that time span. Nevertheless, inequality in pay continues in 2008.

Evidently, women in managerial jobs earned more than women in factory labor but always less than men. This economic inequality is largely covered up by the use of job titles such as bank manager or vice president. Katz,

Stern and Fader show that the inequality of earnings for women and men is not related to a lack of education inasmuch as women earned less than men at every educational level and even when women had more education than men. Clearly, bigotry is a principal factor in producing this discrepancy. This inequality is gradually lessening as indicated by the difference in the ratio of women's earnings to men's by birth cohort. Women born between 1946 and 1955 earned 62 percent of men's earnings in 2000. Those born two generations later earned 82 percent of men's earnings in 2000. In sum, the rewards of work remain less for women than for men, even at the beginning of the 21st century.

Differentiation

Katz et al. report that by 2000 women's occupations ranged from the top of the income scale to the bottom. This therefore led to social stratification, which in the United States is mainly based on occupation.

Accordingly, physicians outrank all other American occupations in achieving a prestige score of 86, followed by lawyers with a score of 75 and professors with a score of 74. As we have seen, one-third of all American physicians and one-third of all American lawyers are women. Women have made similar gains in the academic world, so that the prestige of women has risen with their entrance into these professions. Women have entered into pharmacy in large numbers. That profession ranks eleventh among 70 occupations included in the National Opinion Research Council's assessment of occupational prestige. Jobs which are typically female do not rate very high on the NORC prestige scale Social workers, librarians, dental hygienists and secretaries cannot compete with architects, dentists and psychologists, all of whom are given considerable social honor by the American public. As these occupations become less and less male dominated, women attain the satisfaction of a high standing and solid prestige in American life.[19]

Banking is the best example of an industry which feminized during the 20th century. In 1910, 95 percent of bank employees were men. By 1960 the majority of bank employees were women, although they were then mainly clerks. By 1980, 39 percent of bank managers were women, and in 2000, 55 percent of bank mangers were women. In 2005, male managers were earning somewhat more than $39,000 while women earned only $36,000. In finance and insurance, men earned a median income of $66,241 in 2005; women earned only $36,692 in that occupation in that year.[20]

American Women in Two World Wars

During the short participation of the United States in the First World War (1917–1918) and the much longer involvement of the U.S. in the Second World War (1941–1945) American women were recruited to work in factories and offices as substitutes for men who were employed in the service. Before 1917 hardly any middle or upper class women worked outside the home. It was considered shameful for women in these social strata to be gainfully employed. It was generally believed that only the poorer classes employed women outside the home because those women had no choice but to augment their husband's minimal income. The First World War changed this somewhat and the Second World War changed this a great deal.

These changes were that working women who had their own income increased their economic and political bargaining power. They demanded the vote and in 1920 they did vote for president of the United States for the first time. Second, women enlarged their vocational opportunities as they could now point to work experience as a basis for gaining a foothold on better work. Third, women improved their freedom to decide their sex lives, both within and outside of marriage, with the consequence that all of these changes altered the family life of Americans forever.

From the end of the First World War in 1918 until the beginning of the Second World War in 1939 American women lost almost all the gains they had made during the brief war interlude since 1917 and 1918. Women continued to work in all female occupations such as nursing, social work, office work, and teaching, which were gender segregated and paid low wages. Women also entered into a good deal of volunteer work or club activities such as the League of Women Voters and the Parent-Teacher Association.[21]

During the economic boom years just prior to the stock market crash of 1929 some American women gained a minor liberation from traditional sex roles, which confined female sexual expression to marriage alone. This liberation did not last long although the Second World War gave women some economic freedom and therefore allowed them a somewhat more relaxed approach to female sexuality. However, the years from 1945 to the middle of the '60s locked women into the same straitjacket which had always been their role before the voting rights of women were recognized in 1920.

During the Second World War, and particularly after the Japanese attack on Pearl Harbor (December 7, 1941), a large contingent of women assumed industrial work and performed as well as men had done prior to the war. In addition, they worked for less than men. Therefore it is surprising that directly after the war women relinquished their just gained advantages and returned to traditional female employment and to the role of housewife.

During the Second World War approximately 12.5 million men were enrolled in the U.S. armed forces. Therefore the government recruited women with such patriotic slogans as, "What job is mine on the Victory line?" The slogan was aimed at middle class housewives who were not working already. Since women in the working class were employed even before the war, the middle class housewife was the most probable source of recruitment for war work. It was of course assumed that these women would be more than glad to relinquish their income to men once men returned from the war.[22]

This theory was upset by reality. In the first place, 61 percent of women who worked in well paid industrial jobs during the war had already been working in poorly paid jobs before the war. These women saw an opportunity to earn more money and learn new skills. Seventeen percent of those women who worked in war production plants during World War II had been students or were unemployed looking for work or were too young to work before the war. That left 22 percent who had been housewives.[23]

After the war more than 80 percent of women who worked in industrial plants during the war wanted to remain on the job. This was also true of 58 percent of housewives who had never worked outside the home before the war. Nevertheless, employers dismissed almost all the women who had worked in industrial plants during the war as soon as men returned to claim their old jobs. These layoffs of women were not produced by any failure of women's efficiency. In fact, a survey taken at the Ford Motor Co. in 1943 showed that women out-produced men and another study of 174 firms in New York concluded that women's productive efficiency was the same as or better than that of men.[24]

Nevertheless, employers as well as labor unions wanted to eliminate female employees from union organized work. While the unions were committed to organizing new workers at all times, this did not include women. Unions viewed industrial jobs as male bastions whose aim was to preserve the family wage. Men were viewed as earners and women as spenders. Furthermore, masculinity was defined by the tough job men were doing, so that the entrance of women into these jobs appeared as an insult to that masculinity to many men. Therefore, the recruitment of women into so many men's jobs during the Second World War challenged these assumptions, so that men were anxious to rid themselves of female competition directly after the end of the war in 1945.[25]

This anxiety to keep women at home while also seeking to increase the power of unions by increasing their membership created a dilemma which unions sought to resolve by pretending that women who worked were forced to work because men's wages were too small to support the post-war family adequately. This fiction permitted men to continue the myth of male domination and female dependency. The facts were that directly after the Second World War prices rose faster than wages and women needed to work in order to maintain the standard of living demanded by their families. This appeared like an assault on masculinity but could not be avoided.

American Women in the 1950s and 1960s

The decade of the 1950s exhibited the first stirrings of female independence in the United States. Divorce, widowhood and the decision to remain single led a minority of women to resist the common belief that family life was American and that the single lifestyle was suspicious and unpatriotic. Because the nuclear family was believed to be the only decent way to live, the few women who decided otherwise were viewed as outsiders and a direct threat to the security offered by the family and the dominance of men. Single women proved that it was possible to live without male protection. This rebellious attitude was bitterly resented by established women and led to such attacks on the single woman's lifestyle as an article in *Harper's Bazaar* called "Live Alone and Loath It."[26]

In the 1950s young women were taught female subservience to men and to be interested in domesticity, which consisted of making a man feel good through her cooking skills, sewing ability, housekeeping and willingness to listen to all male complaints. Single women were therefore viewed as incomplete and annoying. The happiness of men was viewed as more important than that of women, whose sole purpose in this world was viewed as the support of men viewed as a master. This advice was given by the famous actress Marlene Dietrich in *The Ladies' Home Journal*.[27]

Married women were viewed as models of virtue in the 1950's but single women were assumed to be lesbians or loose morally. It was widely believed that single women lured married men away from their family responsibilities and that single women were irresponsible infants.[28]

Even now, in the 21st century, single women are still stigmatized, although that stigma is not nearly as demeaning and debilitating as was true in the 1950s.

The 1950s view of women as supporters of men without any standing of their own ended when in 1961 President Kennedy appointed the Presidential Commission on the Status of Women. That commission precipitated the founding of the National Organization for Women, promoted the Equal Rights Amendment and gave inspiration to Betty Friedan's revolutionary book *The Feminine Mystique*.

The Commission on the Status of Women was formed with Mrs. Eleanor Roosevelt as chair. The commission of twenty-six leaders included women and men of all races and religions such as Arthur Goldberg, the secretary of Labor; Abraham Ribicoff, secretary of Health, Education and Welfare; and Ms. Dorothy Height, president of the National Council of Negro Women as well as the executive director of the National Council of Catholic Women. Absent were representatives of the ordinary woman who worked in a factory or served as housewife.[29]

The commission issued its report after a 22 months study on October 12, 1963. The principal recommendations of the commission were that women seek higher elective and appointed offices; that more women gain a college education, that the law force employers to pay an equal wage for equal work; that paid maternity leave be instituted; and that child care be supported for working women.[30]

These recommendations were converted into law when the Civil Rights Act of 1964 included non-discrimination on the grounds of sex in Section 703. That was the first time in American history that a law existed giving women equal rights with men.[31]

Subsequently, a number of the members of the Commission on the Status of American Women founded the National Organization for Women. This organization sought to create a private non-government pressure group similar to the National Association for the Advancement of Colored People, as it was thought that the U.S. government would not act on behalf of women unless pressured to do so by citizens' action. The principal effort by the National Organization for Women has been to pass the Equal Rights Amendment to the U.S. Constitution, which was first proposed in 1923 but was never ratified by a sufficient number of states. On March 27, 2007, the Equal Rights Amendment was reintroduced into both the House of Representatives and the U.S. Senate. Since passage depends not only on congressional action but also on the agreement of two-thirds of all state legislatures the outcome of this effort is by no means certain. Thirty-five states have ratified the amendments as proposed in 1923 and again in 1973. While earlier attempts to bring about the ratification of the amendment by 38 states was dependent on a seven year deadline imposed by Congress, no such deadline was included in the 2007 proposal.[32]

The Natural Superiority of Women and The Feminine Mystique

In 1952, Ashley Montagu (Israel Ehrenberg) published *The Natural Superiority of Women*. The book was published in five editions through 1999, the year Ehrenberg-Montagu died. At its inception the book was given scant attention outside the academic world because it did not fit into the popular assumptions concerning sex and gender at that time.

Ehrenberg-Montagu begins by pointing to the centuries old male argument that men must be superior to women because men are larger, have more muscle, more height and a larger brain. He calls this the "might makes right" argument. Yet, Ehrenberg-Montagu argues that women have a more powerful immunological system than men, which gives them more protection against illness, shock and starvation. He further shows that the woman's smaller brain has more neurons in the corpus callosum, resulting in better coordination between the hemispheres, therefore allowing women to think more soundly. Women have more stamina than men and live longer and "stand the test of time" better than men. Women, says Ehrenberg-Montagu, are the true carriers of humanity, as seen in the love of a mother for her child.[33]

While *The Natural Superiority of Women* was hardly noticed in the popular media, the opposite was true of *The Feminine Mystique* by Betty Friedan. Not since Harriet Beecher Stowe wrote *Uncle Tom's Cabin* in 1852 has a book had so profound an influence on any American social movement. *The Feminine Mystique* was published in 1963 and almost at once sold one million copies. The reason for this astounding success was and is that Friedan identified and labeled "the problem that has no name," the condition of women in the 1950s. This problem, said Friedan, was that women were told and believed that their existence is limited to the role of spouse, mother and housewife without any chance of ever gaining any other role. Evidently only single women willing to remain in that state were able to express their needs and wishes without having to worry about the approval of men. The vast majority of single girls, however, were limited to attracting a man, getting married, having children and pleasing the husband forthwith. Wives were told to bolster their husbands' careers but not their own.

Betty Goldstein had graduated from Smith College in 1942 and married Carl Friedman in 1947. He dropped the m from his name and it became Friedan. She divorced Friedan in 1969. In 1957 Betty Friedan attended the 15th reunion of her Smith College class and discovered that many of her classmates were as dissatisfied with their housewife roles as she was. She administered a questionnaire to her classmates and used it as the basis of her book. The book describes how magazines devoted to female readers had no contents concerning ideas, politics or anything not related to homemaking or marriage. In short, Friedan found that women had to give up their identity and draw all satisfaction from the man's identity. The media portrayed women as "The Happy Housewife Heroine."[34]

In 1966 Friedan went on to become the first president of the National Organization for Women, which had a membership of 500,000 in 2007.

The Sexual Revolution

When Alfred Kinsey published *Sexual Behavior in the Human Male* in 1948 his book was viewed with alarm by the mid-century puritans.[35] Then, the zoologist Kinsey published *Sexual Behavior in the Human Female* in 1953 and continued the assault on "know nothing" sexual beliefs begun by Sigmund Freud a half century earlier.[36]

Together, these books became known as "The Kinsey Report." These studies were the product of numerous interviews by Kinsey and his associates and showed that the popular belief that sex was commonly conducted only by married people and that women had no sexual interests other than procreation were false. For example, Kinsey showed that 92 percent of men and 62 percent of women had masturbated and that 68 percent of males and 50 percent of females had engaged in premarital sex. Such findings flew into the face of true believers who knew that masturbation causes blindness. Yet, where were all the blind people?

Indeed, Kinsey's studies were limited to white, middle class, college educated Americans. Nevertheless, the studies were of great importance because they were conducted by highly trained interviewers using a face-to-face method. The studies aroused the anger of the Family Research Council, a group devoted to the suppression of sexual behavior *ipso facto,* and led to all kinds of *ad hominem* denunciations. Nevertheless, it has endured as the foundation of the scientific study of sex in America.

Subsequently, numerous sexologists made considerable progress in studying human sexuality. Notable among these is Vern Bullough whose 1973 book, *The Subordinate Sex,* was a direct attack on the inequality of women. Bullough also wrote *Sexual Variance in Society and History, Homosexuality: A History,* and *Contraception Today,* as well as books on prostitution and other sexual practices. By the end of the 20th century a veritable flood of books and articles on sex became commonplace in America, so that sex education was hardly questioned and college courses on the psychology of sex, sexual behavior, the sociology of sex and gender, etc., became standard offerings in American institutions of higher education.

The sexual revolution affected a good deal more than just academics. As birth control methods improved and attitudes towards sex became more liberal, the number of single mothers increased as well. In 1970 there were 3 million single mothers in the U.S. That increased to 10 million by 2000 and beyond. The proportion of births to unmarried women increased from 34 percent in 2002 to 35 percent in 2003. In 1980, only 18 percent of infants were born to unmarried mothers but the number reached 33 percent in 1994. This may mean that many Americans did not use birth control or that it failed its users.[37]

The sexual revolution also changed the generally held view that male sex is dominated by lust and that for women sex is a lesser interest and an appendage to romance. Prior to that revolution girls were forced to pretend that they had no sexual interests. Those who admitted to such interests were viewed as prostitutes. After the sexual revolution of the 1960s women were more free to discuss their own sexual needs, so that premarital sex, unmarried cohabitation, extramarital affairs, homosexuality and pornography became common topics of conversation and discussion. In short, less rigidity concerning sex has been in vogue since 1980 and will continue to be ordinary practice for the foreseeable future. While there was a time when sex was a taboo topic, this is no longer the case. Now money is off limits, as no one will willingly reveal the contents of his bank account.[38]

Much of the change in attitudes toward sex is due to the pill. Prior to the pill and its success, single unmarried women were viewed as dull old maids. This view has changed to viewing single women as independent, sexy and capable of defending themselves against marauding men. The popular TV series *Sex and the City* was a reflection of this view. The sexual revolution therefore deviated from the traditional belief that sex is only for reproduction to the view that sex for the sake of sex is acceptable and even desirable.

This means that the invention of the pill was the principal catalyst for the gender revolution of the forty years beginning in the 1960s, as visible by the fact that in 1960 only 18.4 percent of professionals were women and that by 1998, 36.4 percent were women. The Food and Drug Administration approved the pill in 1960. That resulted in changes in the law which gave minors more rights and lowered the age at which social maturity is attained from 21 years to 18. This came about when the 26th Amendment to the Constitution was adopted in 1971. The pill also increased the age at first marriage because it allowed women to gain an education without having to choose between celibacy or unwanted pregnancies. That this choice was no longer necessary became evident when colleges, beginning in 1971, distributed contraceptives to female students. No doubt abortion, legalized in 1973, also contributed to later marriage, although it is by no means as powerful a catalyst for delayed marriage as the pill.[39]

Because social movements engender a backlash it is not surprising that this also affected the sexual revolution, which came to an end in the 1970s. This does not mean that the gains achieved since the 1960s were abolished. Many of the changes in sexual behavior became permanent. However, the reactions to some of these changes were negative. A consensus developed that sex with children is unacceptable and that those who engage in this are dangerous criminals. A sex police was developed in the United States, mainly directed at sexual violence, and including pornography, which has expanded from magazines for men to similar magazines for women such as *Playgirl*.[40]

Among the young, the sexual revolution has led to a decline in the traditional dating process to give way to hooking up, which describes a short run sexual experience dependent on making contacts through the Internet. Consequently, most American adolescents report at least one sexual experience before graduating from high school.[41]

There are therefore many adolescents who avoid dating because they do not want to get involved in a long term relationship. They view those who date as losers and hooking up as a winning strategy. Sexual partners found on the Internet are labeled friends with benefits. The sites used by teenagers to meet such friends are also rating sites because the participants post their pictures and other information which any viewer can then rate on a rating scale.[42]

The Legal Revolution

In 1972, Congress amended the Civil Rights Act of 1964. Included in that amendment was Title IX, which refers to students and employees of educational institutions. This section of the amendment reads: "No person in the United States shall, on the basis of sex, be excluded from participation in or be denied the benefits of, or be subject to discrimination under any educational program or activity receiving federal assistance."

Although the law addresses all aspects of education in all schools at all levels, regarding counseling, housing, financial aid, scholarships and numerous other educational services, its greatest impact has been on athletics. The law requires that schools receiving federal funds provide equal opportunity for members of both sexes. This law was augmented with The Equity in Athletics Disclosure Act of 1994 which made it mandatory that colleges and universities spend as much money on women's sports as on men's in the areas of recruitment, scholarships and budgeting. This evidently reduces the contributions a school can make to its football team. As a result there are today 600 more women's teams than men's teams in the National Collegiate Athletics Association.[43]

Although domestic violence is as old as marriage and victimizes women far more than it victimizes men, no federal law protecting women from spousal abuse existed until 1994, when Congress passed changes to the Gun Control Act and the Violence Against Women Act. Seeking to relieve the overburdened state courts concerning domestic violence, the law now prohibited some domestic abusers from possessing guns in certain situations. Although the majority of domestic violence cases are still handled by state and local jurisdictions, the Federal Gun Control Act of 1996 made it a felony to cross state lines in order to injure or stalk or harass an intimate partner. This also applies to Indian territory. Furthermore, someone subject to a protection order or someone convicted of a domestic violence crime may not possess firearms. The law also provides a domestic violence hot line and the right for a victim to confer with a government attorney.[44]

The reason these laws finally protected women and some men and children from domestic abuse may be understood by reviewing the literature concerning such violence. For example, a 1996 study of all 50 states and the District of Columbia reveals that 25 percent of women and 7.6 percent of men were raped or physically assaulted by a spouse, date or cohabiting partner in a lifetime. In any one year, 1.3 million women and 835,000 men are physically assaulted by an intimate partner. In 2001 intimate partner violence made up 20 percent of all violence against women, excluding homicide. In 2000, 1,247 women were killed by an intimate partner. Forty-nine percent of the 3.5 million crimes committed against family members were against spouses. Males were 83 percent of spouse murderers.[45]

Additional crimes against women include stalking and various forms of harassment. These offenses are largely reduced by the issuance of protection orders by the courts. According to James Placek, 86 percent of women who received a protection order found that the abuse stopped or was greatly reduced.[46]

Rape shield laws are another effort to protect women. These laws are intended to defeat the efforts of a defense attorney to put the rape victim on trial by claiming that the rape victim consented to the activity. Defense attorneys seek to discredit the victim by insinuating that the victim has a bad reputation on the grounds of having had sexual contacts with various men. The mental condition of the victim is also an issue defense attorneys like to raise. By embarrassing the victims and denouncing them publicly, defenders of rapists have succeeded in reducing rape accusations to 60 percent of their actual occurrence.[47]

To counteract these disadvantages for rape victims, Michigan created the crime of criminal sexual conduct in 1975. This law replaced the traditional rape laws. The law distinguished four degrees of sexual assault, depending on the amount of force used, the infliction of injury and the mental condition and age of the offender. It is further proposed that rape should be covered by the general assault laws so that the emphasis in a court would be on the offender, not his female victim. In states where rape shield laws are in use, the victim is no longer required to reveal her sexual history. Corroboration is no longer required in states with rape shield laws and some states have voided the ancient law exempting husbands from the charge of rape by the wife.[48]

There are numerous other state laws pertaining to the rights of women. These laws and regulations are mostly state labor laws and pertain in the main to work related issues such as maternity leave, equal pay provisions and the physical conditions of employment.

The Political Revolution

On August 18, 1920, the sixty-sixth Congress of the United States ratified the 19th Amendment to the Constitution. That amendment resolved that "the right of citizens of the United States to vote shall not be denied or abridged by the United States or by any State on account of sex."

This amendment finally recognized women as independent voters not dependent on their husbands for their political opinions. It was long in coming. In fact, it took 131 years for Congress to give women the right to vote since the first Congress met in 1789. Since then, women have slowly gained a foothold in American politics.

In 2007, there were 86 women in the U.S. Congress. Of these, seventy were members of the House. As late as 1915 there had never been a woman in Congress. Then, in 1916 there was one woman in the House. She was the first woman to be elected to the House of Representatives. Her name was Jeanette Rankin. A Republican, she was elected from Montana in 1916 on a platform of staying out of the First World War. She also campaigned for prohibition of alcohol, against child labor and in favor of universal women's suffrage. She was elected again in 1940 after an absence of 22 years from the House, as she was not re-elected in 1918. She was the only member of the House to vote against the declaration of war against the Japanese in 1941 and was therefore not re-elected in 1942.

In 2008 there are 16 women U.S. senators. Yet, it wasn't until November 21, 1922, that Rebecca Latimer Ferguson of Georgia became the first woman to serve in the United States Senate. She had been appointed to fill a vacancy and stayed in the Senate only 24 hours. The first woman to be elected to the U.S. Senate was Hattie Wyatt Caraway. A Democrat, she was also appointed to serve the vacancy caused by the death of her husband in 1931. In 1932 she was elected on her own and continued in the Senate after she was re-elected in 1938. In 1944 she was defeated by J. William Fulbright. Thereafter, Franklin Roosevelt appointed her to a number of offices.

Of the 16 female U.S. senators in Congress in 2008, the career of Senator Hillary Rodham Clinton is indeed unusual. She is the only first lady to run for an elected office. As first lady in her husband's presidency she took an active part in the administration, with particular reference to health care. A Democrat, she was elected in 2000 as a senator from New York. She therefore became the first New York woman ever elected senator. She was re-elected in 2006. In 2007 she announced her candidacy for the presidency of the United States.

In 2007 nine women served as governors of American states. Nineteen twenty-four was the year in which two women reached the position of state governor. The first governor of an American state was Nellie Tayloe (not Taylor) Ross. She was elected in a special election following her husband's death. She ran on the promise that she would carry out her husband's policies. She served only two years and was defeated in an effort to gain re-election.

Sixteen days later, Miriam Amanda "Ma" Ferguson became the first woman governor of Texas and the second woman ever to be governor of an American state. In 1924 her husband, James Ferguson, failed to get his name on the ballot after being impeached during his second administration as governor. Thereupon Mrs. Ferguson announced her candidacy for the office of governor. Accused of all kinds of fraud and kickback schemes, she did not run for a second term in 1928 but was re-elected in 1932. Defeated in an effort to regain the governor's job in 1940 she nevertheless received more than 100,000 votes that year.[49]

Of the nine women who served as governors in 2007, Linda Lingle of Hawaii is indeed remarkable. She is the first Republican elected governor in forty years. She is the only Jewish governor Hawaii has elected and she is the only woman ever elected to that position. She had been mayor of Maui County and council member as well as chair of the Hawaii Republican Party before becoming governor. In each of these elections Lingle succeeded despite predictions that she had no chance of winning. Her great popularity came about because she succeeded in creating a state surplus of $750 million in her first term as governor after inheriting a deficit of $250 million. She won a second term in 2006 with 63 percent of the vote to 35 percent for the Democratic candidate.

In 2007, seventy-seven women held statewide elective executive positions across the country. This constituted 24 percent of the 315 available positions. Likewise, 24 percent of all state legislative positions were held by women in 2007, meaning that the number of women in state legislatures more than quintupled since 1971.[50]

Some Consequences of the Feminization of America

Because the education of mothers has increased considerably since the 1960s, the median age of educated American mothers rose from 26 years in 1970 to 32 in 2000. This was not true of women with lesser educational attainment. The median age of mothers on the bottom of the socio-economic scale is 23 and has remained there for forty years.[51]

Another consequence of the increase in female employment has been the increase in family resources, which mainly benefited children of educated mothers. Both material goods and social advantages are more available to children and adults in two income families, particularly among those whose women earn the incomes associated with the professions. While only 12 percent of educated mothers of small children worked outside the home in the 1960s, this rose to 18 percent in 1970 and to 65 percent in 2000. Therefore, the gap between the upper middle class and the poor has widened considerably because of the rise in female education and employment.[52]

A further consequence of increased education by American women is that educated women are more likely to marry and are less likely to divorce than is true of those with little education. Indeed, divorce increased for all women from 1960 to 1980. Thereafter, divorce rates fell among the college educated while these rates continued to rise among lesser educated women. This contradicts the popular belief that economically independent women choose to be single and choose to be single mothers.[53]

We have already seen that feminism provided women with an identity other than wife and mother and therefore promoted egalitarian marriages, and, as we shall see, a reversal of power in some families from patriarchy to matriarchy. All this is of course dependent on new birth control technology in the form of the pill. This is an oral contraceptive which is taken every day. It stops ovulation, thickens the cervical mucus, and releases hormones which prevent fertilization. This, together with the legalization of abortion, has given women much greater control over fertility, leading eventually to the increase in female entrance into professional schools.

Yet another consequence of female emancipation from the kitchen is the ever increasing failure of men to support their children. There are evidently a good number of fathers who can shirk their responsibilities regarding out-of-wedlock children because they believe that mothers can support such children themselves. Furthermore, the pill has allowed women to have sex with men who did not promise marriage, which of course lowered the bargaining power of women who wanted marriage and children. In addition, public opinion no longer rejects single mothers and their children, giving single mothers total control over children in the absence of so many fathers.[54]

Beginning with the 1970s, income inequality between those with a college education and those without became an incentive for women and men to succeed in higher education. The income for college educated men exceeded high school educated men by about a third by the 1980s. Among women the increase was even greater. As more and more women entered the labor force with a college education, the wage gap between the genders decreased as the prospects for men without a degree worsened. That became true because educated women now found educated men who gave them the emotional support needed to promote their career and help with child rearing as well.[55]

A further result of the entrance of women into higher education and the professions has been the proliferation of women's studies at American universities. Such studies did not exist in 1967, while at the beginning of the 21st century hundreds of colleges teach courses in women's studies and many give degrees in this area. For example, the University of Wisconsin at Madison has promoted a women's study curriculum since 1977, including courses in U.S. women's history, European women's history and, more recently, courses in Latin American women's history and the history of African American women. Thirteen courses regarding women are taught each year at the University of Wisconsin at Madison.[56]

The University of Arizona announced in 2007 that the board of regents has approved a new Ph.D. program in women's studies. The curriculum includes women's health, sexuality, race, nationality, history, sociology, film, literature and writings of women. There are, in addition, fourteen other universities in this country who confer doctorates in women's studies.[57]

The Criminality of Women

There are those who believe that the criminality of women has increased because women have achieved so much in the quarter century since 1980. Inspection of the Uniform Crime Reports as issued by the F.B.I. reveals that the overall crime rate for women for the decade 1996–2005 rose by 7.4 percent. Meanwhile the crime rate for men fell by 7.6 percent during the same ten year period. It should be understood that men commit far more offenses than women as indicated by the size of the group charged with 31 different offenses as reported by the Department of Justice. Thus, 6,261,672 men were charged during 2006. In that same year only 361,643 women were so charged. Among men, embezzlement increased by 7.8 percent, drug violations increased by 21 percent and all other offenses increased by 6 percent in the ten year period from 1996 to 2005. Among women embezzlement increased by 33 percent and the possession and receiving of stolen goods increased by 19.3 percent. Even aggravated assault, which saw a male decrease of 14 percent, increased among women by 5.4 percent. Other increases in crimes by women were: burglary, 5.4. percent; motor vehicle theft, 5.2 percent; violent crime, 4.4 percent; other assaults, 15.4 percent; forgery and counterfeiting, 3.0 percent; vandalism, 10.2 percent and sex offenses, 2.6 percent.[58]

A number of explanations for the criminality of women have been promoted for over a century. Currently, the increase in female criminality is attributed to the rise in female involvement in the economic and social world. The argument here is that the greater participation of women in the financial activities of the American community allows women the same opportunities to steal and embezzle as was true of men. More women are now subject to the strain and anxiety which men have experienced for centuries and which fuel the temptation to use illegal means to succeed. Women are now far more often in positions of trust than was true heretofore and therefore have opportunities not available to them prior to the ascent of women in the 21st century. The opportunity to be an insider trader on the stock market requires that one be on the inside like Martha Stewart, who was convicted of charges related to that offense and imprisoned in 2005. These views are mainly supported by the criminologists Freda Adler and Rita Simon who hold that the increase in female crime is limited to white collar crime. However, an inspection of F.B.I. statistics for the decade ending in 2006 indicates that aggravated assault, burglary, violent crime, other assaults, offenses against the family and children and drug offenses have also risen considerably among women in those years.[59]

It is notable that recently a number of adult women have been convicted of sexual assault because they became sexually active with underage boys. Inspection of the Lexis-Nexis Web site reveals that in 2006 alone, there were 15 reports in American newspapers concerning sexual encounters between adult women and young boys. Included are Amy Burke, who, at age 36, was charged with aggravated sexual assault for having sex with an underage boy in the school in which she, a married mother, was teaching.[60]

Deanna Bobo, a Little Rock, Arkansas, teacher, was convicted on two counts of sexual assault for having sex with a student on several occasions, both in her car and in his home.[61]

Rebecca Poole, a married drama teacher, was convicted of having sex with a 15-year-old student in her husband's Porsche car at least six times,[62] and Melinda DeLuca, 30, of Salt Lake City, described as "a married church going woman" with two daughters, was charged with having sex with a 16-year-old male student at the school in which she taught.[63]

These and a long list of other such female sexual offenders indicate that sexual behavior not commonly approved among middle class moralists is far from unusual among women as well as men and that the erstwhile absence of such known conduct is best explained by the general repression imposed on women prior to the end of the twentieth century. It should also be noted that American society has never been able to resolve the sexual issue balanced between the demands of puritans for suppression and abstinence and the demands of the pornography industry for indulgence and participation. This issue is discussed as length by Vance Packard in his *The Sexual Wilderness*.[64]

Summary

Nineteenth century American women were expected to live by Victorian views of sex and marriage, as schools were segregated by gender. The two world wars demonstrated that women could work efficiently in industrial production, leading to a more equal distribution, differentiation and reward system for women in the employment market. The ascent of women into a better economic position than was previously available was also helped by law and by the publication of books favoring women's emancipation. Consequently women entered higher education in greater numbers, achieved professional standing and benefited from gaining political power. These changes had repercussions in all American social institutions, including the family, which is the topic of our next chapter.

CHAPTER 3

The Families of Women Achievers

Achievement in education and subsequently in science and in the humanities is mainly dependent on the family in which we are raised. Therefore, the achievement of American women at the end of the twentieth century and the beginning of the 21st century is largely the product of the role of women in the American family, which has changed considerably since the beginning of the 20th century. Then, almost all American families were a patriarchy, because that type of arrangement had been traditional for centuries among Europeans and their descendants in this country. Indeed, the black family was different then and now because the black family has a different history than the European American family. Therefore, as we shall see, the black family was and is more often female governed than was true of the European American family.

Because Europe includes numerous cultures, all families of European origin did not treat women the same. Depending on the ethnic group from which a family came, the position of women in the American family at the beginning of the 21st century differs, so that we cannot speak of one American family but of many kinds of American families.

Sexual differences guarantee differences of social standing between women and men. Mothers are not fathers or vice versa so that each sex has experiences which the other cannot share. These differences have given rise to cultural inventions "which have been used to prevent women from undertaking many things of which they are perfectly capable."[1]

Because ethnic differences largely dictate the role women play in their families, I shall undertake to discuss several American families which represent the status of women in each of these ethnic groups. We shall begin with the Anglo woman because women descendants of English speaking immigrants have achieved an almost total role reversal in the century ending in 2008.

The English Woman in America

There is a considerable literature describing the lives of women in colonial America. Among those who contributed to this literature is Abigail Adams, the wife of John Adams, who became the second president of the United States. Because John Adams was seldom home during the ten years of the Revolutionary War, a good deal of correspondence between Abigail and John Adams is available and reflects the position of women in early America.

Undoubtedly, that position was that of a supporter subordinate to men, a position as ancient as mankind itself and reinforced by the Puritan tradition of New England since the early 17th century.[2]

When Anne Hutchinson was expelled from the Massachusetts Bay Colony in 1632 for preaching doctrines which seemed to undermine male authority, the position of women in the Puritan community was made most clear and served as a warning to women everywhere not to rebel against men. The New Testament had already made this most certain, as can be seen in 1 Corinthians 7:9; 11:3 and 14:34, which tells us that women should not speak in church and should ask their husbands at home to answer any questions they might have.[3]

Therefore the ascendancy of American women in the 21st century constitutes a revolutionary role reversal which women of an earlier age could not have imagined and which men would never have allowed.

In light of the Protestant ethic which the German scholar Max Weber has discussed in his widely read essay "The Protestant Ethic and the Spirit of Capitalism" ("Die Protestantische Ethik und der Geist des Kapitalismus"), the achievements of American women of Anglican origin needed only to wait for the liberation of women, as already discussed.

Weber's analysis contends that Puritan ethics and ideas have influenced the development of capitalism. Since capitalism is the basis of American civilization and depends on hard work, frugality, ambition and individualism, these traits, promoted by the early settlers of Massachusetts, are still with us and fuel the drive to succeed among men and women of every ethnic origin in America. It is not necessary to be of English descent to be so influenced.[4]

At the beginning of the 21st century 75 percent of the population of the United States was composed of Americans of European descent. Twenty-three percent of U.S. residents in 2006 were descended from English speaking immigrants, however distant. Therefore, a considerable majority of Americans are not related to the 17th century settlers in Virginia and Massachusetts. Nevertheless, the influence of Puritan ideas persists and has been responsible for the achieving society which has made the U.S. the most powerful nation now extant.[5]

Accordingly, we find that once women were given access to higher education and other means of furthering their ambitions, women of all ethnic origins, but particularly those whose early American ancestry gave them first opportunities to enroll in the educational elevator, have included more outstanding successes than can be recorded here.

Among these are Grace Murray Hopper, who defied the common belief that only men can contribute to mathematics by becoming the grandmother of the computer age.

Having received her master's degree in mathematics from Yale University at age 23, she began her teaching career at that same university and then earned a doctorate, also from Yale, in 1934. This was truly unheard of at that time. She then served in the Navy during the Second World War, developing aiming angles for naval guns under various weather conditions. After the war she was associated with Harvard University, where she developed a computer language called COBOL.

Re-instated in the Navy, she became the first woman to hold the rank of rear admiral, where she made yet additional contributions to computer science.

Another example of an outstanding woman achiever in the 20th century was Margaret Mead. Daughter of an economics professor at the University of Pennsylvania, she was immersed in scholarship from an early age. Nevertheless, her father needed considerable persuasion to send her to Barnard College for Women at Columbia University. There she became a student of Franz Boas, who may well be called the father of American anthropology. Boas came to the United States from his native Germany in 1899 to escape discrimination based on his Jewish religion.

Mead was influenced by the new anthropology taught by Boas to her and another exemplary student, Ruth Benedict.

Mead was the first woman anthropologist ever to visit Samoa, where she wrote the most influential book in anthropology, called *Coming of Age in Samoa*. Here she described the adolescence of the Samoans, which differed so much from American adolescence. Unlike adolescence in the United States, Mead found that Samoan adolescence does not involve stress and anxiety. She also describes that the native diet may involve cannibalism, that headhunting was then practiced, that infanticide was common and that the natives would bite lice with their teeth.

There can be little doubt that Margaret Mead was one of the originators of American anthropology. Of course, Mead has her detractors, including Derek Freeman, who wrote a whole book denying Mead's claims.[6]

Mead was a prolific contributor to anthropological literature gained mostly from her hands on field work. Of these, *Sex and Temperament in Three*

Primitive Societies sought to dispel the shroud of secrecy which in her time enveloped the very existence of sex. No doubt she contributed greatly to the alteration of this attitude by the end of the 20th century.

Sally Ride is another woman of great achievement. She became the first American woman to reach outer space in 1983. Ride was preceded in space by two Soviet women. She was a nationally ranked tennis player as well as a physics student, graduating with a Ph.D. from Stanford University.

She joined the National Aeronautics and Space Administration in 1978 and subsequently participated in two missions of *Challenger* in 1983 and 1984. She then taught at Stanford until becoming CEO of her own company in California.

Ride is a member of the National Women's Hall of Fame and has received numerous awards in the area of aeronautics. She is also the author of several children's books concerning space exploration.[7]

Hispanic Women Achievers in the U.S.A.

The contributions of Spanish speaking Americans and those of Hispanic ancestry are so immense that they cannot be reviewed here. Suffice it to say that in the 21st century the impact of women of Hispanic origin is at least as great as that of any other ethnic group. This should not be surprising. Today, 42.7 million Americans can point to Spanish ancestry. That constitutes 14 percent of the U.S. population. Of course, all people of Spanish ancestry are not the same. We have citizens of South American descent, many who came from Mexico and others from the islands of the Caribbean.

There are also numerous Americans whose Spanish ancestors came in the 16th century during the great era of exploration. When Ponce de Leon came to Florida in 1513 he and his men preceded the Pilgrims in Massachusetts by seven years. Texas became Spanish territory in 1519 and at that time included a good deal more land than it does now. Even California, discovered by Juan Cabrillo in 1542, was a Spanish possession before the English speakers got there.

The Spanish who settled in what is now the United States were, as expected, living in a patriarchal society. Women had large numbers of children and their life consisted of what the Germans call "Kinder, Küche und Kirche," i.e., children, kitchen and church.

Together with other Americans, that has largely changed in our Hispanic American families. Here are three examples of outstanding American women of Hispanic origin.

Dolores Huerta was born in 1930. She became a major labor union leader in this country. Together with Cesar Chavez, she founded the United Farm Workers union in 1962. She did this because she had been a teacher and saw the children in her class coming to school hungry and without shoes. Huerta herself has eleven children.

In 1965 Huerta organized a grape strike which showed growers that the union had muscle. This strike led to the first union contract ever in the grape industry and finally gave the near slave agriculture workers a voice.

In 1972 Huerta became the co-chair of the California delegation to the Democratic convention. This gave her enough prominence to put pressure on Congress to give farm workers unemployment insurance, collective bargaining rights and many other rights

The famous folk singer Joan Baez is of Mexican descent. Born in 1941 on Staten Island, New York, she is the daughter of a physics professor.

She began her singing career in the Boston coffeehouses when she attended Boston University. In 1960 she became a recording artist with Vanguard records and then toured with Bob Dylan (Zimmerman) in the 1970s. She was always a civil rights protester and a promoter of non-violence. Joan Baez has one daughter by her ex-husband, David Harris, who made a name for himself by going to jail as a Vietnam War protestor.

Joan Baez is known today for her historical songs and for political songs. She has also recorded country songs and general popular music. She is without doubt a principal supporter of all peace movements and an ardent liberal.

As can be expected, all women of Hispanic origin are not Democrats. Outstanding among Republican women of Hispanic origin is Josefina Carbonell, who was appointed by President George W. Bush as assistant secretary of Health and Human Services in 2001.

Before accepting this sub-cabinet post, Carbonell was the chief executive officer of Little Havana Activities & Nutrition Centers in Florida. She founded this company in 1972 and built it into the largest aging, health and nutrition project in Florida. Her company now operates 21 sites and serves more than 55,000 clients.

Carbonell also established the Pro-Salud Clinics in Florida. These clinics provide primary health care, preventive screening and medication for older adults and their families.

Carbonell has been given numerous national awards for her initiative and work. She holds the Claude Pepper Community Service Award, the Social Security Commissioner's Award, the Miami Herald Award and numerous others.

Carbonell is a graduate of Florida International University and has been a fellow at the Harvard University John F. Kennedy School of Government. Finally, Carbonell is an immigrant. She was born in Cuba.

The Jewish Woman Achiever in America

Prior to the development of the American Jewish community, Jewish women were at all times viewed as inferior and subservient to men. These views were rooted in the Jewish religion and were transmitted from there to other religions derived from Judaism. It is therefore not surprising that the Eastern European Jews who arrived in this country between 1891 and 1924 continued to hold this view.

The first Jews to come to the North American continent came from Recife, Brazil, in 1654, because the Dutch colony there had been invaded by the Portuguese who brought the Inquisition with them. Twenty-three Jews traveled to New Amsterdam that year.[8]

These few Jewish refugees were joined by a few co-religionists from Portugal and Spain during the seventeenth century. Following the dictates of Jewish tradition, the women in these families occupied an inferior place in the families governed by their husbands. This continued to be true when between 1840 and 1880 some 250,000 German Jews migrated to the United States. Like all Germans at that time, patriarchy was common in these families, although German Jewish women were the first to challenge the dominance of men in several spheres of family life.[9]

These challenges did not go unanswered. On January 21, 1864, an article, "God's Curse of Womanhood," appeared in the Jewish journal *The Occident*. This said in part: "Now when Eve was created she was made equal to Adam in every respect, and by no means had he any power or authority over her whatever.... But after she had induced him to break the commandment of God, and he was cursed to labor and to toil for his living, and to support her, to supply all their wants through hard work, *she was also cursed by losing her right to be equal to him ... he shall rule over her.*"[10]

The German Jewish American women who challenged male authority were in part successful. However, their numbers were very small and the impact of their attitudes were hardly felt after the vast number of Eastern European Jews arrived in the United States beginning in 1881. That year marked a major turning point in Jewish history. In March of that year the czar of Russia, Alexander II, was assassinated. His son, Alexander III, then ascended the throne and promptly began a brutal persecution of the Jews in his vast empire. This led to a major migration of Jews to Western Europe and from there to America. By the early 1920s when Congress closed the doors to mass immigration, some 2.5 million Jews had arrived in this country. More Jews and other ethnics would have come in subsequent years but could not do so because the Immigration Act of 1924 severely limited the number of Southern and Eastern Europeans as well as Asians allowed into the country.[11]

The Eastern European Jews had three things in common which set them apart from the Portuguese and German Jews already here. Unlike these earlier arrivals, the eastern Jews spoke Yiddish or Jewish. The Yiddish language is written with Hebrew letters but is not Hebrew any more than English is Latin although written with Roman letters. Yiddish is derived from the same root as a number of German dialects, particularly Bavarian. It is not corrupt German, as is popularly believed, but is a branch on the tree of the Germanic languages.[12]

The second difference between the newly arrived Yiddish speaking Jews and the American Jewish community was that the newcomers were destitute. Poor in the realms of the czar, they were even worse off financially in New York or the other East Coast cities where they first settled.

Thirdly, the Eastern European Jews differed from almost anyone then in America because they lived in a sacred community governed by the Almighty. These families were absolutely patriarchal, even if the mother worked outside the home selling food or commodities from pushcarts.

Children in the sacred family treated parents with utmost respect and old age was seen as beautiful, as age was held in high esteem. In turn, children were held to rigid standards enforced by scoldings and beatings. Fathers had near-deity standing in a culture in which there was a sharp division of labor between the sexes. Some families were extended families including grandparents. In that case the oldest male was the head of the household, but women were never the heads of households.[13]

Among the Yiddish speaking Jews marriage was always Jewish and was viewed as a sacred occasion. Marriage to non–Jews was almost unknown, as neither Jews nor Gentiles were normally willing to promote such a union. Normally, marriages were arranged by the father of the bride and the father of the groom. Undoubtedly, mothers maneuvered behind the scene to get their daughters married, but fathers had the final word as to who married whom. Divorce was possible but so rare that it too was nearly unknown. While a man could divorce his wife easily, a wife could not divorce her husband unless the couple visited four rabbis, and even then she could not be certain that a divorce would be granted.

Jewish family life was dictated by the law which dealt with women entirely from the point of view of a patriarchal society. A woman's role in life consisted of caring for her husband, children and home. All her needs were to be met by her father, husband and son. The novelist Anzia Yezietska wrote in her novel *Bread Givers* in 1925: "Only through a man has a woman an existence. Only through a man can a woman enter heaven."[14]

Women in the Eastern European Jewish family were obliged to prepare all food according to the Jewish dietary laws and were also expected to undergo the ritual baths regularly. In court, however, a woman's word was not accepted.

The sex lives of Eastern European Jewish woman was strictly controlled by the demands of a book called *The Set Table*. This book, also called *The Code of Jewish Law*, contains numerous regulations as to chastity, laws forbidding a man to be alone with a woman, laws pertaining to menstruation and laws pertaining to intercourse.[15]

Women in that society shaved their hair and wore a wig instead. The reason for this procedure was that a woman should only be attractive to her husband and not to other men, who might like the sight of a woman's hair.

This, then, was the heritage of the Eastern European Jews and the position of women in those families.

In the 1920s, some forty years after the beginning of Jewish mass immigration to the United States, the orthodox Jewish community experienced a number of changes which altered Jewish family life and finally led to the emancipation of Jewish women from the strictures of the Eastern European environment.

Although there are a few Jews in America at the beginning of the 21st century who still live a lifestyle resembling the Eastern European orthodoxy, the vast majority of American Jews have left these arrangements and have given Jewish women an entirely different status-role.

This new status-role came about through the secularization of the Jewish family in an America which also promoted secular values at the expense of various religious traditions.

The most dramatic difference between the role of the Jewish woman at the beginning of the 20th century and that same role at the beginning of the 21st century is the high intermarriage rate of Jews with non–Jews, which reached approximately 52 percent in 2006. This of course affects men and women and has become the central issue of concern for Jewish survivalists.[16]

An example of the life of a Jewish woman raised by an Ashkenazi Jewish mother and Irish Catholic father was published by Charlotte Green Honigman Smith in 2003.

According to Jewish law, children of a Jewish mother are Jewish no matter the religion of the father. Hence, Charlotte Smith was taught to observe the Sabbath and Jewish holidays, attend Reform religious school and become bat mitzvah. She also attended a rabbinic school and has worked for synagogues and Jewish organizations.

Smith recites how her father was always a practicing Catholic who took her to mass and other Christian events and who lit a Christmas tree in their home every year but that nonetheless she was always Jewish. Contrary to popular opinion, Charlotte Smith was not conflicted about her religion nor did she become an agnostic. She was Jewish in every way, and as a child knew

3. *The Families of Women Achievers* 55

more about Judaism than most children with two Jewish parents and did not suffer the December dilemma.

Smith next shows how she became a Hebrew school teacher and found that a considerable number of children in her class had one non–Jewish parent and said so openly. This represents a huge change from the days of the immigrant Jews of the early twentieth century. In fact, Smith worked for the Jewish National Fund and found that many of the contributors to the Tree in Israel program included names of recent bat or bar mitzvahs such as Rossini, Yamamoto and Chang.

Her principal argument is this: for forty years Jews have worried about losing Jews in the next generation because of intermarriage. Yet, it has not declined. Therefore, the Jewish community needs to do more to bring the children of interfaith marriage into the community instead of assuming that such children are always lost to Judaism.

Smith also shows that her father, a practicing Catholic, participated in the activism that existed with respect to letting Soviet Jews leave the Soviet Union. The point here is that non–Jews have a conscience and are often willing to be supporters of Jewish causes. She even says, "I believe what I take from my Irish heritage makes me a better Jew."

Smith is not alone. Her situation is now common in the Jewish community and depicts a level of self-determination utterly unknown one hundred years earlier.[17]

Eve Rosenbaum is another contributor to the anthology *Joining the Sisterhood*. Once more we see that a Jewish woman at the beginning of the 21st century enjoys self-determination, unlike her great-grandmother. Rosenbaum is a native of the San Fernando Valley in California. Her family came from New York but Eve learned to ride a horse, act in plays, take music lessons and attend High Holy Day services with other once a year Jews.

But after her grandfather died in New York, her father decided the family would become religious and he meant it. Under the influence of the family, Eve Rosenbaum became determined to become a religious girl in the orthodox sense. Associated with an orthodox community and attending an orthodox school in Los Angeles, Rosenbaum became involved in that absolute atmosphere in which those not born into orthodoxy were singled out as outsiders and a bad influence.

In the course of attending a school called Bais Yaakov (The House of Jacob), Eve Rosenbaum discovered that she could not refrain from watching television and talking to boys. It was expected that she should be unemployed because women should not work (outside the house), and should not go to college but get married directly after graduating from high school. She was also told that she shouldn't do anything without the permission of her husband.

When her family moved to New York, Eve Rosenbaum rebelled against the family. She went to college, lived with other students and lived her life without pretenses.[18]

Then there is Lynne Schreiber. She too describes her Jewish life in *Joining the Sisterhood*. Her experiences are so far removed from the immigrant families of the early twentieth century that her Polish Jewish ancestors would never recognize her family.

She met a Catholic man who knew all about his religion. She, however, could not explain Judaism. The family hung a stocking over the mantle lest the children feel different on December 24 and 25 each year. She has an uncle who became a Buddhist and only one aunt still lights Shabbat candles every week. She calls herself "a product of a fast paced *USA Today* world of sound bites and quick bites."

Lynne Schreiber notes how she was dragged by her parents to boring services on the High Holy Days. Her Catholic boyfriend asked her one day how she could be so Jewish without knowing anything about it. This is again a common Jewish American dilemma. The Jews of the early twentieth century knew only Judaism. They knew nothing else. The Jews of the early twenty-first century know everything else, but not Judaism.

Schreiber shows how she left her Catholic boyfriend and became acquainted with Judaism. She associated with Jews committed to modern Orthodoxy, which rejects contempt for women but emphasizes family life and the meaning of the Scriptures. (Torah). She is an exception among American Jews because she came from secular confusion and found security in her heritage.[19]

The difference between the lives of Jewish women who have come of age at the beginning of the 21st century as compared to the immigrants of the 20th century is evident. Now, self-determination is the rule. Women of all faiths decide for themselves whom to marry and what career they wish to achieve. It is no accident that it was a Jewish woman, Betty Friedan (Friedman), who wrote *The Feminine Mystique,* nor was it an accident that the National Organization of Women was headed by several Jewish women. Jewish women have been in the forefront of those who demanded equal rights, and Jewish women are disproportionately represented among the professionals of this country.

In the family, too, women have become dominant. This is best illustrated by the story of the boy who comes home from school and tells his father that he has been given a part in a school play. "What is the part?" asks the father. "A Jewish husband," answers his son. "Tell the teacher to give you a speaking part," says the father.

No doubt, Jewish women have liberated themselves from the near slavery of a century ago. This also cost the Jewish community. The Jewish birth rate is only 1.4, so that the American Jewish population stands at zero population growth. The intermarriage rate for Jews is 53 percent, so that the chances of Jews having Jewish grandchildren are severely diminished.

There are numerous Jewish women who have become prominent in politics. Among them are the two senators from California, Barbara Boxer and Dianne Feinstein. Jewish women have also risen to prominence in the academic world, in the arts, in business and in almost all major endeavors in this country.

The best example of a Jewish woman scientist who rose to prominence in her field, physics, is the Noble Prize winner in physiology and medicine of 1977, Rosalyn Yalow. Confronted by the usual anti-woman prejudices, she was offered a teaching assistantship at the University of Illinois in 1941 when most men had gone to war. She attributes her employment to the lack of men.

After marrying Aaron Yalow in 1943, she earned a Ph.D. in physics in 1945. Thereafter she became employed as a medical physicist in a Veterans' Hospital in New York City where she developed radioimmunoassays, a technique used to measure circulating insulin and other biological substances. This method has been cited as a revolution in biological and medical research by the Swedish Karolisnka Institute, which awards the yearly Nobel prizes in medicine.

There are millions of Americans who have one or several Jewish ancestors but are not Jewish themselves, like the former candidate for the presidency of the United States, the senator from Massachusetts, John Kerry. In fact, until he became a presidential candidate and his life was scrutinized by the media, Kerry was thought to be of Irish descent.

The Irish American Woman in America

It has been estimated that between 1860 and 1920, 1.2 million Irish women migrated to the United States. Of these, over a million claimed that their occupation was domestic service, so that in 1920 they held 15 percent of all domestic service jobs nationwide. That meant that 60.5 percent of all Irish women then employed were working as domestic servants.[20]

Unlike the Jewish and Italian immigrant women who came to America at the end of the nineteenth and beginning of the 20th century, Irish women who came here were mostly single. This gave them a level of freedom which the young married women in the Jewish community did not have until the end of the 1970s and beyond.

The reason for this rather free existence of Irish women in America was first that in Ireland marriage was generally postponed into the late twenties or early thirties and that many Irish never married at all. Even married Irish women in America saw themselves as autonomous individuals. Evidently, many Irish women did not marry because they wished to preserve their independence.[21]

Hasia Diner, in her book *Erin's Daughters,* shows that the majority of the single Irish women in this country sent home a large amount of money earned in the domestic service or in the garment and textile industries. Furthermore, Irish American women were active in the labor movement in the 20th century and rose to teaching and nursing jobs in the second generation.[22]

We have already seen that marriage was often delayed by Irish men and women because they considered it important to gain a solid economic base before tying the knot. Today, delayed marriages are not as common as they were in the Irish American community in the early twentieth century even as divorce, once utterly prohibited, has gained more acceptance among Americans of Irish heritage. Furthermore, Irish American women and men are much more likely to intermarry with partners not of Irish descent.

Traditionally, Irish American families have been large. Irish American families, like all families, raise their children not only in a manner reflecting their ethnic group, but also treat children differently according to social stratification. Mothers, in Irish American families are almost alone in raising their children, fathers having a minor role. Irish American women are very active in civic affairs, participate in politics, run for office, gain higher education in large numbers and display a great deal of independence just as their domestic servant ancestors did. Brendan Rapple writes: "This will and determination remains one of the most dominant character traits of contemporary Irish-American females." Therefore Irish American women are about the best example of women who have attained high status work such as physician, lawyer, academic or elected official.[23]

The Italian American Woman in America

Between 1901 and 1910 nearly nine million immigrants came to the United States; 3,800,000 of these immigrants came from Italy, making Italians the largest ethnic group to arrive here.[24]

Italian women, like Jewish women, came mostly with their families, although there were some single women who had the courage to migrate far from home to work in American factories, mostly along the eastern seaboard. Unlike Irish immigrant women who were in the main single, Italian women were generally married and therefore did not engage in domestic work outside the home, although this kind of employment was common in Italy.

The majority were either married on arrival or married men of Italian heritage in the U.S. Generally, these women and their families came from a rural background in Italy. They were almost always quite poor, and had little education and many children. In fact, the Italian American birth rate was a good deal higher than that of any ethnic group then in America.

In 1940, married women born in Italy who were then 65–74 years old had 5,439 children per 1,000 women compared to 4,153 per 1,000 foreign born women not from Italy and 3,544 among native born European American women.[25]

Another measure of the extraordinary fertility of Italian American women in the early 20th century is the crude birthrate of Italian American women then living in New York City. Since New York had the highest number of such immigrants at that time, the comparison between the Italian American birthrate of 52.6 per 1,000 population in the Italian American community and the balance of the white population of 23.8 per 1,000 is indeed striking.

One consequence of this high birthrate was that many Italian American girls who grew up in these large families did not go to high school because they had to work at home at piecework jobs until they were old enough to enter garment factory work. Once they were married they left the factories and returned to doing piecework at home while raising children. This lifestyle meant that Italian American women, like many other women in the pre–1960s era, lived lives of drudgery and hard work.[26]

As labor and school laws were enforced more and more in this country and more and more office jobs became available, many Italian American women left the factories and worked in better and safer surroundings, mostly in offices.

By the 1950s Italian women, like so many other immigrants, resisted male control. Their birthrate declined even as more and more girls from Italian families attended high school and some became college students. The result of this increase in education became visible almost at once, when the birthrate among Italian American women fell to less than that of non–Italian women in the general white population.

This was undoubtedly the result of the heavy concentration of Italian Americans in urban areas, particularly New York City. Urban women traditionally bear fewer children than the European peasant women who were the mothers and grandmothers of the Americans of the 20th century.

As the Italian American family became smaller and families were more willing to invest in the education of girls, American women of Italian descent in the third generation exhibited the same enterprise and achievements as other American women.

Outstanding among such women is Ella Tambussi Grasso (1918–1981) who became the first female governor of Connecticut. Unlike some women governors who inherited the job from their husbands, Grasso was elected to this position in her own right after serving in the Connecticut state legislature and as Connecticut secretary of state. Thereafter she was elected to the U.S. Congress and then held the governor's position for two terms.[27]

Geraldine Anne Ferraro is another outstanding example of the success American women of Italian descent have achieved. She is the only woman ever to run for the office of vice-president of the United States. She was asked to do so by the Democratic presidential candidate Walter Mondale. She and Mondale lost the election of 1984 to the Republican candidates.

Before becoming nationally known as the vice-presidential candidate, Ferraro, also known as Mrs. John Zaccaro, had represented the Ninth Congressional District in the House of Representatives from 1979 to 1985.

Ferraro was raised by her seamstress mother, as her father had died when she was only eight years old. An outstanding student, Ferraro finished high school at age 16 and went to college on scholarships. She then worked as a second grade teacher while attending law school at night.

Catherine De Angeles, M.D., became the first woman to edit the *Journal of the American Medical Association* in its 116 year history. She is the vice-dean of the Johns Hopkins University Medical School and the editor of *Archive of Pediatrics and Adolescent Medicine* from 1993 to 2000.

De Angelis was born and raised in a coal mining town in Pennsylvania. Despite a lack of money, she became a nurse and then paid her way through medical school at the University of Pittsburgh by working in a laboratory and a hospital library. Among her subsequent achievements are specialization in pediatrics and faculty appointments at the University of Rochester and a faculty appointment at Johns Hopkins University. She is also the author of 11 books and holds a master of public health degree from Harvard University. She has published over 200 articles in scientific journals focusing mainly on women in medicine.

Her astonishing career is undoubtedly the product of the family support she received, which allowed her to overcome obstacles only an iron willed determination could master.

The African American Family

Because racism is so explosive a word and politically correct speech is imposed on the media and academics as well, it is sometimes difficult to discuss the African American family in an objective manner.

Nevertheless, Kay S. Hymowitz has written extensively on the black family in *The City Journal,* including statistics which some want to deny or blame on the system. Hymowitz wrote in 2005 that nearly 70 percent of black children in America are born to single mothers who are poor and are most likely to pass on their poverty to their children. Hymowitz argues that politicians, the media and educators refused to recognize the work of former senator and Harvard professor Daniel Patrick Moynihan, whose 1965 book *The Negro Family* showed that unmarried motherhood was and is the prime reason for poverty in the black community. Single parent families are so common in the African American family that only a minority of children grow up with their fathers present. This means that generally, African American families are headed by women, so that both boys and girls seldom understand the male role in family life.[28]

Considering these handicaps and difficulties it is indeed astonishing that women raised in these circumstances can nevertheless rise to considerable success.

One such success was Eula McClaney, who was raised a sharecropper in Pike County, Alabama, and became so successful in the California real estate business that she lived in a mansion in Beverly Hills and rode about in a Rolls Royce. She wrote a book about her achievements called *God, I Listened.*[29]

Most of the great black female contributors to American culture made their mark in entertainment and sports. Included are Aretha Franklin, Natalie Cole, Ella Fitzgerald, Patti LaBelle and Tina Turner, all in music; Valerie Hooks, Carla Dunlap, and Jayne Kennedy in sports; Oprah Winfrey, Lena Horne, Whoopi Goldberg (Caryn Johnson) and Debbie Allen in entertainment and Shirley Chisholm, Barbara Jordan and Katie Hall in politics.

The most prominent African American woman at the beginning of the 21st century is Condoleezza Rice. Rice became U.S. secretary of state on January 25, 2005, when she was sworn in by President Bush. Prior to attaining this position of power and influence, Rice was national security advisor to the president. She had been provost at Stanford University for six years. Earlier she was a professor of political science. She is the author of a number of books on foreign policy and she is also a concert pianist.

Rice was born in 1954 at Birmingham, Alabama.[30]

There are of course many others who have managed to deal with the peculiarities of the black family and the disadvantages which poverty and racism put in their way.

The Asian American Woman Achiever

Asia is a large continent containing many nations, languages and cultures. It is therefore unfortunate that many Americans, not acquainted with the multitudes living there, presume that all Asians are of the same origin.

The United States population actually includes people who came from such diverse places as China, Japan, Korea, Taiwan, Vietnam, Cambodia and the Philippines or who are descendants of such immigrants. Furthermore, Hawaii, although an American state, includes citizens of Pacific Island origin, as does Samoa.

Like women in almost all the world, "Asian women have been taught from childhood to be unassuming, and to work quietly and well" without complaining or seeking advancement.[31]

The achievements of Asian American women are as impressive as those of other ethnic origins. Most recently, Angela Warnick Buchdahl, daughter of a Korean Buddhist mother, became a rabbi and is now serving a congregation in Westchester County, New York.

Born in Seoul, South Korea, she moved to Tacoma, Washington, with her family when she was five years old. Her father is Jewish and her mother remains a Buddhist. This led a number of her co-religionists to question her authenticity as a Jew even as she is also marginalized by reason of her racial features.

On a trip to Israel at age 21 she decided to become a rabbi. She attended Hebrew Union College in Cincinnati, Ohio, where she was ordained a rabbi and also a cantor. She then married Jacob Buchdahl and has one son.[32]

Maya Lin was born in the college town of Athens, Ohio, where both her mother and father were members of the Ohio University faculty. Lin's family had fled China in 1949, leaving behind a prominent family known for a number of professional achievements, including architecture.

Maya Lin, an architect, won the national design competition for a Vietnam War veterans memorial in Washington, D.C., when she was only an undergraduate architecture student at Yale University in 1981. She won over 1421 other entries. The memorial was completed in 1982 and became the most visited memorial in the city.

This memorial is unique because the names of all the servicemen who died or are missing in action in Vietnam are inscribed on it. Because the names are recorded in the order in which they died from 1959 through 1975 the memorial produced a sense of history not known in the usual memorial depicting a heroic figure.

Lin has since then designed other memorials, including a sculpture honoring the women of Yale University and her Civil Rights Memorial in Montgomery, Alabama.

She now owns and operates Maya Lin Studios in New York City. She was featured in an award winning documentary, *Maya Lin: A Strong Clear Vision*, in 1994 and in 2000 published a book *Boundaries*. Since then Maya Lin has served on numerous boards including the governing board of her *alma mater* and was elected to the National Women's Hall of Fame in 2005.[33]

Amy Tan is a novelist and story writer. Her book *The Joy Luck Club* was included in the *New York Times* bestseller list for eight months. The paperback rights sold for $1.23 million and the book was translated into seventeen languages. Thereafter she wrote *The Kitchen God's Wife*, again a great success, as were several more novels and children's books.

In an interview in 1996, Tan described the pressure her parents placed on her when she was quite young. They wanted her to be a doctor and a concert pianist. This kind of pressure is by no means uncommon in the Asian American community. Asian American families are known to make considerable demands on their children, both with respect to school achievements and the professional world. The line of communication in these families is one way, i.e., from parents to children. In addition there is an American myth contending that Asians are smarter and harder working than anyone else. This myth adds to the pressures which are responsible for an unusually high suicide rate among American youngsters of Asian descent.

The suicide rate for all minority women in the United States is 3 per 100,000. For women of Asian descent the suicide rate is 5.4 per 100,000. This is about the same as the white suicide rate but evidently far higher than that of other minorities. As the pressure to succeed mounts, suicide increases as well.[34]

Native American Women Achievers

Only 1.5 percent of Americans, or 4.1 million, are Native Americans. Victims of a concerted effort by European Americans to destroy them, their numbers declined immensely during the eighteenth and nineteenth centuries. Reduced to so-called reservations, Native Americans suffered poverty, segregation, ignorance and bigotry, including such myths as the belief that Indians were always drunk, that Indians were savages and that Indians needed to be wards of the U.S. government.[35]

In light of these unusual barriers to success in American culture, it is remarkable that even these obstacles have been overcome by some Native American women. Among these is Dr. Zoe Locklear, dean of the School of Education at the University of North Carolina. A Lumbee-Cheraw, she is a native of North Carolina, where she earned her undergraduate degree and master's of education degrees as well as her Ph.D. from the University of North Carolina. She served as superintendent of schools in one school district and then became associate superintendent of the North Carolina Department of Public Instruction. In addition she has been a member of numerous boards, committees and task forces, and was named outstanding alumnus by the University of North Carolina Alumni Association in 2003.[36]

Wilma Mankiller was born in Tahlequah, the capital of the Cherokee Nation in Oklahoma, in 1945, and became the first woman chief of the Cherokees. The Cherokees were the victims of the infamous Trail of Tears in the 1830s.

In the 1950s Wilma Mankiller and her family were moved to California by the Bureau of Indian Affairs with empty promises of work and housing, none of which materialized. She attended California schools where her name became a cause of ridicule and aggression, a common experience for children who are in any manner different in our schools.

Inspired by other native American activists, Wilma Mankiller divorced her husband and moved back to the Oklahoma reservation, where she worked for the Cherokee Nation writing grant proposals aimed at improving Cherokee life.

Despite a number of physical ailments and a bad injury in an auto accident she succeeded in raising enough money from grant sources to direct the laying of a pipeline which supplied water to a small Cherokee village 16 miles from the water source. It was a major achievement for her. As a consequence of numerous actions on behalf of her people, Mankiller was repeatedly elected chief, leading her to develop industries including an electronics plant, a bank and other construction. She raised millions for the development of a Cherokee job training center.

In 1987, Mankiller succeeded uniting all American Cherokee by calling a conference of Cherokees outside of Oklahoma as well as for the majority living in that state. The conference discovered that there were 175,000 Cherokee in all of the U.S.A. who, under the leadership of Wilma Mankiller, have revived their language, their customs and their heritage.[37]

Maria Tallchief is an internationally known ballerina. She is the first American to dance at the Paris Opera despite the arrogant European prejudice that no foreigner could be a major ballet star.

Unlike many Native Americans, Tallchief came from a wealthy Oklahoma family. Her grandfather, who had negotiated the establishment of the Osage Tribe reservation, became wealthy when oil was discovered on his land, leading to the production of vast sums of money for some residents of the reservation.

At age four, Maria Tallchief began music lessons and dancing lessons in

Oklahoma. Because of her evident talent at a young age, the family moved to Beverly Hills in California, where she became the student of the Russian ballerina Bronislava Nijinska.

Consequently, she became a member of the Ballet Russe at age 15. In 1942, Tallchief married George Ballanchine, who later became the most recognized choreographer in America. Subsequently she danced in Europe and Russia. She then moved to Chicago after divorcing Ballanchine and there she organized her own ballet school called The Chicago City Ballet.

She is without doubt a major achiever in her art form as she continues to teach students in her school the lessons she learned from a lifelong career at the top of her profession.[38]

The Sociology of Achievement

Sociologists have studied achievement for many years. Therefore some distinct attributes of achievers are well known. The earliest studies of achievement were made by psychologists such as Francis Galton, who published *Hereditary Genius* in 1870, followed in 1926 by *The Early Mental Traits of Three Hundred Geniuses* by Catherine Cox. It was not until the 1950s that sociologists began the study of achievement, studies which were continued into the next century.[39]

These studies revealed that achievers generally lived longer than the average population. The reason for this is that achievers were usually the children of well-to-do families who had the resources to send their sons to expensive universities. In the nineteenth century and most of the 20th century there were hardly any public universities in Europe or America, so that only wealthy families could afford a higher education for their offspring. Achievers are more often only children than is true of the general population. The fathers of achievers were mostly men who had a profession or were successful businessmen. Many achievers were students of professors who were also high achievers in various sciences or humanities and a considerable number of the men rated as high achievers married women whose fathers had attained a good deal.[40]

Finally, studies of achieving people have shown that until most recently, achievement of an academic or business kind was limited to men. Because families prior to the end of the 20th century would not invest in the higher education of girls, only a very few women were ever among the great achievers at any time.

For example, a study of German Jewish achievers included the great composer Felix Mendelssohn. Felix, like his sister Fanny, showed great musical talent at a young age. Therefore, his parents sent him to Italy and France to study with well known musicians. Not so his sister. Fanny had an equal ability, but she was told to stay at home because girls should not travel or become prominent. She was nevertheless well known as a pianist in her day but lacked the education which helped Felix become so famous.

The rejection of women prior to the end of the twentieth century was so severe that an effort to find the names of the mothers of great eighteenth and nineteenth century achievers led to identifying only one-third of such mothers. In two-thirds of the names investigated in three encyclopedias and numerous old newspapers the names of only the fathers of achievers were given, even posthumously.[41]

Summary

American women achievers come from many ethnic backgrounds. Included here are a few examples of the variety of ethnic groups living in this country. Among these are those of English speaking descent, those of Hispanic origin, Jewish Americans as well as Irish, Italian, African and Native Americans.

With the exception of the Irish and African Americans, these women came from families which were patriarchies a century ago but have experienced a true role reversal since then. This came about in the course of one hundred years, so that at the outset of the 21st century American women of all ethnic groups are contributing immensely to all American institutions including the military, which we shall review in the next chapter.

CHAPTER 4

Women in the Military and the Police — Storming the Last Bastion

Women as a Fighting Force

The Greek historian Herodotus (484–425 B.C.) would have us believe that a nation of Amazons once lived north of the Black Sea and there fielded an army of women who fought the Greeks in several wars and even helped the Trojans. This myth was perpetuated for centuries and included the belief that the Amazons had only one breast so that they could more easily hold a bow and shoot arrows at their enemies. The stories about Amazons are undoubtedly mythological.

Today (2008) there are indeed female warriors but they are not living at the Black Sea. They live in the United States and participate in the wars of this country. Included in such a war were a number of women soldiers who participated in the combat mission of the U.S. armed services in Iraq. That war was the consequence of an attack upon the World Trade Center in New York, the Pentagon in Washington, D.C., and an aborted attack in 2001.

Those who fought in Iraq and are still there also risk dying there so that we now have women as well as men killed for their country in combat. Among these are Adrianna A. Salem, who was killed on March 4, 2006, as a member of the 3rd Forward Support Battalion in the 3rd Infantry. Emily J.T. Perez also died at Al Kifl, Iraq, on September 2, 2006, as did Tatjana E. Reed, a sergeant in the 66th Transportation Company. She was killed on July 22, 2004.

On January 7, 2007, Elizabeth A. Lonecki died when a "vehicle borne improvised explosive" struck her in Baghdad. Jessica L. Cawvey died in Fallujah, Iraq, because an explosive device detonated near her vehicle on October 4, 2006. First Lieutenant Debra A. Banaszak was another casualty on October 28, 2006, as were many more men and women even as the war continues. Additional female fallen heroes are Capt. Gussie M. Jones, 41; Pfc.

Nichole M. Frye, 19; Pfc. Holly J. McGeogh, 19; Sgt. Tamarra J. Ramos, 24; Sgt. Keicea M. Hines, 27; Capt. Kimberly M. Hampton, 27; Staff Sgt. Kimberly A. Voelz, 27; Sgt. Linda C. Jimenez, 39; Chief Warrant Officer Sharon T. Swartworth, 43; Pfc. Karina S. Lau, 20; Spc. Frances M. Vega, 20, Pfc. Rachel Bosveld, 19; Pfc. Annalaura E. Gutierez, 21; Spc. Alyssa R. Peterson, 27; Sgt. Melissa Valles, 26; Pfc. Lori Ann Piestewa, 23; and others. As of June 2007, seventy of the 3,500 soldiers killed in Iraq were women.[1]

This small list of an ever growing array of dead and wounded soldiers includes young women, almost all in their twenties, who have died for their country.

It would have been hard for those who saw the First World War and even the Second World War to believe that women would be fighting and dying in America's wars. Yet this has now become reality as the last all male occupation, that of warrior, is that no longer and women have taken their place in the front ranks of combat soldiers.

In 1995 Mady Wechsler Segal wrote that "the military has been defined traditionally as a masculine institution; it may be the most prototypically masculine of all social institutions."[2] The reason for this erstwhile total masculinity of the military is viewed as cultural by feminists. This means that some social scientists would hold that the sole reason for the exclusion of women from military assignments or even combat is related to the definition of gender in various societies. Such an explanation is commensurate with 21st century technology in that women can operate an electronic device as well as men. The cultural definition, however, overlooks that in earlier societies men used swords and other heavy weapons which only those with male muscles could successfully employ.

In World War I, in which the U.S. participated in from 1917through 18, thirty-three thousand women served in the armed forces. Thereafter, almost 400,000 women served in the U.S. armed forces during World War II. Their contribution was limited to nursing and some office work.

As early as 1938 when the U.S. was not at war, the army nurse corps increased its strength from 600 to 675. When the U.S. was attacked by Japan on December 7, 1941, there were more than 289,000 nurses in the U.S., of whom 100,000 volunteered to serve in the armed forces. Seventy-six thousand were accepted and served in the navy and the army. These nurses came under enemy fire and in the Philippines endured the Japanese attack. This was also true in Europe, where nurses were engaged in front line duty. This was not envisaged by Congress when the Army Nurse Corps was created in 1902 and the Navy Nurse Corps in 1908.[3]

In 1908 the Navy Nurse Corps numbered only 21 nurses, all of whom were assigned to the Naval Hospital in Washington, D.C.

In World War II a new field of nursing, the flight nurse, was established when in 1942 the Air Force Nurse Corps was first authorized by Congress.

The evidence that military nurses faced all the dangers that war implies are the casualties suffered by military nurses. One of these casualties was Ellen Gertrude Ainsworth, who died as a result of injuries received from enemy action near Anzio, Italy, in January 1944. For her courage under fire she was awarded the Silver Star and Purple Heart posthumously.[4]

With the entrance of the U.S. into the First World War, military nurses became casualties alongside men. In that conflict 359 service women died. In the Korean War, 17 women died and eight died in the Vietnam War. Many more became casualties during the Iraq war.[5]

After the Second World War the participation of women declined. Thus, in 1948, there were only 6,000 women on active duty among 1,460,000 enlistees These women constituted only .4 percent of all military personnel at that time. It was in that year, 1948, that Congress passed the Armed Forces Integration Act. That act at first limited the number of women in the services to 2 percent of enlisted strength and the number of female officers to 10 percent of female enlistments. Further, the act imposed a ceiling for women's promotions in that it allowed women to attain no rank higher than lieutenant colonel in the Army or Marines or commander in the Navy.[6]

In 1952, during the Korean War, the 3,504,000 enlistees in the U.S. armed forces included 31,000 women. Thereafter the number of military men and women declined from 2,888,000 in 1956 to 2,489,000 in 1960. Of these, women were only .8 of 1 percent or 21,000 to 22,0000 in 1960. By 1972, the U.S. armed forces enrolled 2,510,000 service men and women, of whom 32,000 or 1.3 percent were women. By 1980 the armed forces had declined further to 2,033,000. The contribution of women to that number had increased by then to 150,000, or 7.4 percent of the total.[7]

By 1989, the number of women in the armed services of the United States had risen to 229,000 or 10.8 percent of the personnel enrolled. About 15 percent of women military personnel were then officers. These officers were and are college graduates. Many are graduates of the service academies, as women were first accepted into these academies in 1980.

When the U.S. invaded Kuwait in 1990 to stop the aggression of Iraq against that country, 7 percent of the service personnel in the area including Saudi Arabia were women.

By 1996 women comprised more than 12.90 percent of the armed forces, although the number of women had declined, as had the number of men then members of any of the branches of the armed forces.[8]

During the conflict in Iraq in 2007 the armed forces had about 2 million members, of whom 150,000 were women.

In 1977 the U.S. Congress voted to permit women to engage in combat. This decision allowed women to participate in missile defense and in other combat support activities. They were then still barred from roles involving the infantry, tanks, combat engineering and other situations which could draw hostile fire. This action opened all but 16 of the armed services' 377 specialties to women. Flying helicopters was also excluded.[9]

In 1990 the advancement of women in the military led Linda L. Bray to become the first woman in American history to command American troops in combat. During the invasion of Panama Capt. Bray headed a 30 member police unit that was ordered to capture a Panamanian guard dog kennel. It was assumed that the kennel would be unguarded. Instead it was heavily defended. Bray led a 30 minute firefight which killed 3 Panamanian soldiers. This was indeed a historic event in military history.[10]

It was also in 1990 that the U.S. Army finally allowed women to pilot C-130 and C-141 transport planes and participate in airdrops.

This was not the only first event in women's military history in the U.S. In 1941 Annie G. Fox was the first woman to receive the Purple Heart medal because she was wounded during the Japanese attack on Pearl Harbor while serving at Hickam Field air base. The first woman to receive two awards was First Lieutenant Cordelia E. Cook, an Army nurse who received both the Bronze Star and the Purple Heart while serving in Italy during World War II. The first woman to receive the Air Medal was Lieutenant Elsie S. Ott for her actions as an evacuation nurse in 1943. There were a number of other firsts prior to 1948 which invariably involved military nurses, as these were the predominant female members of the U.S. armed forces.[11]

In 1994 the risk rule prohibiting women from flying helicopters into combat was rescinded. Also rescinded were rules prohibiting women numerous other roles, so that 91 percent of all career paths in the armed services are now open to women.

The first woman to command a naval warship at sea in the U.S. Navy was Kathleen McGrath. She was commissioned in the U.S. Navy in 1980 after finishing officer candidate school. In 1983 she reported to the USS *Prairie* for a tour of duty to the western Pacific. In 1987 she became operations officer aboard the USS *Cape Cod*. Two years later she participated in Operation Desert Shield and Operation Desert Storm, i.e., the war against Iraq and the invasion of Kuwait by the U.S.

In 1994 Captain McGrath assumed command of the USS *Recovery*, deployed to the Mediterranean and the Caribbean seas. Next she became chief staff officer of Destroyer Squadron Seven, deployed in the western Pacific and the Arabian Sea. In 1998 Captain McGrath took command of the USS *Jarrett* with a crew of 262. They sailed to the Persian Gulf as part of the American patrol in that area. Thereafter Captain McGrath was assigned to the Joint Advanced War Fighting Unit in Alexandria, Virginia. In 2002 she retired because of illness and died soon thereafter.[12]

Women in American Military Academies

In 2007 women made up 14.4 percent of enlisted personnel and 15.9 percent of the officer corps in the 1.4 million person active duty U.S. military. In 1973 only 1.6 percent of the U.S. military was female. One result of this partial feminization of the officers corps has been a somewhat more egalitarian attitude towards enlisted personnel on the part of officers. While it was customary for decades to simply order enlisted soldiers to do something, female officers have been instrumental in asking rather than ordering and in meeting with enlisted personnel to explain various actions.[13]

Technical and tactical skills on the part of junior officers and enlisted personnel have also contributed to the more cooperative method of leadership in the military. Many younger enlistees and officers know more about recent technology than senior personnel learned when they began their careers. It is, however, technology which dominates today's military, so that those who are competent technicians, whatever their rank, are most valuable to the unit to which they have been assigned.[14]

The most important event leading to the advancement of women in the military has been the enrollment of female cadets in the military academies of the United States. In 1976 the U.S. military academies began admitting women. In addition, state sponsored military academies such as the Virginia Military Institute and The Citadel, located in South Carolina, also admitted women after a U.S. Supreme Court ruling demanded this.

The oldest of these academies is the United States Military Academy at West Point, New York. Founded in 1802 when President Thomas Jefferson signed legislation to establish the academy, the academy admitted women for the first time in 1976, as did the other two U.S. military academies, the U.S. Naval Academy at Annapolis, Maryland, and the U.S. Air Force Academy at Colorado Springs, Colorado.

Four thousand men and women are enrolled at the U.S. Military Academy at West Point. These students are known as the Corps of Cadets. Of these, 13 percent are women. While the West Point Academy was originally only a school of engineering, it now has a wide ranging curriculum including foreign languages, humanities and numerous sciences. The U.S. Naval School, was founded in 1845 and named U.S. Naval Academy in 1850. The Naval Academy enrolls 4,300 midshipmen, of whom 19 percent are women.

The curriculum includes foreign languages, mathematics, humanities and a number of sciences.

The third U.S. military academy is the U.S. Air Force Academy located in Colorado. It was authorized by President Dwight D. Eisenhower in 1954 and the first class entered in 1955. As in the other two U.S. military academies, women entered the U.S. Air Force Academy in 1976. The academy teaches flying, navigation, and parachuting, as well as astronomy and the mandatory combat survival training. The curriculum also includes international affairs, political and behavioral sciences and a number of physical sciences. The academy enrolls 4,200 cadets, of whom about 11 percent are women.

In 1839 the Virginia Military Institute was founded by the legislature of that state and is today the nation's oldest state supported military academy. Although VMI made every effort to remain a single sex, male only institution, the U.S. Supreme Court ruled in 1996 that the school could no longer exclude women. As a result the first women to enroll came in 1997. The institute now enrolls 1300 cadets, of whom 100 are women. The curriculum includes engineering, humanities and social sciences and numerous physical sciences in addition to special courses in leadership.

In 1842, the South Carolina legislature passed an act establishing the South Carolina Military Academy called The Citadel.

This institution enrolls about 130 women among the 2,000 cadets. The Citadel was far from allowing women to enroll when the Supreme Court ordered this policy change in 1996. This court order came about after Shannon Faulkner applied and was accepted by the Citadel after she had removed all references concerning her gender from the application. When the admissions office learned of her sex, the Citadel revoked her admission, leading to a two-and-one-half-year legal battle resulting in a victory for Faulkner. Shortly after admission, Faulkner resigned for reasons of health.

Alumni in particular were opposed to the entrance of women into the Citadel. Many protested that women were "ruining the school," although the meaning of "ruining" could not be defined by those who used it.[15]

Sexual Harassment

The entrance of women into the formerly all male military service brought charges of sexual harassment almost immediately upon the arrival of the first cadet on the campus of the West Point Academy.

That this was not caused by the enrollment of women in military schools but had an older tradition may be seen by the so-called Tailhook Scandal, erupting in 1991.

A tailhook is a device which helps stop an aircraft on landing on an aircraft carrier. The pilots who fly planes from the deck of a carrier may be members of a private association of about 15,000 called The Tailhook Association. The association includes active as well as retired naval personnel and holds an annual convention, one of which took place in Las Vegas, Nevada, in September of 1991.[16]

That convention led to charges by several women, both in the Navy and civilians, that 83 women and seven men were assaulted by drunken conventioneers. One hundred and seventeen officers were implicated in one or more incidents of sexual assault or indecent exposure. It was further charged by the inspector general of the Defense Department that 51 individuals made false statements to the IG and that high ranking officers were aware of the misconduct but did nothing to stop it.

It appears that earlier Tailhook conventions were stag affairs and unwritten rules or tradition excluded spouses or other women from these gatherings. Nevertheless, some prostitutes evidently participated in these conventions and were subject to male touching as they walked through the hallways. This conduct became gross during the '91 convention, when women naval officers and enlisted personnel attended and men grabbed women's breasts, buttocks and crotches. Some men also tore clothes from women walking through the hallways. Some men streaked, that is, walked naked about the hallways in front of women, while others mooned or exposed their buttocks. Eighty individuals were known to have exposed their testicles in public and yet others bit the buttocks of females. All of these activities were viewed as assault by the inspector general of the Defense Department.[17]

The Tailhook scandal had several consequences. One of these was that a former Navy lieutenant, Paula A. Coughlin, was awarded $5 million in punitive damages by a jury which convicted Hilton Hotels of failing to provide adequate security during the 1991 Tailhook convention at which Ms. Coughlin was sexually assaulted by other officers.[18]

Another consequence of the Tailhook scandal was that the then secretary of the Navy, John H. Dalton, sent letters of reprimand to three admirals and numerous other senior officers. Such letters resulted in failure to be promoted and a reduction in pension for those already retired.[19]

In 2004, Congress established an investigative committee to examine how sexual harassment and assault are handled by the military academies, i.e., the U.S. Military Academy at West Point, New York; the Naval Academy at Annapolis, Maryland; and the Air Force Academy in Colorado Springs, Colorado. This action was prompted by complaints by female cadets that sexual harassment continued despite the Tailhook scandals and the subsequent decrees, sensitivity training and the ending of a number of careers resulting from those scandals.

The report recommended 44 steps needed to make it easier for victims to report incidents of sexual harassment or assault. Female cadets interviewed for the congressional report continued to believe that they would be the targets of reprisals if they reported aggression against them. The committee listed a number of harassments ranging from derogatory remarks to assault. In fact, at the Air Force Academy, this 2005 study found that there had been an increase of harassment incidents from 59 percent of women reporting such conduct to 79 percent of women reporting harassment in 2005.[20]

Therefore the committee recommended that more women be given officer commissions and that more women be promoted to non-commissioned officers.

Gender Harassment

Gender is a social position derived from sex, which is a physical condition. Therefore, sexual harassment consists of imposing male sexual needs upon unwilling women. Gender harassment consists of the unwillingness of some men to allow women the same rights and privileges which male status guarantees.

Gender harassment is therefore another hurdle women in the armed services need to overcome. According to Miller, some military men perceive women as the powerful group who are oppressing men in the service. Men who believe this may sabotage women or fail to respond immediately to an order given by a woman officer, a behavior Miller calls foot-dragging. Miller also identifies feigning ignorance, keeping a record of any and all mistakes made by women, indulging in gossip and making indirect threats.[21]

Miller's study shows that a good number of military men believe that women take advantage of their sex to promote their own career.

Gender harassment is difficult to discern. It is covert, not overt like sexual harassment. Therefore gender harassment is seldom visible and cannot easily become the focus of a complaint. On the contrary, many a female officer believes that she cannot report un-cooperative behavior by male subordinates lest she be accused of poor leadership ability.

Constant scrutiny, according to Miller, fits into the military organization, which seeks to discover competence at all times. Therefore men who look for errors and mistakes by females in their units are apparently doing the right thing even if their motive is derived from rejection of women in the military.

Army women are also frequently the object of untrue gossip about their sex lives. The phrase "she slept her way to the top" indicates resentment of women who have attained promotion. Such women are referred to as sluts whether they engaged in sexual activity or not. Women who are known not to participate sexually are called dykes by men who resent women, so that female servicewomen can't win among the men who reject women as soldiers.[22]

Miller reports that she found evidence that some servicemen will sabotage women in the armed forces. Equipment may be damaged or the necessary tools are not given to women so that they cannot perform the job assigned to them.

Finally, Miller also found indirect threats used to make life difficult for female enlisted personnel. Male soldiers will tell stories, true or not, about women having been raped during maneuvers or night exercises.

Men who make these threats are often those who are convinced that women can accuse men of sexual harassment, true or not, and win every time no matter what the facts or what a man may testify. Therefore it is the perception of some military men that women have the power to ruin their career any time they see fit.

Colonels, Generals and Admirals

The word oxymoron comes from the Greek and means sharp-dull. In short, an oxymoron is a self contradictory statement. Before 1980, the words "woman general" would have been an oxymoron, as no one had ever encountered a woman in that rank or any truly high command position in the U.S. armed services. Yet, today, in 2007, the Air Force has 24 female generals, the Army has 14, 11 women are admirals, 4 women are Marine generals, the Coast Guard has 3 female admirals and 19 female generals serve in the National Guard.[23]

One example of a woman general is Rebecca Halstead. Halstead is the first West Point graduate to become a brigadier general. This is the lowest ranking general officer who at one time commanded a brigade. Halstead now commands the 3rd Corps Support Command in Iraq. That command is designated to supply everything from bullets to water to the troops while training Iraqi troops to learn to do this for themselves. Halstead served in Afghanistan, Germany and Italy before going to Iraq.[24]

Lt. General Claudia Kennedy retired from the Army in August of 2007. At her retirement ceremony she was greeted by Army secretary Louis Caldera and numerous other defense department officials.

She first joined the Army in 1967 and was commissioned a second lieutenant in 1969. Her military education followed her graduation from Southwestern University, where she earned a degree in philosophy. Subsequently she attended the U.S. Army Command and General Staff College and the Army War College. Born in Germany, she also served as commander at the U.S. Army Field Station in Augsburg, Germany, and later commanded the 703rd Military Intelligence Brigade in Hawaii.

In Washington, D.C., she became director of training for the Joint Chiefs of Staff, then continued in a variety of command posts in the area of intelligence. She has received the Legion of Merit decoration as well as the Defense Meritorious Service Medal and several additional awards and medals.

Before retiring, General Kennedy accused Major General Larry G. Smith, then deputy inspector general, of sexual harassment. This complaint originated in 1996 but was not made public until 2006, resulting in the transfer of Smith to another post. Kennedy claims that sexual harassment is still common in the armed services despite the effort of the Defense Department to eliminate it.[25]

An example of a woman admiral is Veronica Froman. Froman was commander of Navy bases in California and Nevada, including the San Diego naval base. The San Diego base is home to 11,000 sailors. Froman had previously been assigned to the Pentagon, where she worked for the Joint Chiefs of Staff.

After her retirement from the Navy, Froman became chief business officer of the San Diego school district.[26]

When the secretary of the Navy allowed the Marine Corps to appoint women to clerical duty, Opha Johnson became the first woman Marine in August of 1918. Since then, over 1,000 female officers and 18,000 women served in the Marine Corps during World War II. In 1948, after Congress passed the Women's Armed Forces Integration Act, Colonel Katherine A. Towle became director of Women Marines. In 1978, the first female Marine general was Brigadier General Margaret Brewer. In 1996 Major General Carol A. Mutter became the first female two star general in the Marines, only to be promoted to lieutenant general two years later.[27]

The advancement of women in the military is a permanent addition to the American defense establishment. It cannot be reversed but will continue to grow even as women advance in all other American institutions, including law enforcement, a profession closely allied in method and staffing to the military.

Women in Law Enforcement

In 2006 there were 655,000 police officers and sheriffs' deputies employed in the United States. Eighty-four thousand or 12.8 percent of these officers were women.[28]

Compared to earlier years there has been a steady increase in the number of women police officers. In 1987 only 7.6 percent of American police were female; in 1990 this had risen to 5.2 percent, and 8.8 percent of police were female in 1993.[29]

All police departments are not the same. Therefore the proportion of women employed by various police departments depends in part on the size of the community. According to the Bureau of Justice Statistics, 17.3 percent of police employed in large communities are women. As the populations policed decline, the number of women employed as officers also declines: 15.6 percent of police in communities of 500,000 but less than one million are women; 14.6 percent of police in communities of 250,000 but less than one-half million are women. Women comprise 11 percent of police in communities of 100,000 but less than one half million, 8.8 percent in communities of 50,000 but less than 100,000, 8.2 percent in communities of 25,000 but less than 50,000, 6.7 percent in communities of 10,000 but less than 25,000, 6.2 percent in communities of 2,500 but less than 10,000 and only 5.7 percent in communities under 2,500 inhabitants.[30]

The employment of women in police work has been viewed as advantageous by a number of studies reviewing employment and published in academic journals. According to these studies, law enforcement agencies that hire and retain women have benefited in six ways. First, women have been proven to be as competent as men in their activities on patrol, their response to violence, and their performance evaluations on the job. Second, women are less likely to become involved in incidents resulting in excessive force. Third, women are more likely than men to implement community based policing, which involves gaining the trust and co-operation of citizens. Fourth, women police are more competent than men in responding to domestic violence against women, which is the largest single category of calls to police departments. Fifth, as the number of female officers increases, sexual harassment and sex discrimination in any department decline, and sixth, management improves as more women are hired into police departments because a good deal of the crude, loud and gross conduct of police commanders is unacceptable to women and therefore is tempered for men as well as women.[31]

The recruitment and retention of women police is evidently more difficult than it is to recruit and retain men on a police force. This is visible because only 12.8 percent of American police forces are female, although this occupation has been open to women for thirty years.

The major reason women leave law enforcement is sexual harassment and gender discrimination. Studies have shown that 60 percent to 70 percent of women officers experience sexual harassment. Yet, only 6 percent to 7 percent of women so victimized reported this conduct for fear of retaliation in a culture of silence. Evidently, it is difficult to prevent such behavior if the victims will not come forward and denounce the offenders. Here the same problem confronts the police departments internally which also confronts them on the street, when citizens will not cooperate with the police in finding and arresting violent criminals because the community culture views the police as enemies so that no one will talk to them.[32]

This is true despite the fact that police departments generally have a system for receiving and investigating complaints of officer misconduct. Yet, many female officers find that the very tools intended to protect them are used against them. This means that those who complain of sexual harassment are themselves investigated on grounds of false but anonymous complaints.

Because women are a small minority, many women who have accepted a law enforcement job feel isolated and are lacking support. While women continue to be a minority among law enforcement personnel, the civilian employees of police departments are mainly women.

Another reason women leave employment by police departments is pregnancy and child care.[33]

Police departments need to insure that promotional policies do not contain bias against women. This bias is often related to the failure of women themselves to apply for promotion because their family obligations do not allow them the time and effort to compete with the men on the job. This problem exists in all occupations in which mothers of small children have to compete with men who have a wife to do a great deal of domestic work which employed women must do themselves. In addition, and unlike other jobs except the military, promotion in police departments usually rests on heroic conduct in the face of danger or in rescuing a citizen from a dangerous situation. In short, police work frequently involves the use of force at great risk to the officer, whether male or female, so that there has been some debate as to the efficiency of women under such stress. This debate has centered on the argument that socialization for girls differs from socialization for boys so that girls are less likely to use force than is true of their brothers. Hence it is argued by some that women cannot possibly use force as much as is true of men.[34]

It has also been argued that women are less likely than men to project a forceful or threatening attitude and that therefore citizens are less likely to act aggressively when confronted by police. Others have argued that those women who enter police service are more aggressive than most women and that the police culture will in any event lead to an aggressive stance toward the citizens.

The Use of Force by Women Police

As a result of the passage by Congress of Title VII of the 1964 Civil Rights Act in 1972 extending the prohibition of gender discrimination in employment to state and local governments, female officers have become eligible for patrol duty in the nation's police departments. Therefore, the use of force by women police became an immediate consideration as these officers were sent on patrol and had to confront some violent citizens.[35]

Hoffman et al. have studied the issues arising from the entrance of women into the police forces of the U.S. and the impact of policewomen on the use of force. Their findings are the result of a study involving 31,778 arrests made by male and female officers in Montgomery County, Maryland. The principal results of this study are that the television dramatization of police activities are hardly real. Instead, the Hoffman study discovered that force was used in only 5.9 percent of arrests and that the overall rate of force was not significantly different for male or female officers. Hoffman et al. found that the rate of injury for those arrested was slightly less when the arresting officer was a woman but that even that difference was statistically not significant.[36]

A number of other studies support the view that female police are as effective as male police or that female police are even more effective.

While the findings by Hoffman of the participation of women in police patrol duty favor such participation, the views of John Lott and others claim that women police are a danger to male police and to the public. Lott's chief argument is that an increase in the number of women police has contributed to an increase in the crime rate and a decrease in solving violent crimes. This is true, says Lott, because women have a slower running speed than men and are therefore less likely to apprehend offenders running away; that the lesser physical strength of women forces police departments to use two officer cars rather have only one officer per car and save a good deal of tax money; and that women are more likely to use guns when threatened because of their inability to fight physically. Lott also argues that shorter reaction time by women leads to more accidental shootings. Lott uses very sophisticated statistical analyses and concludes that each 1 percent increase in the white female police force leads to a 2.7 percent increase in the shooting of civilians.[37]

The Use of Female Police in Prostitution Assignments

Female police are often used to sting men seeking the services of prostitutes. This is a major departure from the historic method of dealing with prostitution by arresting only women who sell sex. This role reversal has come about because female police are now available to conduct these stings and because nothing has ever eradicated female prostitution, so that this later technique may be more successful than the policy of focusing only on women.

The speculation on the part of law enforcement is that arresting, shaming and deterring the customers should be more effective than playing the revolving door year in and year out. There are a number of professionals in law enforcement who believe that the only means of limiting prostitution is to hold the male customers responsible for these offenses.[38]

Included in the effort to hold men responsible for visiting prostitutes is the revocation of driver's licenses, seizing the vehicle of the customer and putting the pictures of male customers of prostitutes on television. Some cities have established johns schools which force men convicted of solicitation to listen to lectures about socially transmitted diseases and other nasty consequences of dealing with prostitutes.[39]

The majority of women police who play the role of prostitute in order to effect a sting are disgusted with the role and with the clientele they accost. Women officers who play the prostitute role are also afraid that her friends, neighbors and relatives will see them while soliciting johns and then believe that they are indeed prostitutes. Furthermore, some female officers who are not approached by any johns are teased by male officers because they could not attract any men.[40]

In view of the many obstacles that women must overcome to be successful in the law enforcement profession, it is indeed remarkable that in recent years numerous women have risen to high positions in various American police departments, including chief of police.

The Rise of Women Police Officers

When Alice Stebbins Wells was appointed to the Los Angeles Police Department in 1910 she became known as the first policewoman in America, although Marie Owens and Lola Baldwin had preceded her. Owens had been appointed by the Chicago Police Department in 1893 as compensation for the death of her police officer husband who had been killed while on duty. Like Lola Baldwin who was appointed to the Portland, Oregon, police department in 1905, Owens was limited in her assignments to helping women and children acting in a capacity which today (2007) would be that of a social worker. Therefore, Wells, who had police powers, is usually considered the first policewoman in the U.S.A.

Los Angeles continued to lead with respect to the appointment of women to the police force and placed the position of woman police officer under Civil Service protection in 1911. By 1912 Los Angeles had three women officers and three police matrons.[41]

By 1917, thirty American cities had appointed policewomen. After the First World War, in the 1920s, two hundred and twenty towns and cities in America had appointed policewomen, mainly segregated into a Women's Bureau. These bureaus usually had a woman in charge who was given the rank of sergeant. As the number of policewomen increased, the need for an organization of such police employees led to the establishment of the National Association of Police Women in 1915. That association continued only until 1932 when the president, Mina van Winkle, died. The association was not reorganized until 1956 under the new name of International Association of Women Police.[42]

The IAWP developed numerous programs designed to promote the interests of women officers and to bring about the integration of women police into the police departments they serve. As the 21st century proceeded, the IAWP grew with the appointment of more and more policewomen, so that the organization had more than 2,400 members with a view of doubling its membership worldwide within a decade.[43]

These developments led to the advancement of a number of women into the higher ranks of police departments nationwide.

In January of 1985, Penny Harrington became the first American woman to head a major police force when she was appointed chief of the Portland, Oregon, police department. Prior to becoming chief, Harrington had successfully sued in numerous sex discrimination suits during her 20 year career on the force. Harrington remained chief for only six months after her husband, also a police officer, had alerted a suspect in a major cocaine case. She then wrote a book entitled *Triumph of Spirit: An Autobiography*.[44]

Evidently, Harrington had all the same problems as police chief that have always plagued male police chiefs. During her tenure minority citizens demonstrated because a citizen of African descent was killed by a police officer's choke hold. Then there were endless budget problems and the resulting cutbacks in police services together with layoffs of employees.

In 2006, Harrington co-authored an academic book, *Investigating Sexual Harassment in Law Enforcement and Nontraditional Fields for Women*.[45]

Elizabeth M. Watson became the police chief of Houston, Texas, in 1990. She was appointed by the first female mayor of Houston, Kathryn J. Whitmire. Watson came from a family of police officers. Her grandfather, uncles and cousins were police officers, as is her husband, Robert. Prior to becoming chief, Mrs. Watson had been deputy chief, having held the rank of lieutenant and detective in previous years. She resigned in 1992 and has since become a police consultant.[46]

Heather Fong became police chief of San Francisco in 2004. At that time she had been with the department for 26 years, having risen through the ranks until she was appointed acting chief in 2005 and chief at a $210,000 annual salary in 2006. Fong holds a master's degree in social work and speaks fluent Cantonese.[47]

Kathleen O'Toole became the chief of the Boston, Massachusetts, police department in 2004. She joined the Boston police department in 1976 and earned a law degree in 1982 while continuing as a member of the police department. In 1986 O'Toole was appointed superintendent of the Metropolitan Police Department. In 1992 she became a lieutenant colonel in the Massachusetts State Police. In 1994, O'Toole was named secretary of Public Safety by the governor and then became secretary of the Boston College 120,000 member Alumni Association.[48]

Margo Frasier is the first woman to head the sheriff's department in Travis County, Texas. In view of the number of women who have been promoted to police chief this does not seem very remarkable. However, Frasier is openly lesbian, living with a domestic partner and her 11-year-old daughter. There can be little doubt that this kind of arrangement, particularly in rural Texas, would not have been allowed there ten years ago (in 1998). Therefore Frasier is seen as a pioneer among women in policing. She supervised 1,340 personnel since she became sheriff in 1996, a job she held until the end of 2004.[49]

Ella Bully Cummings became the police chief of Detroit in 2003. She is the only woman to be chief of police in the 138 year history of the city. Of African American descent, Cummings has had thirty years of police experience. In 2004 Detroit experienced a considerable decline in violent crimes. She holds a bachelor's degree in public administration and a juris doctor cum laude from the Detroit College of Law.

Although women remain only about 17 percent of the police force in large American cities, they constitute more than 37 percent of police in Pittsburgh, which has been called "the showcase for women in policing." Pittsburgh also has the highest percentage of women in command positions. In view of the declining violence rate which has now been observed in American communities for ten years, there are those who attribute this decline to female communication skills and the extra sensitivity women display towards children and rape victims.[50]

Although women have made some major gains in the law enforcement profession, only 200 of the 18,000 police departments are now (2007) headed by women .[51]

Women Firefighters

There are about 293,600 firefighters in the United States. Of these, only 6,500 are female professional firefighters. Nevertheless, the number of women associated with fighting fires is far greater than this small number would indicate because much firefighting is done voluntarily. It has been estimated that there may be as many as 30,000 female volunteer firefighters. The history of women in the fire service is not known, with the exception of a few women firefighters who had made a name for themselves under unusual circumstances.

One of these women firefighters was Molly Williams, who was an African American slave and was owned by a member of the Oceanus Engine Company #11 in New York City in the early nineteenth century.[52]

Later in the nineteenth century Marina Betts distinguished herself as a Pittsburgh firefighter and in 1859, the San Francisco heiress Lillie Hitchcock Coit became a member of Engine #5, a most exceptional occupation for a wealthy woman then, there and now.

In 1875, Adelheid von Buckow joined volunteer Fire Company #1 in Atlantic City, New Jersey, and remained with that company until it disbanded in 1904. Likewise, Carrie Rockefeller became a member of Engine Company #1 in West Haven, Connecticut, in 1895.

Early in the 20th century Captain Marie Stack was in charge of the Los Angeles first all woman fire company which was augmented later by two more all woman fire companies. In 1915 the town of Silver Springs, MD, formed an all woman fire company. In 1926 Emma Vernell became an active firefighter for many years after her husband died as a firefighter in the line of duty. In 1936, Augusta Chasan became known as "The Fire Lassie of Jersey Homestead" after she volunteered for a job she did until she was 90 years old.[53]

During World War II many women became volunteer firefighters because so many men had joined the armed services. As a result there were some all-woman fire companies in California and in Texas. Also in Texas, in 1967, women formed an all female fire brigade in the town of Woodbine, specifically to defend against brush fires which threatened to burn down their homes. Because the nearest fire department was ten miles away, twenty-three women bought the needed equipment and then trained with the U.S. Forest Service.

That service appointed paid women firefighters in 1971. These women worked for the Bureau of Land Management in Montana. These all woman fire companies became the target of a number of male crews who could not tolerate competition from women. As a result women were gradually included in formerly all male fire companies.

It was Judith Brewer who was the first woman firefighter to make the profession her career. She started in 1973 with the Arlington County, Virginia, Fire Department and retired in 1999 as a battalion chief.[54]

In 1974 the San Diego, California, Civil Service Commission ordered the hiring of women into the fire department followed in 1975 by Petersburg, Virginia; Fairborn, Ohio, Houston, Texas, Fort Wayne, Indiana; and the U.S. Air Force.

The first woman fire chief in the U.S. and probably in the world was Anne Holst, a descendant of the founder of the Factory Mutual Fire Insurance System. She became the chief of the Cedar Hills, Rhode Island, Fire Department in 1931. Since she was also a pilot she was active in the management of forest fires.

Now, in the 21st century, there are a number of women who have risen to high rank in various American fire departments. Coleen Walz is a battalion chief in the Pittsburgh, Pennsylvania, Fire Department. She is a 17 year veteran. The department has only 20 women among 840 members because it is evidently very difficult to persuade women to become firefighters.

Rita Wessel has been a firefighter for 35 years including with the U.S. Air Force and the Pittsburgh Fire Department. She has become an instructor at the Pennsylvania State Fire Academy and says that very few women are willing to enroll because of a cultural bias to the effect that women don't do firefighting. Men are even more reluctant to let women into firefighting than into any other formerly all male occupations.[55]

The highest ranking woman in the 138 year history of the New York Fire Department is Rochelle Jones. That department has 11,500 members, of whom only 24 are women. That is slowly changing, although only about 200 women a year have joined fire departments in this country in the decade ending 2006. Of these, there are 14 fire chiefs in the country, including Rosemary Cloud, who heads the 100 member East Point, Georgia, Fire Department. She is the first black female chief in the country, having spent 22 years as a firefighter.[56]

In 2007 the 12th International Conference on Women in the Fire Service was held in Oakland, California. The significance of these conferences was that this professional organization guarantees the continued access of women into the firefighting profession as yet another example of the entrance of women into the last bastion of male exclusivity.

The latest uniformed service to employ women is the U.S. Border Patrol. In view of the current effort to restrict the entrance of illegal immigrants across the Mexican-American border, the Border Patrol is making a major effort to recruit women into that service. In 2006 only 5.4 percent of the 12,967 workforce was women. The Border Patrol seeks to hire 6,000 additional agents by 2008 with a view of at least equaling the female contingent of the F.B.I. at 18.5 percent, the AFT at 13.3 percent and the Secret Service which employs 10.2 percent women.

The income of Border Patrol agents begins at $35,000 and rises to $45,000 a year after basic training.

Summary

A number of women have been killed in the Iraq war, beginning in 2001. This is no longer surprising, although it was not long ago that nurses were the only military women in America. When women were first admitted to the armed forces their work was restricted and so was their rank. However, the overall female participation rate in the armed forces of the United States was nearly 14 percent in 2007. This increase is due largely to the admission of women to all U.S. and state military academies.

Women in the military have encountered sexual and gender harassment. This is also true of women in law enforcement Nevertheless, women have been promoted in police departments and are also serving as firefighters.

CHAPTER 5

Women in American Religion — The Patriarchy Trembles

The Rabbi Has No Beard

When Sally Priesand was ordained as the first American female rabbi on June 3, 1972, she became the first of 829 women ordained in three American Jewish denominations during the 35 years since that revolutionary event.[1]

Priesand is not the first woman to be ordained a rabbi worldwide. That honor belongs to Regina Jonas of Berlin, Germany. She was ordained privately by a rabbi in Offenbach, a town on the Rhein, on December 27, 1935. Although she had graduated from the Hochschule für die Wissenschaft des Judentums or Higher Institute for Jewish Studies, she was not accepted at any seminary and her status was in question during her short life. She was murdered by the German government in December of 1944 at age forty-two.

Sally Priesand was more fortunate. From 1981 until her retirement in 2006 she was the rabbi of the Monmouth Reform Temple of Tinton Falls, New Jersey, with a congregation of 365 families. It took nine years of working as a part time assistant rabbi before Sally Priesand became the full time rabbi at the Monmouth Reform Temple. There she was highly successful, having relinquished marriage and children because she felt she could not do everything.

Evidently, Priesand's ordination revolutionized Judaism, as a feminist theology emerged which justified the ordination of women, contrary to the age-old traditions which prohibited women from functioning in that status-role. The 829 women rabbis in 2007 represented about 16 percent of the 5,000 rabbis functioning in the United States. Since Orthodox seminaries will not ordain women, the proportion of women rabbis for the three branches of Judaism that do so is a good deal higher. There were about 1,800 Orthodox rabbis in the U.S. in 2008, another 1,800 rabbis serve Reform congregations, 1,175 belong to the Conservative movement and 250 are members of Reconstructionist Judaism. Therefore, women are around 25 percent of non–Orthodox rabbis in America in 2007.

A woman who seeks to become a rabbi must study in a theological seminary for at least five years. It is usually required that the candidate spend one year in Jerusalem, thereby becoming fluent in the Hebrew language. A comprehensive knowledge of the Bible, i.e., the Torah, is required by all denominations, as is a knowledge of rabbinic literature, Jewish history, Hebrew, theology, pastoral psychology and public speaking. Furthermore, an understanding of community service and education is stressed. Some seminaries also provide advanced degrees in Talmudic research and Bible study. Evidently, a great deal is demanded of a woman seeking this profession.[2]

Rabbis earn between $50,000 and $100,000 annually, although some who are employed by very large Reform or Conservative congregations earn more. Rabbis earn additional income by performing ceremonies such as funerals, confirmations (bat or bar mitzvah) and weddings.

There are four major Jewish seminaries in the United States. These are The Jewish Theological Seminary of America (Conservative), Hebrew Union College–Jewish Institute of Religion (Reform), Rabbi Isaac Elchanan Seminary of Yeshivah University (Orthodox), and Reconstructionist Rabbinical Seminary.[3]

The Jewish Theological Seminary had 120 applicants in 2006, of whom 67 were women. The seminary accepted 48 female and 33 male applicants, so that 60 percent of all graduates of the class of 2010 will be women, thereby guaranteeing that women will become the majority of conservative rabbis within another generation.[4]

Women who have chosen to become rabbis or have already attained that status seek to fulfill several roles. One of these is teacher. That is of course understandable since the very word rabbi, derived from "rav" or "more," refers to one who knows more about Jewish law than other Jews and is therefore a teacher of Jewish law, history, theology and customs. Women rabbis also seek the role of community spokeswoman with reference to the non–Jewish community. Other interests of women rabbis are "resource person," "moral voice," or "the moral conscience of the Jewish community."[5]

Although by 2007 the Jewish community has accepted the existence of female rabbis whether in agreement with that position or not, women who entered that calling in the 1970s were almost always rejected by all but a few. At first, women rabbis could hardly find a congregation willing to appoint them. Therefore, the early pioneer female rabbis generally became teachers or associate or assistant rabbis in small congregations.

It has been observed that the sermons of female rabbis generally differ from those of male rabbis in that women resort to a good deal of storytelling while men seek to hold forth, exhort the congregation or pontificate dramatically. While these public appearances seem to be most satisfactory to men who often gain access to larger pulpits in highly paid positions among big city congregations, women seem to gain more satisfaction from counseling and teaching.[6]

One such rabbi is Rachel Bat-Or, who was installed at the Shaarey Israel temple in Macon, Georgia, on August 26, 2007. Like so many women rabbis, she is the first female rabbi in central Georgia.

In 2003, the Central Conference of American Rabbis elected Janet Ross Marder its president. This is not surprising since 377 of the 1,800 Reform rabbis in the United States are women. The CCAR also elected three women rabbis to one-half of the leadership positions in their organization, which reflects that one-half of all Reform Jewish seminary students are women.[7]

Some Jewish women have revolted against the ancient patriarchy by revising the ceremonies of Judaism. Most important of these revisions is the recent introduction of the women's Seder and the Women's Haggadah. The word seder means order and refers to the order of the Passover meal which involves a number of rituals reminding the participants of the Exodus from Egypt as recounted in the Bible. A Haggada is a book of quotations from the Bible, including Exodus, Psalms, songs and blessings. This book is traditionally all male oriented. Therefore, Nomi Nimrod and E. M. Broner rewrote the Haggada, which now refers to "wise women" rather than "wise men," to "the four daughters," not "the four sons," and calls the plagues visited upon the Egyptians "the women's plagues." The stories concerning the prophet Elijah, traditionally told at the seder, become stories about Bella Abzug, a one time member of Congress and feminist leader.

Feminists, who abhor the Jewish patriarchy, point to Jewish Scripture to defend their case. Their argument is that there is an egalitarian core in Judaism which has been covered up by male arrogance which has distorted the egalitarian message of the Torah, i.e., the Bible. One example is the manner in which the matriarch Rachel pushed forward her son Jacob in defiance of patriarchal custom. A further example is the rescue of the baby Moses by Pharaoh's daughter and Miriam, Moses' sister. Then there is the book of Judges in which Deborah is displayed as the only female of the twelve judges who then follows in the tradition of Moses. Likewise, the story of creation includes women as well as men and asserts that both are made in the image of God (Genesis 2:7–24). Then Exodus 20:12 and Deuteronomy 5:16 both exhort children to honor their father and their mother. The command that men and women be fruitful and multiply (Genesis 1:28) evidently concerns women. In sum, all of these biblical verses which concern Jews as well as

Christians justify a feminist approach to both religions and stand directly opposed to the ancient patriarchy which has ruled both communions for so long.

Reaction of the Orthodox Jewish Community to the Ordination of Female Rabbis[8]

While the ordination of women rabbis was at first entirely ignored by the Orthodox (straight belief) Jews who resist women in the clergy, it has been noted and disputed by that community after the Conservative movement also ordained women. The reason for this change in perception is that Reform Jews are not considered Jewish at all by the Orthodox so that anything they do is given no notice. When, however, the Conservative Jewish Theological Seminary ordained the first woman rabbi, Amy Eilberg, in 1985, the Orthodox community not only took notice but protested vehemently. The Orthodox now accused the Conservatives of seeking to next ordain non–Jews because they believed that the Conservatives had entered upon a path of a gradual movement toward the Reform community. This seems to them to be the case because in 1955 women were first allowed to read the Hebrew Torah (Bible) in public, and in 1978 women were first counted as a quorum of ten worshippers. Among the Orthodox and earlier among the Conservatives a required quorum for public worship consisted only of men. Then in 1974 women were allowed to be witnesses before a Conservative Jewish court of law, a practice utterly prohibited among the Orthodox.[9]

The Orthodox community denies that women are treated in an unequal manner despite the separation of the sexes during synagogue services in that women must sit in a balcony or behind a partition so as not to be seen by the men on the main floor of the synagogue. The argument by the Orthodox community is that women have a different but nevertheless equally important role to play as men. Household chores, particularly concerning kosher or ritually pure food, are such a female issue and are considered most important by Orthodox Jews, as are child rearing and the preparations for the Sabbath.

Nevertheless, this rejection of women as rabbis and therefore as unequal can be challenged from Scripture itself. First there is Genesis 1:26 which holds that each person, not only the man, is created in the image of God. Then there is Joshua 1:8 which commands that "you shall study it day and night" meaning the Torah or Bible. By "you" is meant everyone, not only men. Both of these texts can of course be negated by pointing to Genesis 3:16 which tells women that their husband shall "rule over you." Then there is another source of dispute. While Orthodoxy denied for centuries that women could study and comprehend the Torah and the Talmud (Learnings) it is now proved that women can in fact be experts in both, as there are female Talmud and Torah scholars in Israel and in the United States.[10]

The Orthodox Jewish community lives by Jewish law, which has traditionally created a number of disabilities for Jewish women. This may be seen in the wedding ceremony in which the husband places a ring on the finger of the bride or gives her a coin, saying: "You are sanctified to me by this ring according to the Laws of Moses and Israel." The bride makes no such pronouncement in traditional Jewish law but is passive throughout the ceremony. A second example of the disabilities placed on Jewish women by traditional Jewish law is the status of agunah. An agunah is a woman deserted but not divorced from her husband. According to Jewish law only men can get a divorce. However, later practice has altered this position, so that divorce requires the consent of both parties. Therefore neither woman nor man can get a divorce if deserted and therefore cannot marry again. It is true that men deserted by their wife would be in the same position and could not remarry. Nevertheless, this law usually operated against the interests of women who were far more often deserted by husbands than vice versa. Furthermore, Jewish law allows a husband to force a divorce upon his wife. A woman cannot force a man to give her a divorce.

Traditionally, at the death of a husband, the wife does not become the guardian of her children. Instead, a rabbinic court can appoint a man to be the children's guardian. Also, at the death of a husband, Jewish law does not consider the wife the legal heir, although at the death of a wife, the husband inherits all of her property. Daughters cannot inherit the property of their deceased fathers because only sons inherit such property.

Jewish law provides that a man can divorce a wife who has become insane. A wife, however, cannot divorce a husband by reason of insanity. There are numerous other disabilities imposed on women by Jewish law. In sum, all of these disabilities are upheld by "Torah true" Jews, so that the notion of a woman rabbi is abhorrent to those who cling to these beliefs.[11]

These laws plainly indicate that Judaism has for thousands of years been defined in terms of male experience only. Therefore it is necessary for women rabbis and students to absorb a curriculum reflecting the interests of men but not women. One of the consequences of the inclusion of women into the rabbinate will be a change in that curriculum. This concerns the liturgy which refers only to men, although among some Conservative congregations an effort has been made to include women. For example, the 18 Blessings which are recited at every Jewish service have heretofore referred only to "the God of Abraham, Isaac and Jacob." More recently, in the English version reference is also made to "the God of Sarah, Rachel, Leah, and Rebecca."

Women who study the Jewish texts are confronted with the fact that these texts never mention them, so that indeed women do not exist in the ancient and medieval liturgy with which women theology students must contend. This includes the traditional Hebrew daily prayer book, which summarizes all of these disabilities in a blessing said only by men: "Blessed art thou, Lord our God, King of the Universe, who has not made me a woman."[12]

Women rabbis are of course confronted with the same issues which confront all employed women with children. Because the rabbinate is a twenty-four hour, seven days a week job, men have traditionally been supported in the rabbinate by a wife called a rebbitzin. The traditional rebbitzin not only insured that the rabbi need not deal with family issues or take the garbage out, she also participated in caring for the congregation by supporting the bereaved, attending confirmation ceremonies, listening to congregants' problems and standing up for their man in the many disputes which are inherent in the rabbi-congregation relationship. Today, in 2008, the role of rebbitzin as unpaid helper is largely confined to the Orthodox. Women rabbis, moreover, are deprived of a rebbitzin *ipso facto*. They do have husbands and children who need attention and take much time to meet their legitimate demands.[13]

The demand for time to devote to their families is called balance. This is a concept seldom promoted by men or even mentioned, despite the evidence that men too need private time with their families or even with themselves. This is very difficult to achieve for rabbis of both sexes but vital for working women.

Female rabbis are not all married. Therefore, the younger rabbis seek to date Jewish men but are seldom successful because men find it intimidating to romance a rabbi. This means in practice that men avoid dating women rabbis in favor of women with more normal occupations. It is also true that many men are unwilling to date women doctors, executives or lawyers who may have more money and more education than they have, so that it is more difficult for women with that much education to marry at all. It is therefore not surprising that as of 2007 about 25 percent of married women earn more than their husbands.[14]

Women rabbis, as late as 2007, are seldom senior rabbis in large congregations. By large is meant a congregation with more than 350 members. This is also true of the Protestant clergy.

The Minister Wears Skirts

It has been estimated that there are about 400,000 non–Catholic Christian clergy in the United States. This number refers to Protestants, or followers of Martin Luther (1483–1546), as well as such non-Catholic Christians as the Eastern Orthodox Church and the Anglican Church. The Eastern Orthodox communion originated in 1054, long before Luther was born. The Anglican communion dates to the life of Henry VIII (1491–1547), king of England, who made himself head of the then English branch of the Catholic church. There are other Christian communions such as the Coptic church in Egypt, which are neither Protestant nor Catholic.

In 2006 the Presbyterian Church and the United Methodist Church marked the 50th anniversary since women gained full clergy rights in these denominations. While few women were recruited into the clergy of these communions before 1980, the number of women who have become ministers since the '80s has steadily increased, so that some commentators believe that at least the Presbyterian ministry will soon hold a majority of women.

Likewise, the Episcopal church has ordained 3,482 women priests, up from 94 in 1977 and therefore reaching 20 percent of all Episcopal priests in 2007. Women are also the majority in Protestant seminaries at the beginning of the 21st century. These changes in the gender of Christian clergy appear to contradict the words of St. Paul, who wrote in 1 Corinthians 14:35 that "it is a disgrace for a woman to speak in church." Recent interpretations of this verse seek to understand this as a comment only concerning women who disrupt church services.[15]

Women Religious Leaders in the 18th and 19th Centuries

In the middle of the Revolutionary War, a group of English believers led by Ann Lee, also known as "Mother Ann," arrived in America. Ann Lee had declared that she was "the second coming of Christ." She organized the Shaking Quakers and settled in upstate New York. Although the group was able to attract a number of new members in the 19th century, the Shakers declined severely thereafter because they practiced celibacy and therefore could not survive. Moreover, the Shakers danced and shouted during religious services, a practice not approved by established Christian denominations. These views led mainstream Christians as well as the press to denounce the Shakers, who then retreated to isolated communities. Together with a lack of offspring, these denunciations led Shakers to almost entirely disappear from the United States by the end of the 20th century.

Mary Baker Eddy was born in 1821 in Bow, New Hampshire. She became the founder of Christian Science, also known as the Church of Christ, Scientist. Home schooled by her brother, Albert Baker, she married George W.

Glover, who died six months after the wedding. She then married a dentist, Daniel Patterson, whom she divorced in 1873. Her third husband was Asa Gilbert Eddy. During all these romantic adventures, Mary also became interested in mental healing as taught by Phineas Quimby in Massachusetts. Subsequently she founded her new church by publishing a book called *Christian Science*. She also founded a newspaper, *The Christian Science Monitor*.

Eddy taught that she had found the final revelation of God to mankind. She therefore wrote *Science and Health with Key to the Scriptures*, a book which showed that she was the key to unlocking the Bible which she called "the dark book." She also claimed to have restored the original Christian church. Her doctrines include the notion that death is an illusion and that healing is accomplished by correct thinking along the lines of Christian Science principles. Numerous other doctrines were also taught and are still part of the dogma of Christian Science.[16]

In 1853, Antoinette Brown was ordained a minister and pastor of the Congregational church in South Butler, New York, thereby becoming the first clergywoman in the United States. Her attainment of that status was by no means easy. Although she was admitted to religious studies at Oberlin College in Ohio, she was refused a degree. Her ordination was equally difficult. No Congregational minister was willing to preside over the ceremony. Therefore a Methodist minister inducted her. Brown left the South Butler pulpit in less than a year and then married Samuel Blackwell, with whom she had seven children. Not satisfied with a housewife role, she participated in anti-slavery and anti-alcohol crusades despite her expulsion from a temperance convention which was dominated by men who would not let her speak.

In 1878 Antoinette Brown became a minister to the Unitarian Association. She resumed preaching and lecturing and briefly served as minister to the Unitarian congregation at Elizabeth, New Jersey, in 1903. She lived to be 96 years old. At age 95 she was elected to the American Association for the Advancement of Science on the strength of her book *The Sexes Throughout Nature*, a book devoted to evolution and the equality of women. She also wrote a novel and published a book of poetry.[17]

Another Christian denomination which has ordained women since the 19th century is the Salvation Army. The Salvation Army was founded by William Booth and his wife, Catherine, in London in 1865. Therefore, this denomination has both a male and a female founder so that women were always welcome to preach within the Salvation Army, as best seen in the efforts of Evangeline Booth, the daughter of William and Catherine, who preached in the streets of London. Later she became territorial commander in both the United States and Canada and rose to the rank of general in the Salvation Army.

In 1880, the Salvation Army began its work in the United States when George Railton and seven Salvationist women arrived in New York City. In that same year, Eliza Shirley and her mother, Annie Shirley, opened a Salvation Army mission in Philadelphia. These women and men were evidently quite successful in that 228 corps (churches) with 569 officers (clergy) had been established in the United States when William Booth first arrived in America in 1886.[18]

The Salvation Army is strongly committed to social services, including help to unmarried mothers, alcoholics, drug addicts and others frequently ignored by mainline organizations. Traditionally, social services have been carried out by women, so that this phase of the Salvation Army's work is most responsive to female interests. The Army has also been one of the leaders in the fight for women's rights. Research has shown that Salvation Army followers are more willing to accede to women's rights than most other groups. For example, 91 percent of Salvationists agree that women are "emotionally fit for politics." Only 61 percent of liberal Protestants agree to this proposition, and only 42 percent of conservative Protestants hold that view. More recently, sexist language was removed from Salvation Army literature.[19]

Outside the Salvation Army and the Unitarian and Congregational churches women did not become clergy in Protestant denominations until the 1980s. Those who did admit women to seminaries seldom granted them degrees or diplomas, even as women who had studied at seminaries were not appointed to serve American churches. In fact, it was not until the 1980s that women were finally accepted in small numbers in the mainline churches as divinity students and pastors.

Inspired by the secular feminist movement begun in the 1970s, women clergy rejected such male terms as "God the father" and rang bells every time someone used a male pronoun at church conventions. Over the years such militancy has largely disappeared as denominations with a good sized female clergy contingent become accustomed to living with women in the pulpit. The need to accept women as clergy became most important as women rose to higher positions in some denominations, so that the United Methodist Church has 20 female bishops today. In that church 53 percent of seminarians are women, although only 20 percent of those ordained are women.[20]

Women have entered the ministry in larger numbers since the 1980s not only because gender discrimination is on the decline, but also because Protestant denominations were facing a shortage of male pastors as the 80s progressed. There are several reasons for this shortage. No doubt the first and most important is that almost all professions pay more than religious work. For example, small Lutheran churches pay only $36,000 per year while independent churches pay even less.

Then there is burnout, which may be described as need to remove from the pressures confronted by pastors, whether rabbis or ministers. Furthermore, the cost of studying at a seminary can be $400 per semester hour or more. In addition, clergy have recognized that the secularization of the United States leaves them on the fringes of occupational prestige and influence.

There is then a real shortage of clergy among the mainline churches in America, including Lutherans, Presbyterians and Episcopalians. This has led to the appointment of women to the Episcopal priesthood in America, beginning in 1975 when the General Convention of the Episcopal Church first permitted the ordination of women as priests.[21]

The seminary experiences of the pioneer generation of women in the clergy were usually uncomfortable if not hostile. While outright hostilities to female clergy are not as frequent as was true in the early days of this development, the number of female clergy who have advanced in the profession is still small despite the appointment of women as bishops in the Episcopal and United Methodist churches. In 1990, Nesbitt found a gender gap to persist in the Episcopal Church, which experienced an increase in the ratio of female to male clergy. Such a gender gap, leaving women in lower level positions throughout their careers, meant that women had little influence on change within the church because they could not occupy positions of power sufficient to influence events. In fact, research has shown that the higher the ratio of women to men in some denominations the greater their increase in staff and lower level positions. Those who are opposed to women clergy say that they are worried that women will diminish the economic opportunities of men. This appears to be an unfounded fear, alone because there is a shortage of non–Catholic clergy which is similar to that among Catholics and Jews.

On November 4, 2006, the 2.4 million member Episcopal church of the U.S. installed Katherine Jefferts Schori as the first *presiding* bishop of the Episcopal Church U.S.A. She is the first and only woman to hold such a post in the 77 million member Anglican communion worldwide. Her installation led to some controversy, as a number of American bishops and Anglican bishops elsewhere refused to recognize her role on the grounds that she is open to gay marriage and the inclusion of homosexuals as clergy.[22]

Although Schori is the first female presiding bishop in the Episcopal Church, it is Barbara C. Harris who was consecrated a bishop of that church in 1989 and served as such in Massachusetts until 2003, when she became the assistant to Bishop John B. Chane in Washington, D.C.[23]

Women clergy of all denominations have career experiences that differ from those of men for the same reasons that all working mothers have different experiences than fathers. Women clergy tend to move into alternatives to parish ministries because they generally must care for husbands and children. The round-the-clock demands which most congregations make upon their pastors usually do not accommodate working mothers. Most churches also do not have institutionalized maternity leave plans. Furthermore, women find that jobs in non-ministry positions are easier to find than pastoral appointments. In addition there are usually vocal minorities in every church who oppose the appointment of a woman minister.[24]

Such opposition becomes problematic for those churches who have been unable to recruit a sufficient number of men into their congregations. A good example is the Anglican Church, whose American branch are the Episcopalians. That church would face a grave shortage of priests if it were not for women who are filling pastoral vacancies in ever growing numbers. One reason for the decline in male participation in the pastoral role is that more than one-quarter of all Anglican clergymen are over 60 years old and ready to retire. Simultaneously, men do not enroll in the seminaries in sufficient numbers to fill the vacancies.[25]

A good number of Protestant female clergy are former Catholics. This is not surprising because the Roman Catholic Church will not ordain women, so that women seeking to enter the clergy are of course constrained to convert to a non–Catholic Christian denomination. The Episcopal Church is the most likely to receive such converts as its clergy are priests and the mass is said in Episcopal churches. This means that the rituals of the Eucharist (good gift) or Communion has as much prominence in the Episcopal Church as in the Catholic Church, although it is also practiced among Lutherans. In short, the Episcopal Church appears to be familiar territory for ex–Catholics. A detailed study of this issue by Paul Perl reveals that the Episcopal Church does indeed attract a plurality, but not a majority, of former Catholic women who have entered the Protestant clergy.[26]

Likewise a number of former Catholic women have become Lutheran ministers. There is no one Lutheran church in America. However, the majority of Lutherans belong to the Evangelical (good message) Lutheran Church in America, which predominates with 4.78 million members. The Lutheran Church Missouri Synod has about 2.5 million members and 410,000 Lutherans belong to the Wisconsin Evangelical Lutheran Synod.

The Evangelical Lutheran Church in America encourages full participation in the life of the church by women. Consequently, women have not only been ordained as pastors but eight women have become bishops in that church. Among these is Marie C. Jerge of West Seneca, a suburb of Buffalo, New York, who was chosen as new bishop of the Upstate New York Synod of the Evangelical Lutheran Church in America on June 3, 2002.[27]

The Rev. Jerge was installed on September 21, 2002, by the presiding bishop of the Evangelical Lutheran Church in America and two bishops of the Episcopal Church. The reason for this collaboration lies in an agreement between both denominations to the effect that Episcopal bishops participate with Lutheran bishops in these ordinations.

The Rev. Jerge served as pastor for ten years at an upstate New York church and was dean of the Southwestern Conference for six years. She holds a master's degree in divinity and a B.A. degree from Smith College.[28]

When the Rev. Cynthia Burkat was elected bishop of the Southeastern Pennsylvania Synod of the Evangelical Lutheran Church, she became the first woman to hold that position. A former assistant administrator of the previous bishop, she founded 12 new churches in that synod, which has 95,000 members in 174 congregations. Burkat is the eighth woman to become a Lutheran bishop. In that position she will have to deal with the issue of ordaining gay and lesbian Lutherans.[29]

The Experiences of Protestant Women Clergy

The Hartford Institute for Religious Research has published a study, *Clergy Women: An Uphill Calling*. This study is the result of a survey of 16 Protestant denominations which ordain women and men. At the time of the study, the United Methodists had the largest number of women clergy, although the Unitarian-Universalists had the highest percentage (30 percent) of ordained women.

Because women are still the targets of unequal treatment in the majority of churches, women clergy frequently resort to finding non-parish ministries. Nevertheless, the financial compensation paid to female clergy has risen in recent years, so that those younger women ordained most recently earn an average annual salary of $48,318 while men earn $46,916. That this is a recent development can be seen by referring to the age of the clergy as reported in the report of the Church Pension Group as of 2006. The report further shows that men age 35 to 45 at ordination were paid an average of $48,050 and women were paid $45,432. At age 45 to 55, men earned $47,395 at ordination, women earned only $43,186. The biggest salary differential between men and women Protestant clergy can be found in the age group over 55. In that group new male ordinands earn $43,643 and new female ordinands earn $33,547.[30]

This increase in financial compensation and the rise of women to higher offices in the church hierarchies indicates that at the end of the first decade of the 21st century the churches may finally systematically support women clergy. This is not to say that passive hostility is no longer in evidence with reference to women pastors. Like the military, religious organizations also include some parishioners who seek to remember every failure, every dispute and every shortcoming of female clergy.

Although some women have now risen to the position of bishop, the career path of clergywomen differs from that of most men in that women are far more likely than men to earn to lower salaries, have less responsibility and fewer benefits. This discrepancy should disappear as more and more women are raised to higher levels of authority in the church with the hoped for consequence that women bishops will not perpetuate the discrimination heretofore practiced. This will depend on recognizing that many of the difficulties exhibited by women clergy are not caused by individual failures but are inherent in the system which far more often fails the female clergy than the other way around.[31]

In 2005, 22 percent of clergy serving the Disciples of Christ were women. Among Episcopal priests, 20 percent were women and 18 percent of the Presbyterian clergy were women in 2005. The United Methodist Church's clergy was composed 17 percent of women and both the American Baptists and the Evangelical Lutheran Church in America employed 13 percent female clergy.[32]

Roman Catholic Women and the Drive for Ordination

No issue so agitates American Catholic women (and some men) than the refusal of the Vatican to permit the ordination of women and their entry into the priesthood. This has become particularly poignant because Episcopal and other Christian churches have acceded to these demands for some years so that it appears to many American Catholics that Pope Benedict XVI and his predecessor, John Paul II, have been unnecessarily conservative on this and other issues.

The views of both popes has been and continues to be that the ordination to the priesthood is not open to women. The principal teaching of the pope concerning this matter is that "the church is not free" to ordain women. This is best understood by reading the Apostolic Letter of May 22, 1994, signed by Pope John Paul II.[33]

That letter presents these reasons for the exclusion of women from the Catholic priesthood. First is the argument that "priestly ordination ... entrusted by Christ to his Apostles ... has in the Catholic Church from the beginning always been reserved to men alone."

The Congregation for the Doctrine of the Faith issued a declaration on the matter of women priests which holds that the exclusion of women was not related to the position of women in the culture of the time when Christ established this rule, but that this rule is independent of any cultural considerations or the prevailing customs of his time. Furthermore, Pope John Paul II relied on the fact that the Blessed Virgin Mary, the mother of God, was not chosen to be a priest. This is viewed as evidence that failure to include women in the priesthood is not a form of discrimination but should be seen as "a plan to be ascribed to the wisdom of the Lord of the universe."

The pope further insists that women are in no sense less than men; their role in the church differs from that of men but that the Gospel "defends the dignity of women." Finally, however, Pope John Paul II wrote, "I declare that the Church has no authority whatsoever to confer priestly ordination on women and that this judgment is to be definitively held by all the Church's faithful."[34]

The Reaction of American Catholic Women to the Exclusion of Women from Ordination

In August 2006, 12 women were ordained priests of the Roman Catholic Church on a riverboat at Pittsburgh, Pennsylvania. This despite the refusal of the Pittsburgh diocese to recognize these ordinations and despite the possibility of excommunication, a group calling themselves Roman Catholic Women Priests danced and sang *We Are Chosen* while holding hands with female bishops also ordained by women or by a few male bishops who conduct such ceremonies in secret.

The leader of this defiance of Roman Catholic church law is Patricia Fresen, who claims to have been ordained by a European male bishop. She considers herself a bishop and, together with other female priests, administers the sacraments such as weddings, confession and the Eucharist (good gift). Baptisms are an exception because even a non–Christian with the know-how can baptize.

Fresen was a Dominican nun for 45 years but was expelled from the order upon challenging canon (Greek meaning rule) law.

The view of the Catholic church hierarchy is that there are many things with which a Catholic may not agree but which are imposed by the church. True Catholics, the hierarchy holds, will act according to church teachings whether or not one agrees. The church rejects the argument that women are not valued. Instead the church argues that Jesus appointed only men as his apostles and that since bishops are the direct spiritual descendants of the apostles, only men can fill these positions. This view may be disputed by holding that Jesus was a Jewish carpenter and that therefore only Jewish carpenters can be priests.[35]

In 1982, Professor Giorgio Otranto published a study entitled, "Notes on the Female Priesthood in Antiquity." This was written in the Italian language and concluded that there were indeed some women who administered the sacraments in the ancient world. According to Otranto, the history of Christianity indicates a continuous debate and ongoing questioning of the role of men and women in the church. Otranto has shown that the reasons for the sharp division of views on this issue are that many of the contestants in this debate overlook or are not acquainted with "testimony of earlier times." Otranto argues that the subjection of women in early Christianity is not certain and that it is not clear that women were always excluded from the priesthood. Otranto then presents a good deal of evidence for this view. Relying on the writings of a ninth century bishop of Vercelli named Atto, a priest named Ambrose asked him how the terms *presbytera* and *diacona* should be understood. His response leaves no room for doubt. He begins by declaring that since in the ancient church "many were the crops and few the laborers" women too received sacred orders. As it attested in Romans 16:1, "*Commendo vobis Phoebem sororem meam, quae est in ministerio Ecclisiae quae est Cenchrae*" or "I commend you to my sister Phoebe who is in the ministry of the church which is in Cenchrae." In addition, Bishop Atto of Vercelli reputedly claimed that in the ancient Christian church "not only men but also women were ordained and were the leaders of the community." They were called *presbyteriae* and they assumed the duties of directing, preaching and teaching, which three roles define the status of priests.[36]

This demonstrates that the argument from tradition can be supported on both sides of the dispute, as best seen by the demands of American Catholics who have been most vociferous in promoting a feminist agenda.

A Brief History of American Catholic Feminism

The effort on the part of women to be ordained has been particularly shrill in the United States as part of the overall activism of American feminists to gain equality with men in the economic as well as educational and political institutions. Feminist consciousness is nevertheless not entirely American. It was also fueled by Vatican II, which declared in 1962 that women should be supported in their effort to gain an education and to be given access to educational and vocational training. The outcome of these new opportunities for women was the then unforeseen revolt of women against many of the strictures to which they had been subject for centuries.[37]

When Pope John Paul II made his first visit to the United States in 1979 he was greeted by Sister Theresa Kane, head of the Sisters of Mercy and president of the leadership conference of Women Religious. Using the opportunity to the fullest and speaking to millions who were watching the event on television, Kane lectured the pope "to be mindful of the intense suffering and pain of many women in these United States ... who are desirous of serving in and through the church as fully participating members."

In 1983 Women-Church was founded in Chicago as a protest group seeking to eliminate sexism, racism and classicism from the church and rejecting patriarchy as well as clericalism. Together with the National Association of Women Religious these groups became active in a variety of pro-woman activities. Some of these activities appeared radical, others were more restrained. This led the Vatican to react by forcing sisters and clergy to resign a number of positions they held which promoted feminine ends. Others were ordered to stay away from politics or be expelled from church orders.[38]

On October 7, 1984, the *New York Times* carried an advertisement signed by 97 Catholic scholars, priests and nuns. This advertisement demanded free and open discussion of abortion so as to exhibit the different views Catholics might have on this matter. As a result, academics who had signed the letter were denied teaching positions in church related colleges. Women living in religious communities were threatened with expulsion. Four years later, in 1988, the Catholic bishops sent a pastoral letter concerning the position of women in the church.[39]

Subsequently, in 1992, a committee of Catholic bishops drafted yet another letter concerning the role of women in the church. This letter sought to find a middle ground between the so-called liberals and traditional doctrines but the draft was attacked by both sides.

All this points to the inescapable fact that an inordinate number of women have contributed enormously to the church but that the number of nuns has suffered a considerable long-time decline. This was particularly true in the Catholic school system, which provided innumerable advantages both to the students and the nuns who taught them.

Additional frustration affected nuns after Vatican II because that conclave permitted nuns to become pastoral ministers, although they are not allowed to carry out the functions which they teach. This means that nuns can prepare converts for baptism, teach new communicants how to receive Communion, teach laity how to participate in liturgical worship, and prepare engaged couples for the sacrament of marriage. Nevertheless, as of 2008, nuns cannot perform any of these rituals. This situation as well as the general rise in feminism has led to a considerable decline in the number of nuns in American Catholicism. Since 1965, the number of Catholic nuns in the U.S. declined from 179,954 to 67,773 at the end of 2006. As a result, the average age of nuns today is 69. It is unlikely that this decline by nearly two-thirds will be reversed soon if ever. Nevertheless, it should be noted that in recent years more young women and even widows with adult children have joined some convents, bringing on a minor reversal of the decades old trend of rejection of the religious life.[40]

During August 17 to 19, 2007, the Women's Ordination Conference celebrated its 25th anniversary in Chicago. Even then, Pope Benedict XVI had not permitted women to enter the priesthood on the grounds that no pope is authorized to allow women to enter the priesthood. This conference has now given rise to the Young Feminist Network, which represents younger women in the Catholic community devoted to the feminist cause and seeking to deconstruct the barriers which tradition has imposed on them.[41]

The effort to ordain women is, as we have seen, primarily an American demand. Since American Catholics are only 60 million in a church with more than one billion members worldwide, it becomes problematic to consider the effect of female ordination on such areas as South America or Asia where women have few rights. Would Catholics in Brazil or Vietnam accept the ordination of women in cultures which know no feminism? It is of course possible that such ordination would promote women's rights in other areas of life or it could lead to mass defection from Catholicism in such patriarchal societies.

It should also be considered that if women may be priests, then women could also be bishops and a woman could, in that event, become pope. In any case, there is nothing in the Gospels that endorses the subordination of women. In fact, in Luke 10: 38–42 Jesus reveals his identity to both men and women and also in Luke 10: 38–42 Jesus says Mary is justified in leaving her traditional role of serving and cooking. Even Galatians 5: 22–23 which lists "the fruits of the spirit" makes no distinction between women and men.

Muslim Women in America

The number of American Muslims is uncertain. Muslim organizations claim that 6 million Muslims live in the U.S. as of 2008. Others believe that this number has been inflated for political purposes and that the true number of Muslims is far smaller. It needs to be understood that all Muslims are not natives of the same country or even the same region. There are Muslims born in the U.S. Most of these Muslims are of African descent and are likely to belong to such militant groups as the Nation of Islam. That group was founded by Louis Eugene Wolcott, who calls himself Louis Farrakhan.

There are also Muslims in the U.S. who come from such diverse places as Morocco, Indonesia, Saudi Arabia or Pakistan, and who differ immensely in culture and socialization.

At the center of Muslim life is the Quran (recitation). That book is regarded as sacred scripture by Muslims and includes a number of prescriptions concerning the lives of women. Accordingly, Muslim women are expected to dress in a manner which does not call attention to them. Yet, that very dress code does precisely the opposite in the United States, where a veil, an Iranian *chador*, a Moroccan *jalaba*, or a Sudanese *tobe* leads to stares and discomfort.[42]

Muslim beliefs concerning girls also conflicts with the physical education program in American schools. It is commonly expected that female students wear shorts and athletic shirts during physical education classes. The Muslim religion prohibits such dress, so that this requirement alone insures conflict with school authorities and classmates. In addition, the Muslim religion requires that girls and women cover their hair in public. Yet, the wearing of scarves or hats in court or in places of employment is viewed as disrespectful in American society, so that some Muslim women have been unable to gain employment because of these practices.[43]

Because some Muslim countries follow the practice of female circumcision or mutilation, American immigration judges have attempted to protect Muslim women and girls in this country by negating deportation orders against such women on the part of the Immigration and Naturalization Service. One example is the request by a Somalian woman living in Buffalo, New York, who was granted asylum by an immigration judge on hearing that this woman faced the forcible slicing off of the outer genitals without anesthesia if she were to return to her home country.[44]

Likewise, a Minnesota woman was spared this horrible mutilation when the 8th District Court of Appeals overturned a decision by the Board of Immigration Appeals to deport her to her native Kenya where her family was ready to mutilate her.[45]

In 2006 a Georgia man was convicted and sentenced to 10 years in prison for the genital mutilation of his 2 year old daughter. Khalid Amed was found guilty of aggravated battery and cruelty to children. Amed used scissors to remove the child's clitoris. Federal law prohibits this practice and some states have banned it as well.[46]

Despite these disabilities imposed on Muslim women by the patriarchy, it can be shown that the Quran makes no such distinctions. The religious obligations of Islam, also known as the Five Pillars of Islam, concern women and men alike. They are: the unity of God and the acknowledgment of Mohammed as his messenger; praying five times a day; giving alms to the poor; fasting during the month of Ramadan; and one pilgrimage to Mecca in a lifetime. While feminism is only beginning in Muslim society and has as yet few followers, it can be justified according to Muslim scripture. In sum, the arguments for patriarchy are not sustained by the doctrines of the three Abrahamic faiths, so that it may be expected that in the hands of Americans that patriarchy will soon come to an end.

Summary

There were 829 female rabbis in the U.S. as of 2007. Furthermore, women are the majority in the Jewish Theological Seminary, the Conservative branch of Judaism. Because the Jewish scriptures address women and men equally, feminists rely on this literature to promote their cause. Orthodox Jews reject feminism but claim that women have equal standing as men but different duties.

Non-Catholic Christians were traditionally as patriarchal as Jews and for the same reasons. Beginning with 1956, such clergy, usually called Protestant, have proliferated among several denominations, notably the Episcopal, the United Methodist and the Lutheran. This has been welcomed because there is a shortage of male pastors in Protestantism. The Protestant segment of American Christianity has also produced such religious founders as Mary Baker Eddy and Antoinette Brown.

American and other Roman Catholic women have agitated for some time to be allowed to become priests. This proposition has not been accepted by any pope, including John Paul II and Benedict XVI. Nevertheless, a Professor Otronto has written a book in Italian which demonstrates that he has evidence, written in Latin, which shows that women were in fact priests in the Roman Catholic Church in the first century.

The issue of female priests will continue to plague American Catholics even as a pronounced decline in the number of nuns is now in evidence in the United States.

Muslim women in the U.S. are confronted with some hostility because of their dress which can include a face mask, a long gown and a veil. Muslim girls cannot meet the dress code for using athletic equipment or attending physical education classes. This, together with the wearing of a long gown and the practice of female circumcision, has marginalized Muslim women in America.

CHAPTER 6

Women in Science

Myths and Realities

Prejudices die hard and bigotry usually outlasts the facts. This is called culture lag and applies to the beliefs about female scientific ability as well as any other unfounded belief. Because, to paraphrase W.I. Thomas's theory of sociology, that which is believed is real is real in its consequences the opinion that girls and women cannot do well in science has held half the population back in applying their talents to scientific work.

According to the National Science Foundation, a number of myths concerning the ability of girls and women to work in mathematically based sciences persist despite evidence to the contrary. Among these beliefs is the view that most girls have less of an interest in science than boys from the time they start school at age six. Yet, a recent study of fourth graders has shown that 66 percent of girls and 68 percent of boys reported that they liked science, even though second graders, when asked to portray a scientist, draw a picture of a white male in a white lab coat. The few children who drew a woman scientist depicted a severe woman with an unhappy face. Evidently, girls and boys learn about the stereotypes early, so that by eighth grade there is indeed a female attrition induced by prejudice. Science, technology, engineering and mathematics therefore include fewer women than men, although, as we have seen, this is gradually changing.[1]

A second myth concerning girls in science is the argument that boys are turned off if girls are encouraged in these areas. Researchers have found the opposite, namely, that interventions designed to interest girls in science also increase the interest of boys in science.[2]

Recent evidence reveals that despite the effort of government researchers and others to end the bias toward girl students regarding science and engineering, teachers continue to interact mostly with boys with respect to these subjects. For example, teachers are likely to help a boy do an experiment in a physics lab by giving him hands on experience. When a girl asks for the same help, the teachers usually do the experiment while the girl watches. In addition there is a myth which holds that parents cannot motivate girls to become interested in science if they don't like science. Yet the opposite was found by the National Science Foundation. Parents who seek to influence girls to be positive about mathematics and science have a good deal of success. So much so, that girls who come from homes where science is given a good deal of attention are as likely as boys to be interested.[3]

Younger students also exhibit a good deal of similarity in mathematics proficiency between the sexes. Using the National Assessment of Educational Process mathematics scores, the NAEP found in 1973 that among 13-year-old children, males exceeded females by only four points on a scale ranging from 0 to 500. In 2004 the difference favored male 13-year-olds by only four points. Among 17-year-olds males again outranked female students by only four points on a scale of 0–500. In short, the male advantage in mathematics is negligible among high school students and remains so throughout college.[4] Despite the evidence that mathematic ability is not limited to males, the record shows that girls begin to lose interest in science and mathematics in middle school. Two international studies have shown this trend. One is the Program for International Student Assessment and the other is the Trends in International Mathematical and Science Study. Therefore, first year male college students choose engineering and other mathematics based curricula twice as often as is true for female students. Sociologists have found that female students view engineering and other technical fields as unattractive socially in that few opportunities for social interaction are available among those practicing these scientific areas. This may be a matter of perception and not based on reality. However, that which is believed to be real is real in its consequences. Furthermore, many girls doubt their mathematical ability despite the higher grades achieved by girls in both mathematics and science courses.

Evidently, then, girls are overtly and subtly persuaded by family and teachers not to pursue a career in these areas and continue to be victimized by the stereotype which predicts that women are better qualified as nurses and secretaries than as engineers and chemists.[5]

As we have seen, the gap between the genders with respect to math and science is slowly closing but continues despite the fact that girls achieve better grades than boys in math and science courses.

Dr. Leonard Sax has examined this issue in his book *Why Gender Matters*, and concluded that girls' brains differ from boys' brains and that therefore the methods used to teach girls need to differ from the teaching methods applied to boys. Sax found that teachers need to use girl friendly strategies such as looking them in the eye when teaching. While the suggestions of Sax have given rise to some dispute, it can hardly be denied that some female role models can go far in convincing girls that math and science are also for them.[6]

Finally, the National Science Foundation study revealed that those who seek to weed out poor students in science and mathematics will inevitably find a disproportionate number of girls to push out the science door. Obviously, the weed out mentality is already convinced in advance that girls and women somehow cannot do scientific work.

The Contributions of American Women to Scientific Inquiry

In 2005, the then president of Harvard University, Lawrence Summers, made some remarks concerning women in science. These remarks were made at a meeting of the National Bureau of Economic Research and were interpreted to mean that Summers believed that innate differences between the sexes might explain at least some of the failure of women to close the gender gap between male and female scientists. These remarks led numerous politically correct Harvard faculty to denounce Summers as a sexist, leading to his eventual resignation.[7]

A fairly objective review of the evidence concerning the differences between the sexes by a number of scientists leads to the conclusion that differences in brain size, neurons in the brain and tissue between neurons do exist, but that these neither preclude nor promote performance in science. In sum, researchers find that boys and girls are quite similar in mastering new tasks related to cognition, although there are differences in the parts of the brain used to attain the same results. Therefore it is reasonable to conclude that the fact that boys have outscored girls on the mathematics part of the Scholastic Aptitude Test for the past thirty years has to do with social factors and is not inborn.[8]

A good measurement of the increased participation of women in American science is the aggregation of doctorates in the physical sciences earned by women. This shows that in 1992 American women earned 28.7 percent of doctorates in the sciences and engineering. In 2001 this had increased to 36.5 percent. In 2005, 10,533 women received a doctorate in science or engineering, marking an increase of 6.9 percent over 2001.[9]

The attainment of the doctorate in science and engineering by women is the consequence of the greater interest of undergraduate women in enrolling in these areas of academic study. In 2004 women received 50.7 percent of all bachelor's degrees in science and engineering fields and are now closing the gender gap in master's programs as 44 percent of such degrees were awarded to women in 2006, up from 34 percent in 1990.

Nevertheless, women are still underrepresented in Science and Engineering employment. Three times as many men than women are professionally employed in science and engineering jobs. This may be in part the result of the income gap between the genders in science and engineering. Men earned an average salary of $70,000 in these occupations in 2006 but women with the same qualifications earned only $49,000.[10]

Over the past century, women scientists have made some major contributions to advances in science and technology. This has occurred in the United States as well as some European and Asian countries.

In the United States membership in the National Academy of Sciences is viewed as a most prestigious honor, conferred only on the most important achievers in science each year. The National Academy of Sciences was founded in 1863 by Abraham Lincoln. Its charter requires that the academy advise Congress each year concerning the latest scientific developments.[11]

The National Academy accepts about 60 to 70 new members annually. While in earlier years women were hardly noticed among the newly elected members, in 2003, 17 of the 70 new inductees were women. In 2004, seventeen of the 72 new members were women, in 2005 nineteen out of 72 new members were women and in 2006 thirteen of the 72 new members were women. In 2007 eleven women were so elected. While the 23 percent of women to all newly elected members appears small, it is a considerable number compared to the nearly total absence of women from prominence in science before the 21st century.[12]

Helen Hobbs is only one example of the excellence which women with scientific credentials have achieved. Hobbs is a doctor of medicine whose research has shown that genetic makeup has a major influence on heart disease. This refers to variations within genes which are associated with low density lipoprotein which may build up plaque which in turn can clog artery walls. Her work in identifying these genes laid the groundwork for developing new cholesterol lowering drugs.

She succeed in this research because she had been given an opportunity to work in the laboratory of two Nobel Prize winning investigators, Michael Brown and Joseph Goldstein.

As a consequence of her success she set up her own laboratory at the University of Texas Southwestern campus in Dallas, where she also runs the Dallas Heart Study, which has already led to distinguishing the reasons for different heart disease levels among African Americans and European Americans.

Hobbs is a professor of internal medicine and molecular genetics and director of several clinics in the Dallas areas.[13]

Another outstanding woman scientist recently admitted to the National Academy of Sciences is Laura Kiessling. She is a professor of chemistry and biochemistry at the University of Wisconsin where she studies protein interactions that differentiate humans from other forms of life. Kiessling designs and synthesizes molecules which are introduced into various bodily processes. Her work has led to advances in treating rheumatoid arthritis and reduced swelling in the sites of injuries.[14]

Ursula Bellugi is a pioneer in the study of the biological foundations of language. She was elected to the National Academy of Sciences in 2007 for her finding that the left hemisphere of the human brain has an innate predisposition for language. This finding became possible when Bellugi traced the influence of individual genes on the development and functions of the brain. She therefore succeeded in showing how changes in brain structure function to shape behavior.

Bellugi is a professor of biological studies at the Salk Institute in La Jolla, California. She is one of fourteen members of the 59 strong faculty who are also members of the National Academy of Sciences. She has received multiple honors for her work, including the Javits Neuroscience Investigator Award. She was recently designated Distinguished Woman of the Decade by the City of Los Angeles.[15]

In October of 2007, Pamela Fraker was elected to membership in the National Academy of Sciences. She is professor of molecular biology and biochemistry at Michigan State University, East Lansing. A pioneer in nutritional immunology, Fraker studies the impact of zinc and other nutrients on immune defense systems. Because zinc deficiency accompanies many chronic diseases including AIDS, Crohn's disease, pancreatitis, renal disease and sickle cell anemia, underdeveloped countries suffer more than the citizens of the U.S. from these problems. Fraker is today the foremost nutritional immunology scientist in the world.[16]

Eve Marder is a professor of neuroscience at Brandeis University. In 2007 she was elected to the National Academy of Sciences in recognition of her work on the dynamics of small neuronal networks. Her work showed that neuronal circuits can be reconfigured. Her laboratory produced the dynamic clamp and she is focused on studying how stability in networks arises in developing and adult animals.

A fellow of the American Association for the Advancement of Science and the recipient of numerous other honors, she is also the reviewing editor of *The Journal of Neuroscience* and serves on the editorial boards of *The Journal of Neurophysiology* and five other journals.

After attaining her Ph.D. at the University of California she spent three years as a post-doctoral fellow at the Ecole Normale Superieure in Paris, France.

Barbara McClintock was 81 years old when she received the Nobel Prize in physiology in 1983. Earlier she had been inducted into the National Academy of Sciences when in 1944 she became the third woman to be so honored. In 1971, President Richard Nixon awarded McClintock the National Medal of Science and in 1981 she became the first recipient of the MacArthur Foundation Grant for her lifetime achievements.

All of these designations were the result of McClintock's work as a plant geneticist. Her concentration was focused on the genetics of maize and how genes in chromosomes could move during the breeding of maize plants. She also showed how genes could turn physical characteristics on and off.[17]

Another Nobel Prize winner is Gertrude B. Elion, who was awarded this honor for her work in chemistry when she was 73 years old in 1988. She was the recipient of three honorary doctorates from Brown University, George Washington University and the University of Michigan. Her research in microbiology led her to a study of biochemistry, pharmacology, immunology, and virology.

She was associated with the National Cancer Institute as well as a number of other scientific organizations and with Burroughs Wellcome and a professor of medicine and pharmacology at Duke University.[18]

These examples of outstanding women scientists are, of course, the exception and not the rule. There are numerous scientists who do not gain access to any academy but who, more than the rare super-achiever, exemplify the rise of women in the American scientific endeavor.

The Inclusion of Women in Health Related Positions

In 2006, 32 percent of all American physicians were women. This is reflected in part by the participation of women on the editorial board of the *Journal of the American Medical Association*. In 2007 the editor in chief was Catherine De Angelis, M.D., the first woman to hold that position. In addition, six of the twenty-four editorial board members were women. While this much female participation may fall short of the exact proportion of female physicians to all physicians, the inclusion of 25 percent women on the board together with the appointment of a woman as editor in chief appears to mean that this one time all male profession has finally accepted women as equals.[19]

The entrance of women into the medical profession has led to some significant changes in the lives of both male and female physicians. In the 21st century it is no longer common for physicians to work to the point of physical and mental exhaustion. This is particularly true of the more flexible residency programs available as part time work. Maternity and paternity leave and tax benefits have become normal expectations in the profession. Furthermore, solo practices are disappearing, as large groups are increasingly providing physicians with coverage and more free time to deal with spouses and children. Furthermore, there are now also all-women practices.

More recently, women physicians have been instrumental in developing the position of hospitalist. A hospitalist works only in a hospital caring for patients sent by a physician who then does not see the patient during a stay in the hospital. The hospitalist decides when a patient is to be released and returned to the care of the primary care physician.[20]

Leadership positions in any profession include membership on the faculties of professional schools. Therefore, it is reasonable that women account for about 30 percent of all medical faculty as the 225,000 women physicians practicing in 2007 constituted about 30 percent of all American physicians. Fourteen percent of women medical faculty were full professors in 2005, 26 percent were associate professors that year, 10 percent were department chairs and 10 percent were deans of a medical school.[21]

Women dentists were almost unknown in 1972 when only 1.9 percent of all American dentists were women. In 2005, 22.5 percent of dentists were women and 42 percent of all dental degrees conferred that year were earned by women. This is well reflected in the presence of three women among eleven members of the editorial board of the *Journal of the American Dental Association*. Moreover, the president of the American Dental Association in 2007 was Kathleen Roth of Wisconsin and ten of the thirty-seven officers of the association are also women.

At the beginning of the 21st century, pharmacy is no doubt the most feminized of the health related professions. Over half a century ago, in 1950, only 9 percent of pharmacy students were women. In 1972 this had increased to 24 percent and by 1980 the enrollment of women in schools of pharmacy had reached 40 percent. A further increase was reported in 2004 when 67 percent of all pharmacy students were women. The consequence of this dramatic gender shift may be seen by comparing the proportion of women in pharmacy employment in 1972, when 12.7 percent of pharmacists were women, to the 48.3 percent share of women's employment in pharmacy in 2005.[22]

Female pharmacists are generally younger than male pharmacists. Fifty-five percent of female pharmacists were less than forty years old in 2006. In that year, 38 percent of male pharmacists were less than forty years old.[23]

The number of women enrolled in advanced degree programs in pharmacy has also risen since 1990 when 38 percent of Ph.D. candidates were women to 49 percent in 2004. Much of this increase in female participation is due to the development of clinical pharmacy during the past 30 years. This allows women the flexible schedule to have both a career and a family. These increases in female participation are not yet reflected in the faculty positions at schools of pharmacy, where 81 percent of pharmacy deans are men and 78 percent of faculty are men.[24]

The entrance of so many women into pharmacy allows for the prognosis that a shortage of pharmacists will soon result from the tendency of women to work only part time because they must raise children and to work less in the course of a lifetime because they have the support of husbands. In fact, female pharmacists are four times as likely to be working part time than is true of men.[25]

Women pharmacists also experience a higher rate of turnover than is true of men because women will follow their husbands to new locations determined by the career needs of husbands.[26]

Average salaries for women and men in pharmacy cluster around $100,000 per year.[27] A woman was president of the American Pharmacists Association in 2007. That year she was the only female officer of the association which had five officers and ten trustees of whom two were women.[28]

Women in Mathematics and Related Occupations

Because mathematics is the language of nature, it is evident that the participation of women in science depends first on the attainments of girls and women in mathematics. The achievements of women in mathematics have traditionally lagged behind boys and men. In recent years, however, this has changed considerably as the gender gap in mathematics is closing fast, so that in some areas girls and women have even exceeded men in mathematics skills.

Looking first at *The Nation's Report Card*, we find that the average scale scores and achievement level results in mathematics show that males achieved two points more than females, i.e., 239 as compared to 237 in basic mathematics skills in 2005. This is a negligible difference and reflects in part a higher achievement in mathematics for both genders as compared to 1990.[29]

College enrollment in mathematics between 1995 and 2005 has remained stable. In 1995, 13,851 bachelor's degrees were awarded in mathematics and in 2004 American colleges awarded 13,755 undergraduate degrees in mathematics. In 1995 46.5 percent of these degrees were earned by women and in 2004 45.9 percent of mathematics degrees were earned by women.

In 1971 the Association of Women in Mathematics was founded by a few women then active in the profession. Shortly after the organization of this association, the name was changed to Association for Women in Mathematics. One of the principal objectives of this group is to insure access of women to the profession by eliminating the age old bigotry to the effect that girls and women are incompetent in this area. The evidence has of course proved otherwise. Nevertheless, the number of women earning Ph.D.s in mathematics is still far less than is true of men, as can be seen by the number of graduate students enrolled in Ph.D. programs as of 2004. In that year, 7,486 mathematics graduate students were women. Male graduate students in mathematics in 2004 amounted to 12,387.[30]

In 2007, the Conference Board for the Mathematical Sciences published a report derived from the 2005 survey of mathematical and statistical sciences at American colleges and universities. This revealed that women received about 30 percent of Ph.D.s in mathematics each year from 2001 to 2005. This is reflected in a 30 percent increase in female mathematics college faculty between 2000 to 2005, as women held 4,346 full time positions in 2000. By 2005 women held 5,641 full time positions in college mathematics departments. Therefore, in the fall of 2005, 23 percent of postdoctoral faculty in mathematics were women. Women also comprised the highest number of part time faculty in mathematics in 2005.[31]

Women in Science and Engineering

At the graduate college level the enrollment of women in science and engineering courses still gave males a slight advantage as of 2004. However, the difference was small. Of 476,331 graduate students in science and engineering, 202,020 students were women that year. This discrepancy is unequally distributed. For example, the biological sciences enrolled 66,520 students, of whom 37,249, or a clear majority, were women. In detail, it appears that women constitute a majority of graduate students in biology, biometry, genetics, microbiology, cell biology, nutrition, and pharmacology. All of these areas are needed to attain degrees in medicine.[32]

Women are not as well represented in engineering as they are in the biological sciences. In 2004, 20.5 percent of undergraduate degrees in engineering were awarded to women. This constituted 13,257 B.Sc. degrees out of a total of 64,675, of which evidently 51,418 went to men. In 2004, 27,318 women were graduate students in engineering in 2004 when 96,383 men were enrolled as graduate students in engineering. Note that we speak of students, not graduates.[33]

Women earned 22.7 percent of master's degrees and 18.3 percent of doctorates in engineering in 2005. In 1998, i.e., seven years earlier, women were awarded only 20.5 percent of master's degrees and only 12.6 percent of doctorates in engineering. Evidently, women have made some gains in attaining equality with men in this area of achievement.

Doctor's degrees translate into faculty appointments. Therefore the percentage of faculty in engineering who are women is a reflection of female achievements in these areas. In 2002, 16.9 percent of assistant professors of engineering were women, 11.2 percent of associate professors were women, and only 3.68 percent of full professors of engineering were female.[34]

The gradual entrance of women in engineering brings about a distinctive female perspective to the profession. Diversity and innovation have always depended on a variety of people with different ideas and thoughts.

To make this possible, attitudes concerning women in engineering need to change. Professors need to realize that they should call on female students in class instead of calling only on men. Employers need to seek out women for work which they can do and employers need to appoint women engineers.

An excellent example of a woman who has contributed greatly to engineering in the United States is Linda Abriola. She is dean of engineering at Tufts University. She has been awarded membership in the National Academy of Engineering and previously held a chair in engineering at the University of Michigan, where she earned the Outstanding Educator Award and the University of Michigan Outstanding Member of the Engineering Faculty Award.

Naomi Leonard is professor of engineering and MacArthur fellow at Princeton University. Her interests include motion control problems for autonomous vehicles. She has designed sensing systems that replicate the coordinated behavior of flocks of birds and schools of fish. She designed self-directed undersea robots. As a consequence of her research, Professor Leonard received a Young Investigator Award from the Office of Naval Research, an award achieved by less than 9 percent of 214 applicants. In addition she has received numerous other awards for her outstanding research ability.

Leonard is the daughter of an engineer who designed jet engines. She plays the piano, and has a great interest in ballet dancing. A major in mechanical engineering at Princeton University, she earned a doctorate at the University of Maryland.[35]

Also at Princeton University is Professor Margaret R. Martonosi, a member of the electrical engineering department. She recently received the Howard B. Wentz Award, designed to assist younger faculty in becoming good teachers. In addition, Professor Martonosi received an award from the National Science Foundation. Her principal interest is architecture in high performance computing.

Cornell University has developed a strong interest in bringing women into engineering. Thus, 28 percent of their 734 engineering students in 2003 were women. Twenty-one percent of Cornell University engineering graduate students are women and women engineering faculty are about 13 percent. The faculty includes Paulette Clancy, who heads the School of Chemical and Biomolecular Engineering, and Teresa Jordan, who chairs the department of Earth and Atmospheric Sciences. Christine Shoemaker is another engineering professor at Cornell University. She is a professor in the school of Civil and Environmental Engineering. She was the first woman engineering professor to be given tenure.[36]

Maria Hough is an engineer who heads a business called Hough Engineering, Inc. A graduate of Michigan State University, she designs airports, transportation, water and waste treatment plants and numerous other structures related to structural engineering. Florida, where Hough practices her profession, has a large number of regulatory demands which engineering firms must meet. Her business yields about $500,000 annually and has remained the same size for a decade because Hough accepts only a limited number of projects and does not seek to expand because she wants to give each project her personal attention.

This, then, is an example of the manner in which some women have entered the engineering profession and established their own business and their independence.[37]

In the late 1940s women engineers began to organize for the purpose of furthering the interests of high school and college students in engineering and to address the gender bias that was then most pronounced. In 1952 the Society of Women Engineers was incorporated in New York City and Philadelphia. The opportunities for women in engineering had come about because during World War II numerous jobs once held by servicemen became available to women. The Society of Women Engineers met for the first time in 1950 although there were few women in engineering at the time. It wasn't until ten years later, in 1960, that engineering schools finally welcomed more women and the membership of the Society of Women Engineers reached 1,200. By 1982 the society had 13,000 members and in 2007 it enrolled 17,000 women.

In addition to the Society of Women Engineers there is also a Women in Engineering Organization which makes considerable efforts to induce high school and college girls to enter the engineering schools and then the profession.[38]

American Women Inventors

Randi Altschul (b. 1961)

In 1999 Randi Altschul invented the disposable cell phone. For some years, Altschul had invented numerous children's toys and produced them. Her company is called Diceland Technology Corporation.

The phone has the trademark The Phone Card Phone and is 3" by 3" and no thicker than three credit cards. The phone has 60 minutes of calling time installed but permits the user to add more minutes or toss it away. The retail price of this device is about $20. Altschul has no electronic education or experience but consulted with others who had such knowledge. Altschul and her partner, Lee Volte, also created a paper laptop computer which will sell for twenty dollars.[39]

Katherine Burr Blodgett (1898–1979)

Blodgett is best known for her invention of non-reflecting glass and the development of the science and technology of thin films together with a color gauge used to make such measurements. She also invented a non-reflecting invisible glass by finding a method that eliminates reflected light. These inventions improved automobile windshields, store windows, camera lenses, telescopes, eyeglasses, picture frames and submarine periscopes.

Blodgett earned a Ph.D. at the British Cavendish Laboratories and at Princeton University. She received many honors during her career, including a medal from the American Chemical Society. She was also an actress and a poet.

Josephine Garis Cochrane (1839–1913)

The dishwasher was invented by Josephine Garis Cochrane in Shelbyville, Illinois, in 1886. Cochrane was a so-called socialite, i.e., a woman who did not work either outside or inside her house. She had servants who chipped the dishes they were washing. Her dishwashing machine became the hit of the 1893 World's Columbian Exposition. Because she was a woman, she faced the usual refusal of manufacturers to even consider her invention until the designs of several men failed. She therefore gave her invention to a temperance restaurant, which led to widespread publicity and acceptance of her dishwasher.

Marion O'Brien Donovan (1917–1998)

Marion Donovan invented the disposable diaper. She was the daughter of the inventor of the South Bend Lathe, which is used to grind automobile gears.

Having earned a degree in English, she became the assistant beauty editor of *Vogue* magazine in New York City, where she married James Donovan and moved to Connecticut.

On having her children, she was faced with the exasperating need to change diapers incessantly and deal with wet sheets as well. This led her to design and perfect on her sewing machine a reusable diaper which she called a boater because it "helped babies stay afloat."

In 1949, Saks Fifth Avenue sold these diapers, which became an instant success. Donovan then invented the disposable paper diaper, which was not easy, as the moisture must be removed from the baby's skin. It took Donovan ten years to convince Victor Mills paper company to manufacture the disposable paper diapers.

In 1958 Donovan earned a degree in architecture from Yale University and then designed her own house. She also invented a 30 garment compact hanger, a soap dish that drained into the sink, an elastic cord that connects over the shoulder to the zipper on the back of a dress and many others. She was awarded over a dozen patents.

Sally Fox (b. 1955)

Sally Fox invented something that could not be done. At least, that was the opinion of all experts who knew that it was impossible to create a naturally colored cotton that could be spun, that is, made into threads on a machine. In 1989, Sally Fox did just that. Before her invention, only white cotton could be commercially spun, although it had to be bleached and dyed. These processes create a great deal of pollution. But Foxfiber, as Fox called her product, needs no dye and no bleach. She first produced celadon green and reddish brown. Since then she has developed a number of new colors.

Fox studied entomology, the study of insects, in college and after graduation joined the Peace Corps and traveled to Africa.

On her return to the United States in the 1980s she found work as a pollinator for the cotton industry. This led to the founding of her own company, which has become a $10 million business.

Fox is the recipient of the United Nations Environmental Program Award, the *Discovery Magazine* Award, *Good Housekeeping*'s Green Award, and was recently recognized by the Massachusetts Institute of Technology.

Betty Graham (1924–1980)

Betty Nesmith Graham was a typist and secretary who invented Liquid Paper, used to cover up typing errors. Prior to the invention of the word processor, electric typewriters made it difficult to erase errors. She noticed that artists do not erase their errors but paint over them. This observation led her to put some tempera water-based paint in a bottle and then used her watercolor brush to correct mistakes in the office.

After five years of making some improvements, she finally marketed her invention under the label Mistake Out but changed that to Liquid Paper when she founded her own company. In 1979, when she employed 200 people, she sold her business to Gillette Corporation for $47.5 million.

Only one-half of her $50 million estate was inherited by her only son from a failed marriage. The other half went to the Council of Ideas.

Ruth Handler (1916–2002)

Barbie is the invention of Ruth Handler, one of the three co-founders of the Mattel Co., the largest toy manufacturer in the United States. Ruth Handler is also responsible for the name Mattel which she created by combining letters from the names of Harold Matson, one of the co-founders, and her husband, Elliot Handler.

Barbie has become an American icon. It was first sold in 1959 and has changed over the years as clothes changed. Barbie has also undergone several facelifts and has more recently appeared in multi-cultural form.

The Mattel Co. first sold only picture frames and then some dollhouse furniture, a business which finally became a toy manufacturer. The Handlers then bought advertising on the Mickey Mouse Show, which increased their business immensely.

The success of Mattel is so great that the company is listed as one of *Fortune Magazine*'s 500, as it already generated $300 million annual revenue in the 1970s.

Amanda Theodosia Jones (1835–1914)

Jones invented vacuum canning of food and the oil safety valve. She first earned her living as a teacher when she was only 15. She was also an author, writing first for *The Ladies Respiratory Magazine.*

Once she had perfected her canning method, called the Ones Process, she patented her invention and then founded a preserving company run entirely by women. She wrote: "This is a woman's industry. No man will vote our stock, transact our business, pronounce on women's wages, supervise our factories."

This was a shocking message in the male dominated society of the nineteenth century.

In the 1880s Amanda Jones moved to the oil fields in Texas. The oil industry needed to burn oil for power to run numerous newly invented devices. Burning oil was then very dangerous because it was not possible to know how much oil would come up from an oil well and how it would light. By inventing the oil safety valve, Jones made it possible to control the flow of oil and prevent a major fire if things went wrong.

Stephanie Kwolek (b. 1923)

Kwolek invented a fiber that is used to make bulletproof vests. Called Kevlar, this material is five times stronger, ounce for ounce, than steel. The material is also used to make radial tires, brake pads, racing sails, fiber optic cable, spacecraft shells and suspension bridge cables. It is also used to make skis, safety helmets and camping gear.

Kwolek has earned a degree in chemistry from Carnegie Mellon University, as it is now called. This led to an appointment to the Dupont Research Division, which then allowed her to experiment with the creation of long molecule chains resulting in petroleum based synthetic fibers. Her work at Dupont led to sales worth millions of dollars worldwide.

Kwolek owns 17 patents and has received numerous scientific awards. She holds the National Medal of Technology and the Lemelson MIT Lifetime Achievement Award.

Hedwig Eva Maria Kiesler, a.k.a. "Hedy Lamarr" (1913–2000)

Hedwig Kiesler invented the Spread Spectrum, which is the technical basis for wireless communications in cell phones, faxes, integrated bar code scanners, modem devices, digital dispatch, faxes, computer mail or multimedia data. Lamarr was assisted in her invention by George Antheil, an American composer.

Originally, her invention served as an anti-jamming device for the use of radio-controlled torpedoes. She became interested in developing such a device when she was married to the Viennese ammunitions manufacturer and millionaire Fritz Mandl, who sold arms to Hitler. At the time of her marriage to Mandl she had begun her movie career and came to the attention of Mandl because of her exceptional beauty. She was later labeled "the most beautiful woman in the world."

Born in 1913 in Vienna, she divorced Mandl when she was 24 years old and moved to London and then to Hollywood, where she starred as Hedy Lamarr in 34 films until her retirement in 1958. She and her co-inventor Antheil donated their invention to the U.S. Navy. They earned no money from this device although they had a patent on what they called "our secret communications system."

In 1942 their invention could not be implemented but came into use during the Cuban missile crisis in 1962, three years after the Kiesler Lamarr-Antheil patent had expired.[40]

Sybilla Masters (d. 1720)

Sybilla Masters was the first American woman inventor. Like so many women who invented in the past, she received no credit for her inventions. Instead her husband was given an English patent when Sybilla found a way of processing corn into many different food and clothing products. The patent was issued to Thomas Masters for "Cleansing Curing and Refining of Indian Corn." A second patent was issued to Thomas Masters for Sybilla's invention called "Working and Weaving in a New Method." This was a new method of making hats and "Bonnets."

These patents were granted by King George I. In the journal *Scientific American* of August 1891 there is an illustration showing the cleaning and another showing the curing process invented by Sybilla Masters. The sheller invented by Masters was worked by a donkey activating a revolving cylinder.

Ellen Ochoa (b. 1958)

A research scientist and astronaut, Dr. Ochoa holds a doctorate in electrical engineering from Stanford University. While there she developed an optical system designed to detect imperfections in repeating patterns. This invention can be used for quality control in the manufacture of numerous intricate machined parts. Later, Ochoa also invented an optical system that can be used to robotically manufacture goods or in robotic guiding systems.

Ochoa has also participated in three space flights, having spent 719 hours in space aboard the shuttle *Discovery* in 1999.

Patsy Sherman (1930–2008)

"Scotchgard" is a method for treating carpets with a stain repellant which has grown into numerous other products known as Scotchgard protectors. This was invented by Patsy Sherman while working as a chemist for the 3M company in Minnesota, where she was born in 1930. Sherman was one of very few chemists to be working in research when she was hired by 3M in 1952 to work on fluorochemical polymers.

Her invention was particularly significant because experts had pronounced such products as Scotchgard as thermodynamically impossible.

Sherman's partner in this discovery-invention is Samuel Smith. Both were inducted into the Minnesota Inventors Hall of Fame.

Valerie Thomas (b. 1925)

Valerie Thomas invented an illusion transmitter which permits television images to be located behind a flat screen so that three dimensional images appear to be "right in your living room."

Thomas had earned a degree in physics when she became a mathematical data analyst for the National Aeronautics and Space Administration (NASA).

There she developed an image processing system on Lansat, the first satellite to send images from outer space. She was associate chief of the Space Science Data Operations at NASA and project manager of the Space Physics Analysis Network. This led to the development of the Internet.

Lisa Vallino

Vallino invented a polyethylene site protector called an IV House because it protects the site when an intravenous needle is inserted into a hospital patient's arm. Prior to that invention, nurses would cut a plastic cup in half and tape it for protection on the site of the IV. The Vallino invention is shaped like a computer mouse, soft, transparent and attached with a piece of tape. The IV House is also safer and less expensive than previous models of IV protection. The Vallino device makes tampering more difficult so that there are fewer re-insertions.[41]

Women in Space Exploration

Twenty-one years had to pass before an American woman flew into space after Alan Shepard had become the first American man in space in 1962. Shepard completed a 15-minute suborbital mission. Two Russian women had preceded her in space when, in 1983, Dr. Sally K. Ride, then 32 years old, flew for 147 hours on STS-7 *Challenger* with four male astronauts. Ride was selected a mission candidate in 1978, the year in which she was awarded the Ph.D. in physics from Stanford University. She flew another 8 day mission in 1984, which included another woman, Kathryn D. Sullivan, Ph.D. She remained with the National Aeronautics and Space Administration until she joined the faculty of the University of California at San Diego as professor of physics in 1989. In 1989 Sally Ride founded a company called Sally Ride Science, which seeks to interest young girls in pursuing a scientific career. She is also the author of five science books for children and in addition to her membership on the President's Committee of Advisors on Science and Technology serves on numerous boards and committees concerned with scientific inquiry.

Dr. Ride is also a member of the National Women's Hall of Fame and has received a number of scientific awards.

Kathryn D. Sullivan, Ph.D., is the first woman to walk in space. She did so in 1984 when she and six others flew on an STS-41G for eight days. Her spacewalk was called extravehicular activity by NASA officials. A geologist, Sullivan conducted a number of experiments including a demonstration showing that satellite refueling is possible. After flying three missions, Sullivan has logged over 532 hours in space.

Her last space flight occurred in 1990, when she participated in launching the Hubble space telescope and conducted a number of scientific experiments while on the spacecraft.

After leaving NASA in 1993, she became the CEO of the Center for Science and Industry in Columbus, Ohio. She is the recipient of numerous honors, including being named to a number of boards and officers of corporations.

On January 28, 1986, two women astronauts and five men died when the Shuttle *Challenger* exploded seventy-three seconds after launch. The two women astronauts were Dr. Judith A. Resnik and Christa McAuliffe. Resnik had earned a Ph.D. in electrical engineering at the University of Maryland in 1977 and was selected as an astronaut candidate by NASA in 1978. Her first spaceflight came in 1984, when she was a mission specialist on the *Discovery*.

In addition to her scientific accomplishments, Resnik was also a classical pianist and experienced aircraft pilot.

Christa Corrigan McAuliffe was a history teacher who was nevertheless accepted for training by NASA after her name was chosen from among 11,500 applicants to be included in the space program. The idea was to have a teacher talk to children from space and McAuliffe had the bad luck to be so appointed.

Unlike all other astronauts, McAuliffe had no scientific education but had earned a master's degree in school administration. Nevertheless, she made every effort to meet the requirements of NASA in their training program and flew to her death with the entire crew.

Eileen Collins is the first woman to have piloted and commanded a U.S.

spacecraft. Retired in 2007, she is a graduate in mathematics from Syracuse University and holds two master's degrees from Stanford University and Webster University. She is an Air Force pilot and was a flight instructor at Edwards Air Force Base before being selected for the space program in 1990.

In 1995 she became the first female shuttle pilot aboard *Discovery*. After several additional missions she became the first female shuttle commander in 1999 on the *Columbia* orbiter. In August of 2005 Collins was the commander on the *Discovery* orbiter after the 2003 loss of the *Columbia* and its crew of five men and two women when the spacecraft broke up over Texas, fifteen minutes before it would have landed in Florida.[42]

When Pamela Melroy commanded the space shuttle *Discovery* in October of 2007 and docked it at the International Space Station, that docking marked the first time that two women were in charge of both the shuttle and the space station. The space station was commanded by Peggy A. Whitson as the station traveled around the earth at 17,000 miles an hour with two female commanders.[43]

Pamela Melroy holds a master of science degree from the Massachusetts Institute of Technology in earth and planetary sciences. Commissioned through the Air Force Reserve Officer Training Program, she served as pilot and commander in the first Iraq war with over 200 combat hours. In December of 1994 she was selected by NASA and was trained as a shuttle pilot. She has spent more than 570 hours in space and also held a number of administrative positions with NASA.

Peggy A. Whitson, Ph.D., earned that degree in biochemistry at Rice University. She worked for NASA as a researcher in the biochemistry laboratory which led to her appointment as project scientist of the Shuttle-Mir program in 1992. In turn she became commander of the International Space Station for a six month tour of duty. This is her second such assignment.

Together with a number of other women now employed in the American space program, these female astronauts have demonstrated that gender is no longer a criterion for success in scientific endeavors nor in the military. While those older Americans who lived at a time when women were given no consideration with reference to scientific achievements of any kind may find these women astonishing, the time has arrived when female participation in all aspects of scientific work is a matter of course, as is also true of the entrance of women into the political life of the nation.

Summary

Although the ancient prejudices against women scientists persist, women have made great progress in every area of scientific work over the thirty years ending in 2007. The prejudice against female efforts in mathematically based sciences is already visible in some grade schools when teachers call on boys but not girls in science recitations. Yet, there is no evidence that there is a true difference in scientific ability based on gender. On the contrary. The increase in the number of women earning doctorates in numerous sciences has persisted over thirty years, as has the acceptance of women into the National Academy of Sciences.

The greatest advances in scientific occupations made by women have been in such health related occupations as physician, dentist and pharmacist. Additional improvements have been made by women in mathematics and in engineering. There are also numerous women inventors and most recently women who have flown into space and have even commanded spacecrafts.

Chapter 7

Women in Government and Politics

Women Govern States

Whether or not the 44th president of the United States is a woman will make a difference only in the sense that such a victory would culminate a long struggle for gender equality in the United States. The election of a woman to the presidency or at least the candidacy of a woman for that great office signals that the American people have expanded the political rights of all Americans over the 219 years since the first Congress met in New York City and Philadelphia in 1789.

Then, only propertied men could vote in any election in any state of the Union except New Jersey. There women voted from July 2, 1776, when the New Jersey Constitution was adopted, until 1807, when the New Jersey legislature deprived women of that right.

Meeting in Burlington, New Jersey, in 1776, the Provincial Congress of New Jersey adopted a constitution which included this paragraph: "All inhabitants of this Colony of full age, who are worth fifty pound proclamation money, clear estate in the same, and have resided within the county in which they claim a vote for twelve months immediately preceding the election, shall be entitled to vote for Representatives in the Council and Assembly and also for all other public officers, that shall be elected by the people of the county at large."[1]

In 1844 the women of New Jersey were excluded from voting, as the revised Constitution of New Jersey followed the example of the New Jersey legislature by using just one sentence in that constitution to deprive women of voting rights which had already been exercised for 68 years. That sentence read: "Every white male citizen of the United States ... shall be entitled to vote."[2]

Note that blacks were also excluded from voting in New Jersey in 1844. Nevertheless, the fact that both groups had at one time voted in New Jersey provided part of the impetus for the suffragists who later fought to restore that right in New Jersey and make it universal in all of the United States by 1920.

Before 1920 some of the western states also allowed women to vote in local elections. Wyoming was the first to do so in 1890 and others followed in the succeeding years.

Today, women not only vote in large numbers, but women are also elected to major state and national offices. For example, between January 18, 1994 and January 31, 2004, Christine Todd Whitman was the 50th governor of New Jersey. Then she was appointed administrator of the Environmental Protection Agency by President George W. Bush and served in that capacity from January 2001 to June 2003.

Whitman is the descendant of two politically active families, i.e., the Todds and the Schleys. She graduated from Wheaton College with a degree in government and promptly worked on the Nelson Rockefeller campaign in 1968. Her husband, John R. Whitman, is descended from the former governor of New York, Charles S. Whitman. She is also related to the Bush family.

Early in her political career, Whitman worked at the Office of Economic Opportunity, which was then headed by Donald Rumsfeld, later to become Secretary of Defense. She also worked for the Nixon administration and the Republican National Committee. Later she was appointed to the cabinet of Governor Keane of New Jersey, leading to her candidacy and election to the position of governor.[3]

Additional female governors have been Sarah Palin of Alaska, Janet Napolitano of Arizona, Jodi Rell of Connecticut, Ruth Minner of Delaware, Linda Lingle of Hawaii, Kathleen Sebelius of Kansas, Kathleen Blanco of Louisiana, Jennifer Granholm of Michigan and Christine Gregoire of Washington.

These nine women constitute 18 percent of all state governors as of 2007. In view of the American sex ratio which favors women over the voting age of 18 by 2 percent in younger years and by 33 percent among the oldest Americans, it is to be expected that the low level of female participation in state government will wane in the next decade so that eventually one-half or more of our 50 governors will be women.

In earlier years of the 20th century, a number of women were also elected governors of several American states, although this was most unusual. Then only Nellie Ross replaced her husband in Wyoming from 1925 to 1927 as did Miriam "Ma" Ferguson in Texas in 1925 and Lurleen Wallace of Alabama in

1967. Wallace belongs to the second half of the 20th century, which saw the election of Ella Grasso of Connecticut, who was the first woman ever elected governor in her own right and without a husband. Then, Dixy Lee Ray became governor of Washington in 1977, Vesta Roy assumed the governor's position in New Hampshire in 1982, in 1984 Martha Collins became the governor of Kentucky and Madeleine Kunin became governor of Vermont in 1985. Twenty states have had female governors over the years so that the voters in thirty states have yet to do so. One of these states is New York, which has never had a female governor but whose voters elected a woman senator in 2000 and again in 2006.

The First Female President?

Hillary Rodham Clinton is therefore the only New York woman among 63 men from New York ever elected to the Senate of the United States. In 2006, Senator Clinton announced her candidacy for the presidency and therefore is also the only woman ever to attain serious consideration for that office. She follows Geraldine Ferarro, who was nominated vice-presidential candidate on the Democratic slate in 1984 alongside Walter Mondale, who was then the presidential candidate of his party.[4]

Senator Clinton deviates from the traditional manner of achieving membership in the U.S. Senate in that she held no elected or appointed office before reaching the U.S. Senate. Nevertheless, as a senator from New York she is undoubtedly eligible to become president, as have a number of U.S. senators in earlier years. In the 20th century, Warren G. Harding (1865–1923), the 29th president, served in the U.S. Senate from 1915 to 1921. Prior to his election to the Senate he had been lieutenant governor of Ohio and Ohio state senator. When he became president, Harry S. Truman (1884–1972) had served in the U.S. Senate for ten years, from 1935 to 1945. In that year he became vice president and on the death of Franklin Roosevelt in April of that year he succeeded to the presidency.

John F. Kennedy (1917–1963) entered the House of Representatives in 1947 and became a U.S. senator in 1953 until his election to the presidency in 1960. Likewise, his successor, Lyndon Johnson (1908 to 1973), had served in the House of Representatives from 1937 to 1949 and thereafter became a U.S. senator from 1949 to 1961 and on the murder of John F. Kennedy advanced from vice president to president in 1963.

In sum, it is evident that all who had entered the Senate and then became president had previous political experience as elected officeholders.

Members of the U.S. Senate from New York serving in the past were also elected to lesser offices earlier in their career. For example, Senator Charles Schumer was elected to the New York Assembly in 1950, entered the House of Representatives in 1980 and became a U.S. senator in 1998.

Senator Daniel Patrick Moynihan (1927–2003) became senator from New York in 1977 and served until 2001. Earlier he had been secretary to Governor Averill Harriman and ambassador to the United Nations. Likewise, James Buckley had been undersecretary of state in the Reagan administration before becoming a senator from New York in 1971.

Numerous other examples of U.S. senators elected from any state indicate that almost all had served in an elected or appointed office or were war heroes or otherwise distinguished themselves, as did John Glenn, the first American to orbit the earth. He was also a major war hero in World War II and the Korean War. In 1974 Glenn was elected to the U.S. Senate from Ohio.[5]

Hillary Clinton derives her political experience from her position as the first lady of the United States during the presidency of President William J. Clinton from 1993 to 2001. She is the only first Lady to hold an elective office and the only first lady to become a candidate for the presidency.

During her tenure as first lady Mrs. Clinton chaired the President's Task Force on Health Care Reform but was unsuccessful in bringing these proposals to fruition because of opposition by the insurance industry and the failure of Congress to support the proposals. Nevertheless, this experience and her involvement in numerous other political activities in and out of the White House have given Hillary Clinton a good deal of background as a presidential candidate. In fact, she has been in the White House, not as an onlooker but as a participant in President Clinton's administration.[6]

Senator Clinton is one of 16 female senators among 84 men serving in the 110th Congress. Two of these senators, Dianne Feinstein and Barbara Boxer, are both from California and two more, Olympia Snowe and Susan Collins, are both from Maine. Likewise, Washington has two female senators, Patty Murray and Maria Cantwell. Therefore, only 13 states have female senators.

The First Woman Speaker of the House

At the opening of the 110th Congress of the United States in January of 2007, Nancy D'Alesandro Pelosi became the first female speaker of the House of Representatives. According to the Presidential Succession Act of 1947, the speaker of the House is the second in line to succeed the president of the United States should the vice president be unable to serve in that position on the departure of the president.

The election of Pelosi to this powerful office not only represented a major, visible change in the ascent of women to political power in the country, but it also indicated the end of at least one aspect of ethnic bigotry in the United States. Pelosi is of Italian heritage and a Catholic. This religious and ethnic combination was at one time cause for riots and violence in the United States, as illustrated by the anti–Italian riot in New Orleans in 1890 which resulted from the assassination of the police chief, David Hennessy, and the unfounded assumption that the Mafia and therefore all Italian immigrants were implicated in that murder. A lynch mob attacked a number of Italian immigrants who had nothing to do with the murder of Hennessy and mutilated and killed these innocents among demands to "hang the dagos" and stop all Italian immigration.[7]

Similar riots against Italian and other immigrants occurred in New York City, Philadelphia and Boston.

Pelosi became a member of the House from San Francisco in 1987. Since then she has been re-elected 10 times, receiving at least 75 percent of the votes since 87 percent of registered voters in her district are Democrats. In 2001, Pelosi was elected minority whip, which made her second in command to minority leader Richard Gephart of Missouri. When Gephart resigned in 2002, Pelosi was elected to replace him and therefore became the first woman to lead a major party in the House.[8]

Nancy Pelosi is the daughter of a professional politician. Her father, Thomas D'Alesandro was a U.S. congressman from Maryland and mayor of Baltimore, an office one of her brothers also held. After graduating from college, Pelosi interned for two congressmen. After marrying Paul Pelosi, the couple moved to San Francisco where her brother-in-law was a member of the city's board of supervisors.

This connection allowed Pelosi to enter politics after her fifth child had become an adult. In addition, she benefits from her husband's business acumen, as the Pelosi family is reputed to have $25 million in assets, making Nancy Pelosi one of the richest members of Congress.[9]

The 110th Congress had 435 members. Of these 71 were women from 32 states of the union. Evidently, 18 states have no female representatives.

Women Enter the Judiciary

When Sandra Day O'Connor was appointed by President Reagan to the Supreme Court of the United States in 1981 she was promptly criticized by both conservative and liberal politicians. This criticism was largely motivated by the fact that O'Connor was the first woman to become one of the "nine old men" on the Supreme Court. Now there were only eight men and one woman and some could not reconcile themselves to this arrangement.

Justice O'Connor served until 2005 and then retired because of illness in her family. During her tenure she supported abortion rights. She also decided several death penalty cases in favor of the defendants. She also favored affirmative action and voted in favor of minority rights with reference to college admissions.

In the area of religion, O'Connor drafted guidelines for the use of lower courts to determine whether or not a Nativity scene could be shown.

After her retirement, O'Connor became the chancellor of the College of William and Mary in Virginia. The college was chartered in 1693 by the king and queen of England. After the American Revolution, George Washington became the first American chancellor, followed by numerous celebrities and politicians.[10]

Ruth Bader Ginsburg is the second woman to be appointed to the Supreme Court. She was nominated by President Clinton in 1993. She has been a so-called liberal judge, affirming the constitutional right to privacy and gender equality. She also supports abortion rights. Most controversial has been her advocacy of using foreign or international law. This dispute came about in the case of *Roper v. Simmons* in which the court held that a convict who was less than 18 years old at the time of his crime could not be executed on the grounds that foreign countries are opposed to the juvenile death penalty.[11]

In addition to the incumbency of Justice Ginsburg, numerous women have been appointed and elected to judgeships in this country during the past 30 years. Among these are several women who have been appointed to the Federal Court of Appeals, which is far more often the court of last resort than is true of the U.S. Supreme Court.

Chief Judge Mary M. Schroeder of the Ninth Circuit Court of Appeals is an excellent example of a woman who rose high within her profession.

Schroeder was appointed by President Carter in 1979 and became chief judge in 2000. The chief judge rotates into that position based on seniority relative to judges who are 64 years of age or younger. A chief judge serves seven years or until age 70, whichever comes first. Therefore Judge Schroeder retired in November of 2007.

Her tenure included a 600 percent increase in immigration appeals. She was instrumental in promoting jury reform and dealing with media relations and the health care of judges in her circuit.[12]

Women in the President's Cabinet

When Franklin D. Roosevelt, 32nd president of the U.S., appointed Frances Perkins (1882–1965) to be secretary of labor, Perkins became the first woman to be part of a president's cabinet. The name of such a group of advisors to the president is derived from the small room in which the group met in earlier years.

Frances Perkins was instrumental in bringing about child labor laws, unemployment compensation, protection of women workers, injury compensation, the minimum wage and old age insurance.

All of these programs were part of the Roosevelt New Deal. In her role of secretary of labor, Perkins reformed the board of the National Labor Relations Board. She served in her capacity of cabinet member throughout the 12 years of the Roosevelt administration and then accepted an appointment by President Harry Truman to be a member of the Civil Service Commission.[13]

Thereafter a number of women have served in various capacities in the cabinets of American presidents. In 2007, four of the fifteen members of the cabinet of President George W. Bush were women. Among these was Dr. Condoleezza Rice, the second woman to be secretary of state. The others were Margaret Spellings, secretary of education; Mary Peters, secretary of transportation; and Elaine Chao, secretary of labor.

The appointment of Rice as the 66th secretary of state followed the tenure of General Colin Powell, who held that office during the first four years of the Bush administration.

Rice had an academic career before entering politics. She had been professor of political science at Stanford University where she also acted as an administrator for six years. While there, Rice became a member of numerous boards of directors and in addition published a number of articles commenting on world affairs. She authored or co-authored several books on foreign policy and served President George W. Bush as special assistant for national security affairs.

During her tenure as secretary of state, Rice has traveled all over the world representing the U.S. in numerous international conferences.

While the position of secretary of state was at one time most powerful in that the secretary dealt with the heads of foreign governments on a personal basis, this has been somewhat diminished in the 21st century because electronics make it possible for the president to contact foreign leaders directly from his office. Furthermore, presidents can fly almost anywhere on Air Force One and conduct foreign affairs themselves, as they do frequently.

Elaine Chao, a.k.a. Mrs. Mitch McConnell, is the 24th secretary of labor. She married Senator McConnell of Kentucky in 1993 and thereafter was appointed to the cabinet position by President Bush. Earlier, she had been the director of the Peace Corps and chair of the Federal Maritime Commission under President Reagan and deputy secretary of transportation during the administration of President George H.W. Bush.

A native of Taiwan, at one time called Formosa, she holds an M.B.A. from Harvard. She succeeded William Aramony as head of the United Way after Aramony was jailed for stealing over $1 million from that charity.[14]

In September of 2006, President Bush nominated Mary Peters to be secretary of transportation. Peters had a twenty year career in transportation as federal highway administrator and as director of the Arizona Department of Transportation where she had worked through the ranks for 15 years. Previously she had been a consultant at an engineering firm dealing with transportation issues. Peters advocates bringing private companies into the construction and operation of highways. She also wants to eliminate the use of gasoline taxes for the support of highway construction.

Peters has a bachelor's degree from the on-line University of Phoenix.[15]

Margaret Spellings is the secretary of education in the cabinet of President George W. Bush. In that capacity she is well known as the author of the No Child Left Behind initiative, which became the landmark of the Bush administration's effort to reform American education beginning with kindergarten. The law was signed by President Bush in January of 2002 after the program was authorized by Congress. It was not reauthorized as late as December of 2007, with little chance of passing Congress a second time.[16]

The intent of this act was to require that all public schools teachers be highly qualified by the end of 2006, a requirement not met by even one state a year later. Secretary Spellings did indeed ask all states to submit proposals as to how they would insure that the poorest schools would be staffed by qualified and experienced teachers. This effort has led to a good deal of paperwork but has had no effect on teacher qualifications in the classroom because a good number of inner-city schools continue to rely on teachers who actually failed teacher qualification tests. This is true because the allegedly high standard for hiring teachers is ignored at hiring time because there is no choice. Well qualified graduates of teacher education programs will not apply at inner city schools.[17]

A good example of this dilemma is the approval by North Dakota of 4,000 teachers who were declared insufficiently qualified by federal officials. In addition, Utah lawmakers have denounced the law as "getting in our way," claiming that the method of defining highly qualified teachers is faulty. Numerous other states have similar objections so that the ideal in this case does not meet reality.

Ms. Spellings has been described as a Washington insider. A longtime friend of presidential advisor Karl Rove, she campaigned for George W. Bush when he ran for governor of Texas and when he ran for president. She was a lobbyist for the Texas Association of School Boards. She is known as a bare knuckles fighter who has been known to call political opponents "un–American" and "little children."[18]

Women Ambassadors

Although Perle Mesta was undoubtedly the best known ambassador this country ever had, she was not the first American woman ambassador to a foreign country. That honor belongs to Ruth Bryan Owen, who was appointed minister to Denmark. Minister is a rank lower than ambassador but carries the same responsibilities.

Owen was the daughter of William Jennings Bryan, candidate for the presidency on the Democratic ticket in 1896, 1900 and 1908. Unsuccessful each time, Bryan nevertheless became famous as an orator and as defender of the prohibition of alcohol and opponent of the teaching of evolution in the public schools.

Ruth Bryan Owen married a British citizen in 1910 after divorcing her first husband. This second marriage cost her her American citizenship, as a 1907 law assigned citizenship of married women to the country of their husbands. Thereafter she moved to Florida where her parents were living. In 1926 she ran for Congress unsuccessfully but was elected in 1928. Because the law made her a British citizen she had to persuade Congress that she should be seated and the law repealed as it applied only to women but not to men. Furthermore, the 1925 Cable Act permitted women to reapply for citizenship. Congress agreed and she was seated and served in the House for one more term. In 1932 she was defeated because she was a proponent of prohibition. This, however, did not end her political career. In 1932 she was appointed to represent the U.S. in Denmark. A widow, she married a Danish captain Borge Rohde, and thereupon became a Danish citizen. She resigned her position as minister that year.[19]

Perle Mesta (1889–1975) had the signal honor of having a musical play composed about her by Irving Berlin (1888 to 1989), who was without doubt the most prolific American songwriter.

This musical was first performed in London, England, in 1950 and starred Ethel Merman as the ambassador to Lichtenburg. In fact, Mesta was ambassador to Luxembourg, a European principality bordering on Belgium, Germany and France. The country occupies only 2586 square kilometers or 1,603 square miles.

She was appointed to this diplomatic position by President Harry Truman in 1949 and remained in that position until 1953 when Dwight Eisenhower became president.

Perle Mesta was born Pearl Skirvin, the daughter of a wealthy Oklahoma oilman. She married George Mesta, a steel manufacturer, in 1916, and became his widow in 1925. From him she inherited $78 million which she used to become a socialite in Washington, D.C., in 1940 after changing her name to Perle.

She became known for inviting politicians to lavish parties. An invitation to such a party was regarded as a sign of arrival at the inner circle among politicians. An early supporter of Harry Truman in his bid for re-election in 1948, she was rewarded with the diplomatic appointment to Luxembourg.[20]

Pamela Harriman (1920–1997) was another female ambassador who was best known for having numerous affairs with both married and single men of prominence. Born in England, daughter of the 11th Lord Digby, she was first married to Randolph Churchill, son of the erstwhile prime minister Winston Churchill. She married him in 1939 at age 19 and divorced him in 1941. Thereafter she married Leland Hayward, a Broadway producer, and upon a second divorce married the governor of New York, Averill Harriman, who had also been ambassador to Russia and Great Britain. She became an American citizen and subsequently supported William Jefferson Clinton in his effort to become president. Pam Harriman served as a Democratic fundraiser and contributed large sums to Democratic candidates She became ambassador to France in 1993 and died at her post in 1997.

Women Mayors

In 2007, only 16.2 percent of mayors of American cities with populations over 30,000 were women. The largest city with a woman mayor was Baltimore, whose mayor, Sheila Dixon, presides over a population of 652,000 citizens. Heather Fargo of Sacramento, California; Meyera Oberndorf of Virginia Beach, Virginia; and Shirley Franklin of Atlanta, Georgia, head populations of more than 400,000. All other female mayors were elected to smaller cities and, mainly, small towns.

Since Baltimore has a black population amounting to 65 percent, it is not surprising that the city is governed by a black woman. Sheila Dixon was born in Baltimore in 1953 and holds a master's degree in education from Johns Hopkins University.

She taught briefly in the elementary schools of Baltimore and then found employment in the Maryland Department of Business and Economic Development. In 1987 she was elected to the Baltimore City Council after gaining membership in the Baltimore Democratic Central Committee a year earlier. She was elected city council president and thereafter assumed the position of mayor of Baltimore because the previous mayor, Martin O'Malley, was elected governor of Maryland, effective January 2007.

Mayor Dixon has joined the mayors of several other east coast cities in a Mayor's Illegal Guns Coalition because Baltimore has a murder rate of 43.5 per 100,000 people, which is nearly eight times greater than the national average of 5.6 per 100,000 population.[21]

The mayor of Atlanta, Georgia, is Shirley Franklin. Elected to a second term in 2005, she has a long history in politics. She was commissioner of cultural affairs in the administration of Maynard Jackson in 1978 and became city manager in the administration of Andrew Young. She was a member of the Atlanta Committee for the Olympic Games in 1991. In 1999 she became a member of the Georgia Transportation Authority.

Franklin is best known for cutting the expenses of Atlanta by eliminating hundreds of jobs, freezing vacancies and even cutting her own salary. She holds a master's degree in sociology from the University of Pennsylvania.[22]

There are numerous additional women mayors and officeholders in the United States. Today, in 2008, this is neither remarkable nor surprising as the rights of women to political power are ever increasing as the members of each generation view as commonplace the political scene that they have witnessed since the day of their birth.

There are, however, many Americans who are old enough to know that the entrance of women into politics was achieved after a long battle against established prejudices and culture lag. Yet, as early as the eighteenth century, some women were already demanding political rights and the rights to free speech, then rejected, now assumed as only natural.

A Brief History of Women's Liberation

Anne Hutchinson (1591–1643)

Although Anne Hutchinson was tried and convicted by the General Court of Massachusetts of heresy (1637) it is evident that her preaching was very much in accord with the religious views of her condemners. One year later, Hutchinson was also condemned by a religious court and excommunicated from the Puritan Church. She then moved to Rhode Island, where she became co-founder of a new colony. Thereafter she and her family moved to Westchester, New York, where she was murdered by a band of Indians (1643).

Anne Hutchinson was a Calvinist, as were the colonists of the Massachusetts Bay Colony. She preached predestination as they did, but she digressed from Puritan orthodoxy by claiming that it was a blessing to be a woman. She also challenged the concept of original sin, which all Christians cited as a evidence that women were the source of all evil.

Indeed, Hutchinson was condemned not because of her beliefs but because she demanded a role for women in the colony. She defied male authority and challenged the status of women. Hutchinson was rejected principally because she had a growing following, including men. This challenged the clergy then in power. Hutchinson thereby became the forerunner of the women's rights movement in the United States, as her influence threatened to become a force in Massachusetts politics.[23]

Mary Dyer (1611–1660)

On June 1, 1660, Mary Dyer was hanged in Boston for repeatedly defying a law banning Quakers from the Massachusetts Bay Colony. Quaker is a popular name for the Religious Society of Friends. Three other Quakers had been killed earlier for the same offense, which included studying the Bible in organized groups of women and men.

Like Anne Hutchinson, Dyer preached that God spoke directly to individuals and not only through the clergy. This angered the clergy immensely as it challenged their power, which was both religious and political, demonstrating the danger inherent in the union of church and state.

Although Dyer had been banished from the Massachusetts Bay Colony in 1638 and traveled to England as well as New York, she returned to Boston and deliberately defied the law banishing all Quakers, thereby contributing to her own persecution. Today, a statue of Mary Dyer is located in front of the Massachusetts State Capitol and another is found in Philadelphia.[24]

Abigail Smith Adams (1744–1818)

She was the wife of the second president of the United States, John Adams (1735–1826). It is therefore understandable that her husband had little sympathy for Abigail's views, as he was born in the Massachusetts Bay Colony and held those Puritan beliefs which led to the ouster of Anne Hutchinson a century earlier.

John Adams had been elected a delegate to the Continental Congress, leading Abigail to write extensively to John while he was in Philadelphia. The First Congress met for only one month, from September 5, 1774, to October 6, 1774. The Second Congress met for six years between 1775 and 1881, and

John Adams was frequently absent from home during those years. This led Abigail to write to him about numerous domestic affairs but also about her view of women. Abigail Adams wrote a letter to John called "Remember the Ladies" in which she sought to mitigate the unlimited power of husbands over their wives. Historians agree that Abigail Adams did not advocate political rights for women as she evidently never considered that possibility. She was concerned instead with the legal subordination of women. There are those who today seek to make Abigail Adams a feminist in the modern sense of that phrase. This view seems out of place because 18th century Americans had no such aspirations. It needs to be considered that the lack of birth control, a relatively short life span, reliance on human and animal power, slavery, lack of experience in democracy, and the failure of the economy to give women an opportunity to be self-supporting made feminism unlikely if not impossible until the middle of the 20th century.

Abigail Adams was the wife of the second president and the mother of the sixth president, John Quincy Adams. Her contribution to the eventual empowerment of women lies in the letters she left behind to become useful as historical evidence that women began to recognize their own worth long before Betty Friedan wrote her monumental *The Feminine Mystique*.

Women Seek the Vote

What seems commonplace to one generation has often been achieved with great difficulty and risk by a previous generation whose sacrifices in the name of the cause are then usually forgotten That is the nature of social change as well as the fate of each generation.

It is therefore vital for our understanding of women's political emancipation in the 21st century to review briefly the long struggle to gain female equality in the voting booth. As we have already seen, women were excluded from voting and holding office throughout most of the history of the United States and the British colonies preceding 1789.

Although New Jersey allowed women to vote as early as 1790, this was rescinded by the New Jersey legislature in 1807 in conformity with all other states.

These defeats did not discourage all women in America. Instead, in every generation new challenges to male authority confronted the patriarchy. One of these was the challenge by Frances Wright, a Scottish born American novelist who traveled the country giving speeches which demanded that women be given the right to vote, to have abortions, to have the right to divorce and to hold elected office.

Wright was a well known writer so that her cross-country lecture tours on the subject of women's liberation gained wide attention in the media of the day.

Wright also demanded an end to slavery and she also attacked organized religion. She was followed by Sarah Moore Grimke (1792–1873), the daughter of a South Carolina plantation owner.

Sarah taught Bible stories to her father's slaves and then secretly taught them to read. This was viewed as a rebellion in the slaveholding South as it was feared that literate slaves would revolt against their masters. In fact, teaching slaves to read was a serious offense in South Carolina at that time.

Sarah was also disturbed by the tradition to have slaves baptized, only to then view them as non-persons who were not permitted to join whites in the same worship services.

Sarah Grimke moved to Philadelphia in 1821 and there became a member of the Society of Friends (Quakers), who were active in promoting the abolition of slavery. Together with her sister, Sarah Grimke then attacked slavery in several pamphlets and then demanded the right for women to vote in a series of newspaper articles entitled "Letters on the Equality of the Sexes" which were published in Massachusetts newspapers. She also launched a series of public speaking tours which angered the New England community immensely. It was believed all over the United States and Europe that women should not speak in public.

Once more it appeared that the Grimke sisters had been defeated in their efforts. Yet, today their courage is rewarded by a level of gender equality they never knew and never anticipated.[25]

The fight for women's rights began with the effort to abolish American slavery. This is best illustrated by the experiences of Lucretia Mott (1793–1880) and Elizabeth Cady Stanton (1815–1902). Both had been active in the abolitionist movement in America when they traveled to London in 1840 to attend an anti-slavery convention but were barred from the meetings because they were women.

This exclusion led Mott and Stanton to organize the first women's rights convention in Seneca Falls, New York, in 1848. Stanton had already spent many years advocating abolition of slavery and the prohibition of alcohol, called temperance. She now became the leading spokeswoman for women's rights in America and was joined in this effort by Lucretia Mott of Massachusetts, whom she had met at the anti-slavery convention which denied them the right to participate.

Lucretia Mott was a Quaker, as were so many of the abolitionists of that day. She and her husband, James Mott, were active in the American Anti-slavery Society. Having moved to Philadelphia, Mott traveled throughout the eastern United States speaking to various reform groups. She became a Quaker minister and used her prominence to teach women the basics about representative government and political advocacy. She then became one of the organizers of the first American women's rights convention, where she was one of the signers of the Declaration of Sentiments.

In 1850, Mott published a book, *Discourse on Woman,* and in 1864 she was one of several women who founded Swarthmore College.[26]

Stanton had moved to Seneca Falls in 1847. There she called for a convention concerning women's rights, which resulted in a number of demands, including the abolition of wedding vows in which the wife promised to obey her husband. The convention, attended by only a few women, ended with a Declaration of Sentiments modeled on the Declaration of Independence. This declaration demanded that women be given the right to vote and that married women no longer be called "Mrs. Henry Smith" or "Mrs. John Doe" but were to keep their own name. The convention also resolved that black men and women be called by proper names and not be referred to as "Zip Coon" or "Sambo."

In 1866 Stanton, Mott and others drafted a universal suffrage petition which demanded the right for all women and men, including blacks, to vote. This resolution led to a split in the women's rights movement, as Congress was just then considering the 15th Amendment to the Constitution, which was finally ratified in 1870 but allowed only black men, not women, the right to vote. Some advocates of women's rights were willing to see the passage of this amendment even if it did not include women while others wanted women included or have no amendment whatever.

As it turned out, the effect of the amendment was delayed for a century, as poll taxes and other devices deprived black men as well as women of the vote until the Voting Rights Act of 1965 eliminated these practices.

In later years, Stanton became the first president of the National American Women's Suffrage Association. Stanton also published a Women's Bible in 1895 which sought to translate the story of Genesis in such a manner as to eliminate the charge of original sin against women.[27]

Susan B. Anthony (1820–1906) may well have been the most prominent of American civil rights leaders during the 19th century. It has been estimated that she gave 75 to 100 speeches a year on women's rights for a period of 45 years.

She too was born into a Quaker family in Massachusetts which later moved to New York. Her family followed the liberal wing of the group when the Quakers split into two segments in 1826.

In school she experienced so much gender discrimination that her teacher refused to teach her long division because she was a girl. Nevertheless, she became a teacher. Having been promoted to principal, she fought for the right of women teachers to earn the same salary as men in that profession. Men at that time earned four times more than women for the same work.

In 1848 Susan Anthony attended the Women's Rights Convention in Rochester, New York, where her family now lived. She became a Unitarian and became involved in the anti-slavery and temperance movements. She became secretary of The Daughters of Temperance and in that position learned public speaking.

During the 1848 women's rights convention, Susan Anthony met Elizabeth Stanton and under her influence became a powerful voice on behalf of women's right to vote. This in turn led her to publish a weekly journal in New York City called *The Revolution*. The purpose of the journal was the promotion of the suffrage for women and blacks as well as more liberal divorce laws, equal pay for equal work and a relaxation of religious discrimination against women in church.[28]

It was in 1873 that Susan Anthony provoked one of the most famous trials in American history because she attempted to cast a ballot for a United States representative from New York. This led to her arrest on the grounds that the constitution of New York prohibited her from voting. The court ruled that the privileges of United States citizenship do not include the right to vote. Anthony was fined $100.00.[29]

In 1893, Anthony and Helen Montgomery founded the Woman's Educational and Industrial Union and began to agitate for the right of women to attend the University of Rochester.[30]

In later years Anthony became alienated from Stanton and others over a number of strategic issues concerning the suffrage movement. Between 1884 and 1887 Anthony and two other women published *The History of Woman Suffrage*. She died fourteen years before the 19th Amendment to the U.S. Constitution gave women the right to vote.

In 1979, 1980, 1981 and 1999 the U.S. Mint circulated the Susan B. Anthony dollar, which was later withdrawn.

An opera, called *The Mother of Us All*, concerning the life of Susan B. Anthony, was composed by Virgil Thomson and Gertrude Stein. Her house in Rochester, New York, was declared a National Historic Landmark in 1965 and her childhood home was placed on the National Historic Register in 2006.[31]

The founding of the National Christian Woman's Temperance Union by Annie Wittenmyer (1827–1900) led to a vocal demand for women's voting rights and the abolition of the American patriarchy. This organization viewed alcoholism largely as a male problem and sought to alleviate its consequences by promoting prohibition of alcohol use.

Wittenmyer did a great deal more than push for prohibition of alcohol use. She also organized help for Civil War veterans and was roundly criticized for meddling in hospitals. She succeeded in persuading Congress to give pensions to army nurses and became a major advocate for women's suffrage.[32]

This advocacy, delivered in magazine articles and books, led to ever increasing efforts to secure the vote for American women. These efforts were not successful during Wittenmyer's life. Several examples illustrate these early failures to secure the vote for American women.

In 1874, the Supreme Court ruled that the 14th Amendment does not give women the right to vote. Likewise, in 1887, the Supreme Court struck down a law in Washington giving women the right to vote. Washington was followed by Colorado in 1893 and succeeded in giving women the right to vote. Yet, in California a large effort by the National Suffrage Association failed to give women voting rights.

Then, in 1909 the Women's Trade Union League organized a strike by 20,000 garment workers who were fully supported by the suffrage movement.

From 1910 on, the suffrage of women began to grow, state by state. Washington granted women that right in 1910 and California followed in 1911. In 1912, Alaska did the same in the year in which Arizona became a state and included women in the electorate. In 1914, Nevada and Montana enfranchised women and in 1916, Jeanette Rankin of Montana became the first woman to be elected to the U.S. House of Representatives.

Alice Paul (1885–1997) founded the National Women's Party in 1916 because she viewed the efforts of Susan Anthony and Elizabeth Stanton as ineffective. This party sought to use the same tactics in the United States which had already been in vogue in Great Britain. These efforts included demonstrations, parades, mass meetings, picketing, a suffragette watch, fires and hunger strikes. In addition, the party published the weekly *Suffragist* and because of this aggressive stance received a great deal of publicity from the media, i.e., the newspapers.[33]

Paul was the author of a proposed Equal Rights Amendment to the Constitution. She also picketed the White House to gain the support of President Woodrow Wilson for the suffragette movement. This led to her conviction and a jail sentence of seven months.[34]

On June 28, 1917, additional demonstrations were held in Washington, leading to the arrest of yet more women who were charged with disorderly conduct and were jailed "for their own protection."[35]

Paul was the best educated of the suffragettes. She graduated from Swarthmore College in 1905, and the New York School of Philanthropy (social work), and earned a Ph.D. in political science from the University of Pennsylvania in 1912. In addition she also earned a law degree from American University in Washington, D.C.

Alice Paul lived 92 years. In 1995, eighteen years after her death, a postage stamp was issued honoring her. In 2004, HBO broadcast a documentary concerning the suffragettes and the achievements of Alice Paul. In 2005, Swarthmore College, from which Alice Paul had graduated in 1905, named their new student dormitory after her.[36]

The Representation of Women in the 21st Century

In view of the long struggle for female equality in politics it is surprising that many women do not know how few women, even now, in 2008, hold political office. Those women who are aware of the relative lack of women officeholders are more likely to vote for a woman than those who overestimate that participation.

Kira Sanbumatsu has demonstrated that in 2003 women knew less about politics than men. Therefore, women who underestimate the level of female involvement in politics are more likely to vote for women candidates than those who overestimate such representation. Women are more likely to overestimate the level of women in office and therefore do not support women as much as could be expected. Of course, the number of women elected to office affects policymaking with respect to issues which are important to women. Therefore, the underrepresentation of women in political offices give women's issues far less attention than could result if women were more alert to voting for other women. In sum, women's failure to fully participate in the electoral process inhibits their ability to further their group interests.[37]

An excellent example of this dictum is that women would be much more liberal about abortion if they knew more about politics. It is also evident that women in office do act on behalf of women. Therefore it is not surprising that if more women held prominent political office, the gender gap concerning voting for political interest would close rapidly.

In the American democracy political involvement and the right to vote are the essentials needed to be a full citizen. Women have to achieve this. There is, however, yet another dimension to democracy. That is freedom of speech and of the press as anchored in the First Amendment to the U.S. Constitution. The right to speak and write concerning public issues with particular reference to elected officials guarantees that those who hold public office are accountable to the people who elected them.

Therefore the role of the media and the participation of women in communications is of vital concern to those who look forward to the equality of the genders before the first half of the 21st century has concluded.

Summary

At the founding of the republic women were excluded from voting or holding any political office. Now, more than two hundred years after the adoption of the Constitution, women have achieved the right to vote and hold numerous political offices. These include governors of states, mayors of cities, senators, representatives and ambassadors. The judiciary is also well feminized, although women have by no means achieved equality with men either in numbers or the kinds of offices they hold.

The history of the suffrage movement is indeed a source of inspiration for anyone who supports the expansion of American democracy. That history includes those luminaries who fought for the rights women now enjoy.

At the beginning of the 21st century women's rights are firmly established among Americans. This is due not only to those who sacrificed so much to gain political equality but is also due to the free press and the freedom of the American media to communicate the messages of those who seek their rights in freedom.

Therefore our next chapter will deal with the inclusion of women in the communications industry, which is so vital in preserving the American way of life.

CHAPTER 8

From Walter Cronkite to Katie Couric

Women Anchors

When Katie Couric assumed the position of anchor of the *CBS Evening News* on September 5, 2006, she became the first woman to solo anchor the weekday evening news on one of the three major U.S. broadcast networks, i.e., CBS, NBC and ABC. In that position she is also the managing editor, replacing Bob Schieffer, who served as interim anchor and editor after the departure of Dan Rather on March 9, 2005. Rather held that job from 1981 when Walter Cronkite retired after nineteen years. Cronkite was regarded as the most trusted news anchor during his tenure and was given such high ratings that as late as January 2008 he broadcast the annual concert of the Vienna Symphony Orchestra from that city.[1]

The appointment of Couric to one of the most coveted positions in television journalism was by no means a sudden occurrence. Instead it was the inevitable outcome of feminization in the broadcasting industry. This development can be traced by reviewing the life of Katie Couric, who began her journalism career while still a student at the University of Virginia in 1975. There she wrote for the college newspaper, *The Cavalier Daily*. Upon graduating in 1979, Couric became a desk assistant at ABC News in Washington, D.C., and later joined CNN as an assignment editor. Between 1984 and 1986 she worked as a reporter for WTVJ in Miami, Florida, and then joined a TV station in Washington, D.C., leading to an Associated Press award and an Emmy award, which is sponsored annually by the Academy of Television Arts and Sciences.

In 1989, Couric joined NBC News as deputy Pentagon correspondent (the U.S. Department of Defense is housed in a five cornered building constructed as a pentagon). From 1989 to 1991 Couric also filled in for Bryant

Gumbel as host on the *Today* show and filled in for Jane Pauley, Deborah Norville, Mary Alice Williams, and Maria Shriver on other occasions.

In short, Couric had a good deal of experience as a fill in for numerous broadcasters, both male and female, before becoming the celebrated anchor in 2006. She had also appeared on *Today* and *NBC Now*.[2]

Although no two careers are identical, a number of women have risen to prominence in the television news industry along with Couric.

Janet Peckinpaugh

The effort of women to gain access to television journalism began in the 1970s and, like so many other efforts in other fields of endeavor, was hard fought. As late as 1999, Janet Peckinpaugh was awarded $8.3 million by a federal jury who decided that Peckinpaugh had lost her high paying job as anchorwoman at a Hartford, Connecticut, CBS station because she was a woman. In addition, Peckinpaugh claimed that her age, at that time 48, was also a factor in her dismissal. While the jury found no age discrimination, they did find that Peckinpaugh was the victim of sexual harassment.[3]

During the final decade of the 20th century, numerous women attained prominent jobs in the TV industry. Some of these women are prominent personalities while others, less well known, make up the majority of women in the TV news industry. Among those who have been among the best known news personalities is Connie Chung, who reported for ABC News for decades until she moved to CNN in 2002.

Connie Chung

Chung was co-anchor with Dan Rather at CBS in 1993 but left to do independent interviews when her work with Rather proved unsatisfactory to both of them. As an interviewer Chung gained some attention by talking to people who had gained some temporary notoriety, such as Congressman Gary Condit, whose female assistant was murdered, and Klaus von Bulow, who was acquitted of attempting to murder his wealthy wife.

The next move in her career took her to CNN, where she briefly hosted a show called *Connie Chung Tonight*. This show was unpopular and led to cancellation of her show after the owner of CNN, Ted Turner, called it "just awful."[4]

Chung ended her career in 2003 after having had spectacular success earlier. She had earned $4 million a year while at ABC and was paid between $2 million and $3 million at CNN. Her early prominence came about when she reported on the Watergate scandal during the Nixon administration in the early 1970s.

Chung was born in 1946 in Washington, D.C., the daughter of a diplomat from Taiwan. She was educated at the University of Maryland, where she earned a degree in journalism in 1969.

In 1984 she married Maurice "Maury" Povich, a television personality. The Poviches have an adopted son.[5]

Barbara Walters

Walters has had a long career in the news business. Born in 1929, she is the daughter of Lou Walters, a Broadway producer and nightclub owner. In 1951 she graduated from Sarah Lawrence College with a degree in English.[6]

Walters began her career as a writer for CBS News and moved from there to write and research on NBC's *The Today Show.* Consequently she became a reporter on that show and became the first female host of such a show after the previous host, Fran McGee, had died.

In 1976, Walters became co-anchor with Harry Reasoner on the *ABC Evening News.* This assignment lasted only two years when Walters succeeded in becoming co-host with Hugh Downs of the *20/20* news magazine.[7]

Eventually, Walters appeared on numerous news specials, including presidential inaugurations and the coverage of the attack on the World Trade Center on September 11, 2001. Her numerous interviews with famous people made her a celebrity herself and led to her inclusion on the Hollywood Walk of Fame. Walters also won numerous other awards, including the Excellence in Media Award, The Lowell Thomas Award, The Lifetime Achievement Award of the National Academy of Television Arts and Sciences and many others. Jerry Oppenheimer has written a biography of Barbara Walters, as she became a socialite in New York's achieving society.[8]

Walters has been married and divorced twice. She has one child, a daughter, who lives in the Pacific Northwest.

In 2008, Walters is still the host of a morning show called *The View,* which consists of discussions with a number of women concerning the events of the day or any topic of interest.[9]

There can be little doubt that Barbara Walters is the most famous female TV personality ever to grace the newsrooms of the television industry.

Diane Sawyer

Another superstar of the television news industry is Diane Sawyer. Her multiyear contract amounting to $7.5 million as early as 1989 reflects the importance of news programming to the major networks, which earn 40 percent of their income from such programs.[10]

Sawyer has been a member of the *60 Minutes* group of reporters and has conducted interviews with a large number of celebrities. These included President George W. Bush, Saddam Hussein, Fidel Castro, Robert MacNamara, and Sammy "The Bull" Gravano. She succeeded in these interviews and was subsequently co-anchor with Sam Donaldson of *Prime Time Live*, a news magazine.

She also reported live from ground zero at the time of the attacks on the World Trade Center and reported from Afghanistan with particular reference to the plight of women in Muslim countries, called *Behind the Burqua*.

Sawyer is also an investigative journalist, as she brought American viewers the story of the warehousing of Russian orphans, an expose of a maximum security prison for women, abuse in an institution for the mentally retarded, and a story about pharmacy prescription errors.[11]

Diane Sawyer is a native of Glasgow, Kentucky. She earned a B.A. from Wellesley College in English. She began her career as a reporter in Louisville, Kentucky. She won the America's Junior Miss pageant in 1963 and thereafter joined the staff of the press secretary in the White House during the Nixon administration. After Nixon's resignation she went to California with him and helped him assemble his memoirs.

This small sample of celebrity female television journalists is by no means representative of the over one hundred anchors, both male and female, employed by major networks in the U.S.A. The vast majority of television anchors work in local broadcasting and are unknown outside the areas in which their stations operate.

Women in Electronic Journalism

The Association of Electronic Journalists conducted an annual survey in 2007 revealing that 40 percent of producers and directors in television are women and that 23.5 percent of news directors in radio are women. Women were 31 percent of all announcers in 2007 and 54 percent of news analysts and correspondents. The number of women in the television news force including all kinds of employment was about 40 percent in 2007.[12]

That number is growing rapidly, as fewer men than ever are applying for jobs in the TV newsroom. According to the *Washington Post*, women applicants outnumbered men 3 to 1 in 2007. Although the total percentage of women in the television news force is only 40 percent, the number of women anchors was 57 percent in 2007. As older men retire, the number of women in broadcasting is increasing, as journalism schools awarded two-thirds of bachelor's degrees to women in 2007.[13]

Because TV news employment is a low paying, no growth field, many men are discouraged from entering this work and look for better paying jobs elsewhere. Indeed, the top anchors earn millions and top reporters can earn $200,000 a year. However, there isn't much room at the top. For example, Fox News Channel, the top-rated all news cable network, employs fewer than 100 anchors and reporters. Even large metropolitan local stations employ only 40 to 50 reporters, sportscasters and weather people nationwide. The total employment in the TV news business for all of the United States is only about 25,000. Therefore, newcomers start their careers in small towns where the median annual salary is only $20,000. Because there is little growth in the industry, even the military pays better than newscasting.[14]

Although the industry is rapidly becoming more and more feminized, the top TV reporters as of 2007 were still mostly men. The Network Correspondents Visibility Study found that of 186 reporters on ABC, CBS and NBC only three women ranked among the top 10 reporters. The study was based on the number of stories each reporter had on the air and did not include anchors.[15]

Because women are more willing to accept low paying jobs than is true of men, the employers who hire reporters and anchors for news shows are evidently seeking to appoint women whose good looks will attract a large audience. In short, physical attractiveness is given a good deal of weight in appointing women to newscasting jobs, although this does not preclude experience and education. In view of the large number of women applying, the attractiveness of an applicant can be a deciding factor in getting a job.[16]

Some Career Women

Robin Meade

Robin Meade, Miss Ohio of 1992, is the lead news anchor of the *Headline News* morning show on CNN. She also co-hosts CNN's *Accent Health* program.

Meade was previously co-anchor of the weekend newscasts of the NBC Chicago affiliate WMAQ. In that capacity she covered the 1996 Olympics. In 1995 she won an Emmy award for her work and in 2005 she was inducted into the Ohio Broadcasters Hall of Fame.

Meade began her career in Mansfield, Ohio, and moved from there to Cleveland and Columbus before gaining national recognition. She is a graduate of Ashland University in Ohio.[17]

Bonnie Bernstein

Bonnie Bernstein is one of the few women to become a nationally recognized sports reporter. She is a sideline reporter for NFL broadcasts on CBS, a job many men would kill for.

Bernstein is also host of *Countdown to the Heisman* reports for ABC Sports. She is also one of the rotating hosts for NFL Live, covers major league baseball and reported on NCAA basketball championships. In 2004, during Super Bowl 38, she became the first reporter to report both on network TV and network radio. Her career has been documented in numerous sports publications such as *Sports Illustrated* and *Men's Health*.

Bernstein was born in Brooklyn, New York, in 1970 and graduated *magna cum laude* from the University of Maryland Merrill School of Journalism in 1992. There she was a four time All America selection in gymnastics and received an award for academic and sports excellence.

Judy Wooodruff

Judy Woodruff was crowned Young Miss Augusta in 1963 at age 17 and has been in the limelight ever since. In 1970 she began her career in TV broadcasting at an ABC affiliate in Atlanta, Georgia, and continued on NBC in the Washington, D.C., area. Between 1972 and 1988 she covered the White House and then became the Washington correspondent for the *MacNeil/Lehrer News Hour*.

Woodruff has won numerous awards for her work. These include the News and Documentary Emmy Award. Together with Bernard Shaw she won the Cable/ACE Award for best anchor and best newscaster of 1995.

In 2005 Woodruff left her TV career behind in order to teach and write but returned in 2006 to host *Generation Next: Speak Up*. In 2008 she also reported on the primary election results in Iowa and New Hampshire.[18]

Women in the Newsroom

A survey published in *Communicator* in August 2007 reveals that "there have been no significant changes in women in TV news in years." According to that survey women have been about 40 percent of the TV news workforce for decades. They make up slightly more than one-quarter of TV news directors, or 26.3 percent. The percentage of women in the radio news force, according to *Communicator,* rose from 20.4 percent in 2006 to 23.5 percent in 2007. Women have gradually increased their number among general managers that run local news from 15.2 percent in 2006 to 15.8 percent in 2007.

Fox stations have more women general managers than any other network affiliates.[19]

Bonnie Erbe

An outstanding example of a successful woman in television is Bonnie Erbe, who hosted *To the Contrary with Bonnie Erbe* in Washington, D.C., She has appeared on National Public Radio and numerous cable news networks. She writes a weekly column on politics, women's issues and religion for the Scripps Howard Newspaper chain and opinion for *U.S. News & World Report*.

Erbe has won the Clarion Award from Women in Communication on three occasions, the Grace Award from American Women in Radio and Television four times, the ICI Award from the Educational Foundation and the New York State Society of CPAs award.

Lisa Zeff

Lisa Zeff has been the executive producer of ABC News. She is also known as a producer of cable network programming and home video products.

Zeff came to ABC in 1994 as managing director of news production and became executive producer and general manager in 1998. Her programs have won nearly 100 awards over the years.

Her best known work includes *Trial of Adolf Eichmann*; *The Vietnam War*; more than 200 hours of *Biography*, *Lifetime Live*; and *She TV*. In addition she produced *Nixon in China*; *Wall Street* and *Unlocking the DaVinci Code*.

Prior to coming to ABC, Zeff worked for Time-Warner, producing *Lifetime Magazine*.

Linda Winslow

Linda Winslow is the executive producer of the *News Hour* with Jim Lehrer. She was previously associated with the National Public Affairs Center for Television. In 1973 she produced the McNeil-Lehrer Watergate coverage as well as the House Judiciary Committee's impeachment hearings.

Earlier, Winslow was vice president in charge of news and public affairs for WETA in Washington, D.C., where she produced *Washington Week in Review* and *The Lawmakers*.

Linda Winslow is a graduate of Michigan State University and holds a M.Sc. degree from Columbia University.

Jane Pauley

One of the earliest TV personalities has been Jane Pauley, who began her career as the first female anchor in Atlanta and Indianapolis in the early '70s. Born in 1950, Pauley was introduced to the *Today* show by Tom Brokaw in 1975. Pauley remained with *Today* until 1989, when she was replaced by Deborah Norville and assigned by NBC to her own newsmagazine. In 1992 she hosted *Dateline,* where she remained until 2002. In 2004, Pauley published an autobiography called *Skywriting: A Life Out of the Blue*. Since then she has hosted a talk show, *The Jane Pauley Show*.[20]

Joan Lunden

Joan Lunden, born in California in 1950, became the co-host of *Good Morning America* in 1975. Earlier she worked as a model in Mexico City, where she also attended the University of the Americas. In 1973 she began her TV career in the weather department of KCRA in Sacramento and in 1975 she moved to ABC *Eyewitness News* in New York. She starred in *Mother's Day* from 1983 to 1989 on the *Lifetime* cable network. Subsequently she hosted *Wickedly Perfect* on CBS.[21]

These examples of women participating in the hosting and production of TV and radio programs may be multiplied many times as the number of women in these positions increases year by year.

Women in Print Journalism

The circulation of American newspapers is gradually declining. This makes a career in print journalism more difficult than it was when newspapers did not have to compete with television, the Internet, the radio and numerous other electronic devices.

In 2007 the circulation of the nation's biggest newspapers dropped an average of 2.6 percent. The circulation of 789 newspapers was 45,153,192 in 2006, having declined from 46,347,669 a year earlier.[22]

This continuing decline demonstrates how difficult it is to begin a career in print journalism. Women, as relative newcomers to employment in newspapers, are therefore disadvantaged *ipso facto* because the number of jobs in newspapers that at one time sustained men are no longer available.

Therefore, the careers of female journalists are remarkable alone because the opportunities to gain access to the profession are so few. Some of those who did well in this profession are columnists, sports reporters, foreign correspondents and, more recently, female editors. In 2007, women constituted 54 percent of all editors.[23]

Maureen Dowd

Maureen Dowd has written a column on the opinion page of the *New York Times* two times a week since 1995. Her principal interests are politicians, both incumbents and candidates. She uses numerous epithets to describe the targets of her criticisms, which include presidents and various cabinet members. In 1999 she was awarded the Pulitzer Prize for her reporting on the Lewinsky scandal, involving President Bill Clinton and Monica Lewinsky, who was then an employee at the White House.

The Pulitzer Prize was established by the estate of Joseph Pulitzer (1847–1911). Pulitzer was a Jewish immigrant from Hungary who is viewed as the father of American journalism. The prize is considered the most prestigious recognition a journalist can attain.

Dowd was born in Washington, D.C., in 1952 and graduated from Catholic University in 1973 with a degree in English. She began her career at *The Washington Star* where she worked as a reporter until *The Star* ceased publication in 1981. She then worked briefly for *Time Magazine* and in 1983 joined *The New York Times* as a reporter. In 1986 she moved to the *Times*' Washington bureau, leading to the Breakthrough Award from the Graduate School of Journalism at Columbia University in 1991.

Dowd has been widely criticized for her acerbic writing style and use of parody concerning powerful officials. She has referred to President George W. Bush as "bubble boy," Vice President Cheney as "Tricky Dick Deuce," and former Defense Secretary Donald Rumsfeld as "Rummy."[24]

Ellen Goodman

Ellen Goodman writes a column which appears in 400 American newspapers and is syndicated by The Washington Post Writers Group. A 1963 graduate of Radcliffe College, she began her career at *Newsweek* at a time when only men were writers. In 1965 she became a reporter at the *Detroit Free Press* and in 1967 moved to the *Boston Globe*, where she began to write her column. This led to her achieving the Pulitzer Prize in 1980.

Goodman is also the author of a number of books including *Turning Point, Paper Trail, Close to Home, At Large, Keeping in Touch, Making Sense, Value Judgments,* and *The Power of Friendship.*

In 1980, Goodman won the American Society of Newspaper Editors Distinguished Writing Award as well as numerous other awards dealing with civil rights and women's issues.

Goodman divorced her first husband, Anthony Goodman, in 1963. With him she had a daughter, Katie. Her second husband is journalist Bob Levey, whom she married in 1982.[25]

Jane Bryant Quinn

Jane Bryant Quinn wrote a column on personal finances for the *New York Daily News* twice a week for 27 years. This reached 250 newspapers through syndication by The Washington Post Writers Group. She is also the author of *Making the Most of Your Money,* which became a selection of the Book of the Month Club. Earlier, in 1978, she wrote *Everyone's Money,* which was labeled a best seller.

Quinn is also known as a television personality. She worked for CBS for ten years and *CBS Morning News* and the *CBS Evening News with Dan Rather.* Quinn is the winner of numerous prestigious awards including the Gerald Loeb Award for Lifetime Achievement. That award is regarded as a business reporter's highest honor, having been sponsored by Gerald Loeb, an investment banker and author of several books on finance and investments. Loeb was also a contributor to *The Wall Street Journal* and was called "the most quoted man on Wall Street" by *Forbes* magazine.

Jane Bryant was born in Niagara Falls, New York, in 1939, the daughter of the chief executive of Hooker Chemicals. She graduated from Middlebury College in Vermont, where she earned a degree in English. Her first job at *Newsweek* magazine was as a mailroom clerk because writing jobs were only for men. She therefore turned to the newsletter business and started writing on consumer finance for *The Insider's Newsletter.*

Recently Quinn has stopped writing her newspaper column. She continues to write for *Newsweek* and *Good Housekeeping.*[26]

Judith Miller

"Congress shall make no law ... abridging the freedom of speech or of the press ... etc." (The First Amendment to the Constitution of the United States).

The First Amendment to the United States Constitution appears to guarantee the most basic freedom upon which a democracy depends. That is the freedom to say or write whatever one likes, including words not approved by government bureaucrats.

Judith Miller, a reporter for the *New York Times,* discovered to her dismay and that of all journalists, that the courts don't take the First Amendment seriously, as she was jailed on October 1, 2004, for her courageous defense of press freedom in this country. Miller spent 85 days in jail but in the end acceded to the tyranny of the court.[27]

The court held Miller in contempt because she refused to reveal the source of her information concerning a leak which designated a CIA agent as a covert agent for that agency. Since the person who leaked this information readily admitted doing so and was not prosecuted, the prosecutor sought to find someone to prosecute although he had not leaked the information under scrutiny. The target of that prosecution had met with Miller, who guaranteed him that he would not be named and his name not revealed to anyone. At issue, therefore, was that reporters could not very well gaininformation concerning the misconduct of government bureaucrats if their promise of confidentiality could be voided by any court by jailing any reporter unwilling to betray her source. In short, freedom of the press was at stake.[28]

Judith Miller is a 1969 graduate of Barnard College and earned a master's degree in public affairs at Princeton University. She began her career at the *New York Times* in 1977 after spending some time in the Middle East as a correspondent for National Public Radio. Her experience in that region led to her assignment as bureau chief in Cairo, Egypt, in 1983. In 1987 she became news editor of the *Times*' Washington office. She reported in a front page story that the government of Iraq was preparing weapons of mass destruction. That story was in part used by the U.S. government as justification for the invasion of Iraq after the attack on the Pentagon and the World Trade Center on September 11, 2001.[29]

Judith Miller left the *New York Times* in November of 2005. Thereafter she became a fellow of the Manhattan Institute for Policy Research.

Miller's career has engendered a good deal of controversy. Yet, whatever the merits of her reporting, she will be remembered along with John Peter Zenger, who first defied tyranny and laid the foundations for the freedom of the press in the United States in 1735. She is a true heroine of freedom who acted in the spirit of Thomas Jefferson, whose memorial in Washington, D.C., exhibits these words: "I have sworn upon the altar of God eternal hostility against every form of tyranny over the mind of man."

Lisa Olson

Lisa Olson was born in 1965 and earned a degree in journalism from Northern Arizona University in 1985.

Olson is a sportswriter for the *New York Daily News*. She was previously employed by the *Boston Herald*. In 1990 she sought access to the locker room of the Boston Patriots football team in order to interview the players after practice. This was arranged so that she could talk to Maurice Hurst, who told her he would only be interviewed in the locker room. According to a complaint by Olson she was sexually harassed while in the locker room in that several players exhibited their genitals and made sexually explicit comments. This incident was published by *The Boston Globe* a few days later.[30]

The publicity given this incident by the *Globe* led to harassment of Olson by the Patriots fans, who slashed her tires, sent her hate mail and death threats, and burglarized her apartment. This led Olson to move to Australia, where she worked for *The Sydney Morning Herald,* which accused her of plagiarism in 1995. She returned to the United States in 1998 and assumed a position with the *New York Daily News*. She also settled a lawsuit against the Patriots.[31]

As a consequence of Olson's experience the NFL issued a report which concluded that Olson was indeed humiliated and degraded, and several players were fined, as was the team. The general manager of the Patriots, Pat Sullivan, was fired.[32]

Since that incident, women have routinely visited male athletes' locker rooms. Undoubtedly, such visits expose male athletes to female voyeurism, as it is impossible to change from athletic gear to civil clothes without exposing male proclivities. Under the pressure of time to file stories and in need of their jobs, women have accepted these arrangements, as have the men they interview. Prudery has thus been bested by economics as culture change defeats puritanism.

Ann Coulter

Aligned with Laura Ingraham, who is as insulting as Ann Coulter, Coulter has made a name for herself in American journalism by making such comments as: "My only regret with Tim McVeigh is that he did not get to *The New York Times* building" and "It would be a much better country if women did not vote."

Coulter is the author of five *New York Times* bestsellers. Coulter is the legal correspondent for *Human Events* and writes a syndicated column for Universal Press Syndicate. She is a frequent guest on numerous TV shows, and has been profiled in a number of magazines.

Coulter was born in New York City in 1961 and is a graduate of Dartmouth College and earned a law degree from the University of Virginia. She was an aide to Sen. Spencer Abraham of Michigan and later worked for the Washington, DC, Center for Individual Rights.[33]

Erma Bombeck

In the second half of the 20th century, Erma Bombeck wrote a widely popular newspaper column which dealt mainly with suburban home life. She was a humorist and called her column *At Wit's End*. In these columns she told about herself and her life as a housewife.

Bombeck began her column in one newspaper in 1964. One year later it was nationally syndicated and eventually ran twice a week in 700 newspapers. Her column was collected in bestselling books. Finally a television situation comedy was based on her writings.

Erma Bombeck was born Erma Fiste in 1927. She graduated from the University of Dayton in 1949 with a degree in English. That year she started her career at the *Dayton Herald Journal* as a reporter for four years and then married and raised three children.

She then became a correspondent for the ABC News show *Good Morning America*. She died in 1996 of kidney failure.[34]

Women War Journalists

Elizabeth Neuffner

Elizabeth Neuffner, war correspondent for the *Boston Globe*, was killed in Iraq in May of 2003. Neuffner was not and is not the only female war correspondent in that dangerous area. Neuffner had also reported from Afghanistan, Rwanda and Bosnia, all dangerous combat zones.

Neuffner had begun her career with the *Boston Globe* in 1988. She began as a court reporter but soon covered the Persian Gulf War of 1991 and thereafter reported from Russia and later from Washington, D.C. This led to her assignments in the Middle East and her early death.[35]

Lara Logan et al.

Women reporters who covered combat zones were few until the invasion of Iraq in 2001. Among those who are now so engaged is Lara Logan, who reports regularly from the front in the Iraq War. Logan is a foreign correspondent for CBS News and *60 Minutes* and in that position faces bombs, terrorist attacks and bullets every day. She is joined by Teri Okita of the *Los Angeles Times*, Arwa Damon of CNN and many others who followed in the footsteps of those who paved the way for women war correspondents in earlier wars. Among these was Margarate Fuller, America's first woman war correspondent, who worked for the *New York Tribune* and described the invasion of Rome by French forces in 1849. During the First World War, Mary Roberts Reinhart reported from the front lines and actually advanced to the very barbed wire separating American from German forces in the trenches. Martha Gelhorn covered the Spanish Civil War, the Japanese invasion of China, the American invasion of Europe, the Vietnam War and the Six Day War in Israel. She was the wife of Ernest Hemingway; his novel *For Whom the Bell Tolls* is dedicated to her.

Margaret Bourke-White covered the North Africa campaign in the Second World War and thereafter photographed from the furthest observation point on the Korean front. Margaret Higgins also reported from the Korean War, which led to her gaining the Pulitzer Prize in 1951. She reported on the French defeat at Dien Bien Phu in Vietnam in 1954 and returned to Vietnam in 1963 to report on the American-Vietnam War.

Elizabeth Shepley Sergeant served as a war correspondent in France during the First World War. In October of 1918 she toured the battlefield on the Western Front lying between the American and German forces near the Belgian frontier. There she was severely wounded. Upon her recovery she wrote a book, *Shadows-Shapes: Journal of a Wounded Woman*, which was published in 1920. Earlier she had written a book called *French Perspectives*.

Elizabeth Shepley was born in Massachusetts in 1881. She graduated from Bryn Mawr College in 1903 and then spent ten years in France, where she studied at the University of Paris, called the Sorbonne after its founder, Robert de Sorbon. She returned to the United States in 1913 and thereafter published articles in *The New Republic* and *The Nation*. In 1927 she published a book called *Fire Under the Andes*, which contains the biographies of fourteen famous Americans. She continued to publish magazine articles about famous Americans throughout the 1930s and 1940s and then wrote a full-length biography of the author Willa Cather which was published in 1953.[36]

The first woman correspondent to be killed in action was Dickey Chapelle. She moved in with the Marines under fire in Okinawa during the Second World War. She parachuted into the Vietnamese jungle but was killed by a land mine there in 1965.[37]

Women Newspaper Publishers and Editors

Nearly 57,000 journalists worked in daily newsrooms in 2007. Of these, 21,400 were women, constituting about 37 percent of the entire cohort.[38]

In 2007 women accounted for 42 percent of all copy and layout editors and 34.7 percent of all supervisors. In 1999 women were 40.3 percent of all copy and layout editors and 33.8 percent of all supervisors. Evidently, the number of women working in advanced positions in newsrooms has increased slightly but still lags behind the 37 percent overall employment rate for women in print journalism.[39]

Women Chiefs

Helen Donovan has been the executive editor of *The Boston Globe* since 1993. At that time she was the first to hold such a position in a major newspaper with a circulation of 398,000.

Donovan had joined *The Globe* in 1977 starting as op-ed page editor. Subsequently she was appointed assistant managing editor of the Sunday edition and in 1985 she became national editor. In 1991 she was named managing editor of *The Globe*.

Donovan is a graduate of Mt. Holyoke College with a degree in English literature. She also earned a master's degree in journalism from the University of Virginia. Thus equipped, Donovan began her career at the *Berkshire Eagle* in Pittsfield, Massachusetts, before working as a copy editor at *Fortune*. She then joined *The Globe*.

Donovan views her success as a confirmation that the glass ceiling preventing women from attaining the top jobs in journalism has finally been broken. At a networking breakfast of the International Women's Media Foundation, she and other women journalists still complained about the difficulties women encounter in the profession.[40]

The International Women's Media Foundation was founded in 1990. Its main mission is to remove the obstacles women face in advancing their careers in journalism. To that end the IWMF conducts seminars teaching women how to enhance their careers and move into leadership positions. The IWMF also seeks to construct networks of women who help one another in face of the so-called old boys network.[41]

Katherine Meyer Graham

Graham was the owner and publisher of the *Washington Post*. She inherited that newspaper after her husband, Phillip Graham, committed suicide in 1963. Graham became a celebrity among journalists after she and her staff covered the Watergate scandal leading to the resignation of President Richard Nixon in 1973. Daughter of a Jewish father and Christian mother, she learned the newspaper business by becoming a reporter for her father's *Washington Post*. Her political acumen allowed her to become socially acquainted with several presidents and other elected officials, so that the media labeled her "Queen Katherine." Like Perle Mesta before her, she was a great party giver and knew how to flatter the rich and the powerful. She died from a fall in 2001 while attending a business conference in Sun Valley, Idaho.[42]

Ellen Soeteber

Ellen Soeteber resigned as sixth editor of the *St. Louis Post-Dispatch* in 2006 to become a professor of journalism. She was the first woman in the newspaper's 123 year history to hold that position.

Soeteber was born in St. Louis in 1950 and graduated from the Northwestern University School of Journalism in 1972. She began her career at the now defunct *Chicago Daily News* and at *Chicago Today*. She moved to the *Chicago Tribune* in 1974 where she worked in several editorial jobs. In 1987 she was named metropolitan editor and became assistant managing editor in 1988. By 1991 she was deputy editor and then, in 1994, managing editor of the *South Florida Sun*.[43]

Under her leadership the *Post-Dispatch* won the Pulitzer Prize and numerous other awards.

Margaret Sullivan

Margaret Sullivan is the editor of *The Buffalo News*, which has a circulation of about 235,000. Sullivan is one of 14 women holding the top jobs at the nation's 100 largest daily newspapers.

Born in Buffalo in 1949, Sullivan is a graduate of Georgetown University and the Medill School of Journalism at Northwestern University, where she earned a master's degree in 1980. She started at the *News* as a summer intern in 1980. By 1989 she had been advanced to assistant managing editor and thereafter rose to senior editor faster than anyone else in the history of *The News*. In 2001 Sullivan also became the first female vice president of the *Buffalo News*.

Earlier, Sullivan wrote for *Columbia Journalism Review* and was American editor at the *Washington Post*. Her first journalism job was at Gannett News Service, followed by a reporting job at the *Niagara Falls Gazette*.

Karen Jurgensen

From 1999 to 2004, Katren Jurgensen was editor of America's most circulated newspaper, *USA Today*, which has a circulation of 2,200,000. Jurgensen resigned because she presided over the deception practiced by reporter

Jack Kelley, whose reports from Cuba, Russia, Kosovo and the Middle East were frequently no more than fabrications.[44]

Jurgensen was appointed chief editor at America's largest newspaper in 1999. She was born in 1949, and had been editor of the editorial page of *USA Today*. She first joined *USA Today* in 1982 and became editor of the editorial page in 1991. She had previous experience working for The Associated Press and *The Rome* (New York) *Daily American*. At *USA Today* she held a number of editorial jobs before being named editor-in-chief.

Jurgensen began her career in 1972 in Charlotte, North Carolina, and later worked at the *Miami News*. She earned a degree in English at the University of North Carolina in 1971.[45]

Women Book Editors

The Bureau of Labor Statistics indicates that women outnumber men as book editors in the United States. The occupation of book editor has long been in the hands of women as well as men, so that in 2006 there were 63,000 women and 59,000 men engaged in that occupation.

The median weekly salary for book editors was $938 or $48,776 annually for both sexes. Male editors earned $975 per week or $50,700 annually and women earned $837 weekly, or $43,526 annually.[46]

Because women book editors are by no means new to that area of employment, the number of women editors is too great to list even a fraction of them here. One example of a fiction editor is Carrie Ferron, who edits women's fiction at Avon Romance. Avon is the country's foremost publisher of romance fiction, including books by Susan Elizabeth Phillips, Laura Lippman, Christina Dodd and Pearl Cleage, who was cited by Oprah's Book Club.

The executive editor at Avon is Lucia Macro, who has been in the editing profession since 1983. She joined Avon in 1996. She has acquired leading authors of romance and women's fiction including numerous *New York Times* best sellers. She is also credited with a new line of erotica called Avon Red.[47]

Hope Dellon is an executive editor at St. Martin's Press in New York. St. Martin's is one of the largest American publishers. She graduated from Yale University with a B.A. and an M.A. in English literature and then joined St. Martin's in 1975. She has edited mostly historical fiction with such writers as Margaret George, Anne Perry, and Bernard Cornwell.

Allison McCabe is senior editor at Crown Publishing Group, a subsidiary of Random House. Before joining Crown she was at Penguin where she acquired and edited both fiction and non-fiction. She also worked at

Harper/Collins where she edited books by Susan Isaacs, Jeffrey Archer, Tony Hillerman and Jerry Oppenheimer.

These minimal outlines of some editors' careers are typical of the thousands of women book editors in this country.

Editors and Publishers of Women's Magazines

Oprah Winfrey

There are slightly more than 80 American women's magazines available at any time. Many of these do not last long, but about 25 have survived for years. These 25 women's magazines actually have a larger readership than TV shows targeting women have viewers. This strong interest in these magazines led to a 3 percent increase in ad revenues for the leading 22 women's magazines, even as revenue for all American magazines declined by 14 percent during the three years ending in 2006.[48]

The most recently launched women's magazine is *O*, which was begun by the actress Oprah Winfrey in 2000 with a beginning circulation of 500,000. This magazine had two million readers in 2007 as the number of ad pages doubled and the income quadrupled.

Oprah Winfrey is not only the publisher of *O* magazine but is also the most successful host on a TV show named for her. She was born in Mississippi in 1954 and graduated from Tennessee State University with a degree in speech and the performing arts.

She began her career on WJZ in Baltimore, MD, where she worked as a news anchor and co-hosted a local talk show called *People Are Talking*. Thereafter Oprah Winfrey has collected one success after another. These successes as a movie actress, talk show host and magazine publisher have led to her inclusion in the National Women's Hall of Fame as well as numerous other honors. In 2005, *Forbes* magazine estimated her worth at $1.3 billion, making her the only African American woman to be included in the *Forbes* list of billionaires.[49]

Winfrey has also been listed among the annual *Time* 100 as one of the most influential people in the world. She founded the Oprah Winfrey Leadership Academy and the Oprah's Angel Network. In 2006 she earned an estimated $260 million.[50]

The February 2008 issue of *O* magazine featured articles including "What's Wrong with Being Angry?" "Does Your Underwear Need an Overhaul?" "What is a Healthy Weight?" "Style and the Short Woman," and "The Divine Miss M," meaning Bette Midler.

Kristin van Ogtrop

A rather recent addition to women's magazines is *Real Simple*. This magazine has a circulation of two million and generates about $300 million in revenues.

The editor of this recent success is Kristin van Ogtrop. She began her career as an assistant at *Vogue*. From there she went to *Premier, Travel and Leisure* and *Glamour* before arriving at *Real Simple*.

Van Ogtrop graduated from the University of Virginia with a degree in English and also earned a master degree in English from Columbia University.

Real Simple contains such articles as "Eat Well, Lose Weight," "The Best Headache Cures," "Easy Freezer Meals" and "Secret to a Lasting Marriage." Additional interest is shown in "Products of the Month," "Should You Use Foil or Plastic?" "What is Your Carbon Footprint?" and "Lessons from First Class Flirts."

Glenda Bailey

Glenda Bailey is the editor-in-chief of *Harper's Bazaar*. *Harper's* is one of America's oldest magazines, founded in 1867 as America's first fashion magazine.

Bailey was previously the editor of another fashion magazine, *Marie Claire*. In that capacity she was highly successful by providing the readers with unique ideas such as producing a "What Women Want" event. This event included Oprah Winfrey, Meryl Streep, Sarah Jessica Parker, Trudie Styler and a number of other celebrities.

Bailey has won a number of awards over the years. She was named editor of the year by *Adweek* in 2001 and also won the Community Action Network award in 1998 and 1999.

Glenda Bailey was born in England in 1959. She earned a degree in fashion design from Kingston University and later became editor of *Honey*, a magazine for women. She also launched a new magazine called *Folio*.[51]

Helen Gurley Brown

In 1965, Helen Gurley Brown became editor of *Cosmopolitan*, a job she held for 30 years. During her tenure the magazine increased its circulation from 1 million to 2.8 million as she altered the magazine from a general interest magazine to a women's magazine, including some emphasis on sex. The magazine features some stories dealing with rape, male nudity, sexual proclivities and advice to women concerning male sexuality. In addition the magazine features stories about hair arrangements, the meaning of Pap smears, and urban legends.

Helen Gurley Brown was ousted from the position of editor in 1995. Since then *Cosmopolitan* has had a number of editors.

Brown was born in Arkansas in 1922. She attended Texas State College for Women and the Woodbury Business College. She began her career in the mailroom of the William Morris Agency and then became a secretary at an advertising agency. She was promoted to copywriter, so that by the 1960s she was the highest paid copywriter in advertising. In 1962, Brown authored *Sex and the Single Girl* and thereafter wrote six additional books on similar themes.

Helen Gurley Brown became editor-in-chief of *Cosmopolitan,* one of the oldest American magazines, when the sexual revolution in America was just beginning. Her career led to her earning the Henry Johnson Fisher Award from the Magazine Publishers of America and in 1996 the American Society of Magazine Publishers Hall of Fame Award.[52] She at first shocked her readers with her demands for women's sexual freedom. She promoted "the Cosmo Girl" and had a decided influence on the sexual revolution of the 1960s.

Summary

The appointment of a woman to anchor the news at prime time at a major network was indeed a breakthrough in the television news industry. It came about because a number of women had already established themselves in the TV newscasting business. In addition, a number of women began to anchor several TV shows as early as the 1970s while other women entered the newsrooms of daily newspapers and rose to become editors. These women founded the International Women's Media Foundation. Editors of women's magazines include such women as Oprah Winfrey and Helen Gurley Brown, who edited *Cosmopolitan* and was a great influence of the Sexual Revolution of the 1960s.

CHAPTER 9

The Sexual Revolution

The First Sexual Revolution — The 1920s

Gender is the social position dividing women from men. Sex is our physical differences. We have seen so far that women have attained considerable achievements during the forty years ending in 2007. Many of these achievements have been made possible because of the sexual revolution of the 1960s with some input from the earlier, first sexual revolution of the 1920s. It is our contention that without the sexual revolution, the gender revolution would not have been possible and that the sexual revolution in turn was the product of scientific advances which permitted Americans to alter their views concerning sexual morality.

When Queen Victoria died in 1901, the Victorian age did not cease with her. It continued for at least twenty years after her if we use as the criterion of culture lag the relationship between the sexes. Yet, for many Englishmen and Americans, the Victorian age really did not cease until the second sexual revolution of the 1960s.[1]

The First Sexual Revolution began directly after the First World War in response to the common belief in the U.S.A. and England that ladies have no sexual interests. This is well illustrated by a survey conducted in 1919 by the New York Bureau of Social Hygiene, as well as other surveys, which concluded that American women generally denied feelings of sexual desire and also denied having had an orgasm although married for years.[2]

The sexual revolution of the 1920s became visible only because at that time wealthier and better-educated women participated in activities that had already been common among the lower or working class. However, the working class is usually invisible to scholars and researchers so that the sexual revolution of the 1920s and even the revolution of the 1960s was recorded only when both became upper and upper middle class activities.[3]

Since reproduction and sexuality are bound together, attitudes towards sexuality are inevitably shaped by the physical and economic consequences of pregnancy. Since few couples had access to effective birth control in the 1920s, abortion and abstinence were the only really effective means of preventing unwanted children. Therefore, the first sexual revolution did not succeed because it could not overcome these obstacles. Women were unwilling to become pregnant numerous times despite the pressure to discard Victorian morality. The only effective means of dealing with this dilemma was to control sexual desire.

Therefore it was only after the invention of the pill in the 1960s that a sexual revolution became possible. The pill tricks the brain into assuming that the body is already pregnant, thereby preventing pregnancy *ipso facto*. Thus, for the first time in human history, pregnancy could be separated from sexual intercourse.[4]

The Second Sexual Revolution

The second sexual revolution took place in the 1960s and has altered the sex lives of Americans, at least in popular culture and to some extent among the young and the old. In short, the second sexual revolution belongs mainly to the 1960s and early 1970s.

In October of 1994, *Time* magazine featured a cover story entitled "Sex in America." This story was a report concerning a book by that title, published that year. It dealt with a survey based on a random sample of 3,432 Americans aged eighteen to fifty-nine. The survey came thirty years after the beginning of the second sexual revolution, accompanied by the rise of feminism, the anti-pornography movement and consciousness raising concerning sexual harassment and sexual abuse.[5]

According to that survey, 94 percent of married Americans claimed to be faithful to their spouse. At that time the median number of sex partners reported by women was two over a lifetime and for men it was six. According to that report only one-third of Americans had sex twice a week or more. Married couples claimed to have more sex than singles and 7.1 percent of men and 3.8 percent of women said that they had ever engaged in homosexuality. Additional findings were that 42 percent of women and 63 percent of men masturbated in the course of a year, 23 percent of men and 19 percent of women engaged in oral sex in a year and 54 percent of men but only 19 percent of women said they thought about sex every day.[6]

Ten years later, in 2004, another survey concerning sex in America revealed that in the 21st century the same people who changed sexual expectations with the aid of the pill in the 1960s are changing sexual practices with the aid of potency enhancing medicines for men.[7]

The AARP study of 2004 surveyed a nationally representative group of 1,682 adults aged 45 years or over to measure their attitudes toward sexual expression. This latest survey reveals that more and more men are using pills to defeat erectile dysfunction. The first erectile dysfunction pill, Viagra, came into use in 1998. It was soon followed by several other such products, so that its use increased from 5 percent to 22 percent between 1998 and 2006.[8]

This survey also finds that those who were reputedly the most open minded about sex in the 1960s disapprove of extramarital affairs as much as did their parents. These same baby boomers also say that American popular culture puts too much emphasis on sex.

In addition to the pill and Viagra, the Internet has changed the sex habits of many Americans in the past ten years. According to the AARP study, 22 percent of men and women exchange sexy e-mails.

Because many older women lack partners because men die before them, older women are more likely than older men to say that sex is not important in their lives.[9]

This latest effort to survey American sexual proclivities is far from producing the kind of changes that forty years earlier brought about the phrase sexual revolution.

At first, the sexual revolution seemed to lead to unlimited promiscuity. This fear was promoted mainly by the media, who reported extensively on flower children, homosexual activities and the increasing popularity of pornography.

The Influence of the Sexual Revolution on Homosexuals

As sexual behavior was transformed from the Puritanism of the 1950s to the more open expression of the 1960s, homosexuals became more and more willing to admit to these activities publicly. That exhibition led to public awareness that disease now interfered and halted much of what appeared to be the final liberation of mankind from sexual repression. The advent of Acquired Immune Deficiency Syndrome, or AIDS, reminded those who had already celebrated final sexual license that humans have not been able to defeat social diseases. In fact, gonorrhea and syphilis, which seemed to have been finally wiped out, returned to threaten women and men alike as penicillin and other wonder drugs began to lose their potency. While penicillin and other antibiotics were at one time viewed as final suppressors of these sexually transmitted diseases, the diseases' further decline has been affected by the discovery that they may have become drug resistant and therefore not finally eliminated. Therefore, sexual behavior is limited by nature as humans cannot withstand unbridled promiscuity. Gender changes are therefore permanent in the Western world but changes in sexual behavior are limited and found much more in the province of verbal expression than in conduct.[10]

At the beginning of the 1960s it appeared that the sexual revolution would produce a permanent sexual liberation. That has not occurred because sexual behavior is so limited by biological and psychic vulnerability that the increased talk about sex is not matched by conduct.

Because AIDS threatened to become an epidemic, discussion concerning sexual liberation gave way to the issue of what could have gone wrong in a society which produced that disease. At first, denial was the most common reaction to AIDS. The media and the public sought to blame the victims of the disease by pointing to their alleged promiscuity and homosexuality. Later, blame was attached to the National Institutes of Health and other government agencies for not acting fast enough or decisively enough to do something about this disease. Finally, we have reached the conclusion that research and treatment can advance a possible cure for AIDS even as it is feared that overuse has made penicillin and other wonder drugs less effective in dealing with the traditional social diseases.[11]

In the course of the debate about AIDS, homosexuals have been particularly affected by public criticism and rejection because the disease appeared at first to be limited to homosexual practitioners. This rejection led to a great deal of effort on the part of the homosexual community and its supporters to argue that behavior, not people, should be avoided. Nevertheless, as in all epidemics, many people seek to distance themselves from the high risk groups. Religious organizations in particular have used the AIDS epidemic to promote their cause, arguing that AIDS is divine retribution for sexual sin. Therefore, for a number of years, the homosexual community was unable to deal with the AIDS problem because so many in the health delivery profession refused to deal with AIDS patients or research the problem.[12]

The labels "heterosexual," "homosexual," and "lesbian" are social constructs. It is for that reason that a good number of people in the homosexual community define themselves as heterosexuals despite their homosexual behavior. Such people are therefore less likely than admitted homosexuals to seek medical help concerning their exposure to AIDS. Therefore, behavior, not sexual identity, must determine who is at risk.

A study by Lever reveals that nearly two-thirds of men who practiced homosexual behavior extensively nevertheless viewed themselves as heterosexuals, particularly if they were also bisexual.[13]

The Hispanic culture, which involves about 36 million Americans at the beginning of the 21st century, prescribes a heterosexual role for men even if they are active homosexuals. This supports the view that there can be a true discrepancy between actual behavior and sexual identity because sexual identity is the product of status designation in American culture in which heterosexuals are provided a higher status than bisexuals, whose status in turn exceeds that of homosexuals.[14]

These status discrepancies allowed the police for years to roust homosexual men and beat them, arrest them on phony charges and generally become the victims of police brutality. All of this changed in 1969 when numerous gay men fought the police who were in the process of raiding the Stonewall Inn, a New York City gay bar. Homosexual men had never before resisted such raids, which were predicated on the view that homosexuality is a sex offense and that gay men have no rights.[15]

Stonewall is so important to the homosexual community that it is celebrated every five years by marches and proclamations in New York, San Francisco and foreign cities such as Manila in the Philippines. These parades and marches no longer attract much attention in the 21st century because the rights of homosexuals have been accepted by most Americans. This is without doubt due to the sexual revolution and its success.[16]

An additional outcome of the Stonewall Riots has been the demand by homosexuals that the Universal Declaration of Human Rights be extended to homosexuals. In the United States, proponents of civil rights for homosexuals attempted to expand federal law prohibiting hate crimes based on race or religion to include such crimes based on sexual orientation. This failed in December of 2007 when the House refused to pass the Matthew Shepard Act. That proposed law is named after a University of Wyoming college student who was fatally attacked in Laramie, Wyoming, by Russell Henderson and Aaron McKinney. Both were later imprisoned for life.[17]

Since then several public opinion polls have shown that the American public is more and more willing to accept homosexuality as legitimate. In 2007 the Gallup Poll discovered that 57 percent of Americans agree that homosexuality is an acceptable lifestyle; that 59 percent of Americans think homosexual conduct should be legal; that 46 percent believe same sex marriages should be legal and that 59 percent want homosexuals to have equal job opportunities.[18]

The Influence of the Sexual Revolution on Adolescents and Young Adults

Socialization is the process whereby we learn to conduct ourselves according to that which is viewed as legitimate in the society into which we were born or which we entered at a later date in our lives.

This applies to the sex drive, which is channeled into behavior approved by the culture or subculture to which we belong. We superimpose the requirements of the culture on our biological drives and act accordingly. That was true of the Victorians and is also true of 21st century American adolescents. We can therefore call that aspect of the enculturation process that involves sex the sexualization process.[19]

One aspect of this process is related to the impact of the media on the adolescent's sexual interests. The media impact may be classified as informal sex education, in contrast to the formal sex education included in the curriculum of almost all American schools.

Informal sex education is of course not limited to the media. Parents, peers and all kinds of friends participate in the sex education of American youngsters outside the classroom. This begins with learning one's gender identity. Gender identity is a social issue because the roles played by women and men are determined by the cultural requirements of each society and are not everywhere the same. American boys and girls learn by observation and parental influence what is masculine and what is feminine and that learning includes forming sexual values.[20]

The sexual revolution of the 1960s has therefore contributed to a change in sexual values for many adolescents. Evidence for this change, among other events, is the refusal of some adolescents to date in the traditional manner. Those adolescents who do not want to get involved substitute hooking up for dating. Hooking up is achieved through the internet and is a no strings sexual encounter. Teenagers and others flirt with each other on-line and then meet for a sexual event without romantic overtones. Some participate with the same partner more than once. Such partners are called friends with benefits. It is claimed by some that girls are as aggressive as boys in making such contacts. The sites used by teens to make such contacts are called rating sites because the participants exhibit their pictures on these sites. The pictures are then rated by strangers, who view them with the intent of finding a sex partner.[21]

The sexual revolution has also decreased the age at which sex is first practiced by adolescents in America. Young children are seldom involved, although 3 percent of schoolchildren eleven to twelve years old are reported to have engaged in sexual practices. This increases to 12 percent for males age 13–14 and 8 percent for females in that age group. By age 16, 34 percent of adolescents have engaged in sex.[22]

The sexual revolution has also impacted parenting. The U.S. Statistical Abstracts confirms that in only 26 years the number of couples with children decreased from 75 percent to 56 percent. Meanwhile the number of unmarried couples with no children increased 230 percent and the number of children in single mother households increased 417 percent as the number of children living with neither parent increased 1,440 percent. In 2006, 67 percent of children ages 0–17 lived with two married parents, down from 77 percent in 1980. Ten percent of these parents were not the biological parent, either father or mother. During those years, 1980 to 2006, the percent of children living with a single father increased from 2 percent to 5 percent.

The majority of children living with a single parent were living with single mothers who usually had a co-habiting partner.[23]

The Sexual Revolution and Sex Education

In his State of the Union speech on January 20, 2004, President Bush proclaimed that "abstinence for young people is the only way to avoid sexually transmitted diseases." This message was most welcome among those who believe that there should be no sex outside of marriage but was very much criticized by the Sexuality Information and Education Council of the United States. That group believes that sex education should include information about contraception in addition to fostering abstinence. The council believes that abstinence only is not realistic although some surveys report that abstinence messages may reduce the number of students involved in sex.[24]

Such educational efforts are widely supported by the American public. In fact, six out of ten Americans believe that sexually active young people should be given access to birth control devices. Therefore, public opinion is in agreement with sex education which holds that the abstinence only approach ignores the evidence that other programs are also effective in delaying the onset of sexual intercourse among adolescents. In fact, there is little evidence that abstinence only programs have either delayed or reduced sexual activity. The evidence is that the comprehensive approach to sex education is far more successful than the abstinence only effort because it includes information concerning pregnancy prevention and the threat of sexually transmitted diseases.[25]

In 1981, Congress passed the Adolescent Family Life Act. It included money for the establishment of a counseling and service network designed to provide contraceptive services only to adolescents who already had a child and who were seeking to prevent another pregnancy. Such a network was never established. However, the AFLA subsidized curricula that promote abstinence only education in schools.[26]

As a result more than two-thirds of all American school districts have a sex education program. The remaining third leave sex education to individual schools or teachers. School districts in the North are more likely to have a district wide policy to teach sex education than is the case in the South or in the West.²⁷

Although a large number of teachers believe that sex education should begin in grades seven or eight, and although some children clearly have sexual encounters before then, it appears that in most American schools sex education does not begin until the ninth or tenth grade. There is also a gap between what teachers think should be taught and what is really taught. There is a particularly wide gap between the belief of teachers that students should be told where they can obtain birth control. Yet, that information is only available in only about 48 percent of American schools. There is much more uniformity concerning teaching about AIDS, which is covered by 90 percent to 96 percent of all teachers, with abstinence a close second. Sex education teachers regard interference from parents and school principals as the major obstacles in teaching about sex.²⁸

In California over $200 million was spent between 1994 and 2004 for sex education, leading to a 40 percent decline in teen pregnancy. This caused considerable savings for the California taxpayer in that fewer teen mothers and their babies needed public help. State officials and parents believe that this success is the product of a comprehensive approach to sex education and are therefore unwilling to take federal money for an abstinence only approach.²⁹

The Sexual Revolution and the Media

The influence of the media on American life, including television, the Internet, radio and printed material, is immense. This great influence on sexual behavior can be seen in particular by comparing the depiction of sexual activity in the media of 2008 to the suppression of sex fifty years earlier. When Lucille Ball, at one time a most popular actress, showed her pregnancy during several television episodes in 1953, the producers of *I Love Lucy* would not allow the word pregnancy to be used on the show and made every attempt to cover up the evidence by using clothes that concealed it.

Pornography

In 2008, sexual intercourse is shown on numerous television shows and movies, so that the word pornography has lost its meaning. This came about when in the mid 1970s videocassettes were first introduced into American life. These cassettes became most popular and are found in about 85 percent of American homes. Videocassettes are the dominant provider of pornography in the United States. Together with the Internet it may be said that pornography has become part of American popular culture.[30]

The effort of Congress to restrict access to pornography consisted mainly of the Child Online Protection Act of 1998, which was held unconstitutional by the Supreme Court in 2004. The court upheld an injunction by the Third Circuit Court of Appeals against enforcing the act. That law sought to allow a fine of $50,000 per day and a six-month prison sentence for posting online material "harmful to minors." This was the third decision defeating similar laws passed by Congress in earlier years.[31]

Congress, in passing this kind of legislation, responds to the fears and beliefs of voters. This is demonstrated by Fisher, Cook and Shirkey, who asked citizens in one large Florida county whether or not they support censorship of explicit sexual material. The overwhelming majority said they support such censorship.[32]

A peculiar belief about pornography on the part of those who watch such material is the belief that it should be censored because of its effect on others. This has been called "the third person effect" and has been observed in situations other than those dealing with censorship.[33]

The debate about pornography, then, centers about its outcome. Some believe that pornography encourages rape, the denigration of women and a general breakdown of public morals. Nevertheless, pornography is part of American culture. It has been kept alive because of wide support and the opportunities which technology has afforded it.

Some of those who are concerned with the rights of women contend that pornography insults women and therefore contributes to the continued disadvantages women suffer. This belief has been found to be untrue. In fact, research has shown that in communities which are tolerant of pornography there is also a more liberal attitude towards the rights of women. This is best illustrated by the experience of the Scandinavian countries, whose laws have eliminated all censorship from pornography even as women have attained more there than anywhere else. The argument is not that pornography causes the increase in women's rights but rather than those who exhibit liberality towards pornography are also more willing to practice gender equality.[34]

Whether or not callous attitudes toward women are related to the use of pornography is in dispute. Research in the United States has shown that there is no significant correlation between viewing x-rated material and support for laws punishing rape or assault on women or prohibiting sexual harassment. Likewise, evidence from Denmark has shown that after that country decriminalized pornography in the 1960s the rate of rape and sex crimes decreased significantly even as the viewing of sexually explicit material increased.[35]

Although sex crimes are not associated with pornography, there is some evidence that blatant disrespect for women and an attitude of superiority towards women on the part of male viewers is related to such entertainment. A study by Cowan and Dunn found that blatant disrespect for women is a most prominent theme among those men studied by them. Women are viewed as objects in pornographic materials, say Cowan and Dunn. Furthermore, women are shown as subordinates in such videotapes, which are devoted to "penis worship." It needs to be understood that all pornography is not the same but that in general it is not sex but the status degradation of women that is most objectionable in that enterprise.[36]

Pornography has perpetuated the stereotype of the macho male. This is true in part because men are the major consumers of pornography. Therefore, pornography depicts a sexual reality in which men and women assume inequitable social positions. Women are frequently portrayed as promiscuous and are depicted as behaving outside of the bounds of the cultural norms of most Western societies. Therefore, sex between total strangers is common in pornography while sex among committed partners is rare. This is the opposite of reality for anyone living in the United States or, for that matter, anywhere. In sum, pornography is a fantasy leading to the conclusion that a macho culture is acceptable, if not endorsed, by men who view such material. Because many adolescents and even children view such material there are a good number of children who rely on this to gain an opinion concerning sex.[37]

The Influence of Television on the Sexual Revolution

A content analysis of television programs aimed at children and adolescents concluded that "numerous aspects of sexuality are commonly presented in the television programs children watch the most." According to Monique Ward, 50 percent of television programs dealing with interaction in television programs deal with sex. She recognized that sex as depicted in the media is not reality but a false picture of real relationships. Further, she shows that sex is not discussed nearly as much as pornographic literature would have us believe. Ward further discovered that sexuality on television is depicted as a strategy and form of manipulation in which the contenders for sex must always appear cool, be good looking and be short run hedonists, a lifestyle also taught by other forms of entertainment. Ward also found that even so-called TV situation comedies emphasizing family values are not sex free. Hence, television has become a major source of information about sex for the young.[38]

The Influence of the Computer and Some Other Technology on the Sexual Revolution

In 1996 Congress passed the Communications Decency Act. Signed into law by President Clinton, this act was designed to prevent the sending or display of indecent material online in a way that made the material available to minors. The law made it a crime "to use an interactive computer service to knowingly send or display to a person under 18 a communication that in context depicts or describes in terms patently offensive as measured by contemporary community standards sexual or excretory activities or organs."[39]

In that same year, 1996, under a challenge by the communications industry and civil liberties organizations, a special three judge U.S. District Court in Philadelphia struck down this law on the grounds that it violated the First Amendment to the U.S. Constitution guaranteeing free speech. On June 25, 1997, the U.S. Supreme Court affirmed that decision and voided the United States Communications Decency Act.

The court also voided this law because it had been written in so broad a fashion that, in the words of Justice John Paul Stevens, "the wholly unprecedented breadth" of the law threatened to suppress far too much speech among adults and even between parents and children. Wrote Stevens: "The interest in encouraging freedom of expression in a democratic society outweighs any theoretical but unproven benefit of censorship."[40]

After the Supreme Court invalidated the Communications Decency Act, President Clinton convened a meeting of industry executives, teachers, librarians and parents to discuss solutions to the problem of Internet pornography as it affects children. The group concluded that stricter supervision of children, stronger self regulation by the industry and the development of technological means of blocking pornography would resolve the problem of children surfing the Internet. Evidently, only the last suggestion has any merit because it has been very profitable to the Information Technology Association and because it would not require parents to do much about it.[41]

On June 29, 2004, the Supreme Court blocked the prosecution of operators of pornographic Web sites a second time. This time the court ruled 5–4 that the Child Online Protection Act of 1998 was unconstitutional as it would be a violation of free speech. In the course of the arguments presented, the U.S. solicitor general, Theodore Olson, told the court that he typed the words "free porn" into an Internet search engine and found that there were 6,230,000 sites available.[42]

Another consequence of the computer age is the ability of strangers to chat in cyberspace and become online lovers. Cyber is the Greek word for pilot or steerer and has become a metaphor for describing the non-physical terrain created by computer systems. This allows people to communicate with one another via e-mail by merely pressing buttons on the computer. The term cyberspace was coined by the author of the novel *Neuromancer,* William Gibson.[43]

Chat rooms are largely used to meet single women or men after first meeting them anonymously. However, numerous married folks have also used chat rooms to meet people of the opposite sex whom they did not know and with whom they have carried on a stimulating conversation. Some of those who engage in this activity actually meet the target of their interest in person, leading to sexual encounters in some instances. Pictures and brief descriptions of participants in chat rooms are usually available at such Web sites as MySpace.[44]

There are some adults who have used chat rooms to exploit children. This is viewed a serious crime in the United States and Europe, although Asian countries are less likely to prohibit such activity.

There are several reasons for cybersex. First is the inability of some women and men to develop adequate social skills to allow them to succeed with the opposite sex directly. This failure to be accepted by a woman or man is not necessarily related to physical appearance. Indeed, good looking people have easier access to sex than those not good looking. Nevertheless, the presentation of self in everyday life is more important than looks. There are many who may not be good looking according to Hollywood standards but who know how to sell themselves to lovers. Conversely, there are those who have good looks but are so self negating that they cannot manipulate the social scene except by hiding behind a computer.[45]

A second reason for cybersex is the inability of some users, particularly children, to understand the difference between fantasy and reality. This leads some chat room users to communicate with a phantom of their imagination only to discover that they have communicated with a person who is quite different from the phantom. In fact, the real person may be dangerous, so that those who are motivated to actually meet someone they met in a chat room may be very disappointed if not in physical danger. Finally, there are those who participate in computer sex because they suffer from a sex addiction similar to alcoholism. These are people who cannot control their sexual needs either because they have no physical affection at home or because they are so called Don Juans or nymphomaniacs who need psychological intervention.[46]

The social functions of computer sex are, first, rebellion against the established social order. This is also the message of all graffiti. Computer sex is secretive and therefore avoids social sanctions while allowing the expression of hostility. Further, computer sex permits persons otherwise regarded as deviant to express their preferences to persons of similar interest without fearing retribution from straight people. In addition, the computer has been an agent of social change in that it permits actions which otherwise could exist only in the imagination. Next, the computer is a transmitter and distributor of messages of all kinds, including sexual messages. Because the computer reaches a worldwide audience, it also succeeds to diffuse messages over large areas so that it insures success for those seeking response to their interests. Finally, the computer creates a sub-culture of persons interested in the same activities. This means that the computer functions in favor of social solidarity, as people otherwise isolated meet one another and reinforce their attitudes and beliefs. This is true of sex or any other notion.[47]

The sexual revolution promoted by television and the computer was given some impetus as early as the beginning of the 20th century when the automobile came into use. This afforded couples the opportunity to engage in sexual conduct outside the home where Victorian attitudes made anything past holding hands quite impossible. It was also at the beginning of the 20th century that Edison's invention of the movies, allowed the production of primitive pornography films. The telephone was invented by Antonio Meucci in 1850. Because Alexander Bell was far better financed than Meucci, his name has been associated with that invention, which was credited to him because of collusion with the U.S. Patent Office. The telephone contributed to the sexual revolution in that it is used by women and men to fantasize concerning the opposite sex through paid telephone messages. The citizens band radio is another device used to obtain sexual gratification. Truckers and others use the citizens band radio to call prostitutes who work the interstate throughways. Call girls in Las Vegas and other places use C.Bs to contact their pimps and their customers. Camcorders and other photographic equipment have been used in the service of sexual needs.[48]

The Contribution of the 1960s Sexual Revolution to Recreational Sex

The 1960s saw the development of recreational sex in that public displays of physical attributes previously prohibited became part of the entertainment industry. Thus, the first topless waitresses appeared in New York nightclubs in 1966. While heralded by the media as a sensation at that time, this type of exposure has become so common forty years later that it is now part of the routine of popular culture. Men, seeking to compete for the public dollar, also exhibit themselves as they dance nude in nightclubs. Such clubs may be targeting homosexual men or women. For example, Hunter's Hunks is a male go go dance team who entertain in gay bars. In Los Angeles there are numerous male dance groups, including Latin Connection, who entertain women at bachelorette parties. These men perform strip tease dances and engage in heretofore labeled lewd acts which resemble the conduct of women who have entertained a male clientele with these performances for many years.

Films, plays and books have also contributed to recreational sex in the aftermath of the '60s sexual revolution. Edward Albee's *Who's Afraid of Virginia Woolf* and the lyrics of the Rolling Stones included obscene language. A musical called *Hair* included naked actors singing gutter profanities on the New York stage. Bare breasted actresses also appeared in such movies as *Bonnie and Clyde* and *In the Heat of the Night*.

After 1970, book banning ended in America. Thereupon such erstwhile banned books as *Valley of the Dolls* and *The Story of O* and the works of Henry Miller were sold in corner drug stores and available in most libraries. The English invented the miniskirt and the magazine *Playboy* reached a circulation of 5 million while one of the best sellers of the era was *The Sensuous Woman* by someone called "J."[49]

Charlotte Moorman, a renowned cellist of the 1960s, became involved in the sexual revolution and performed topless on the New York stage. In 1968, the actor Julian Beck took off his clothes in the aisle of a theater. In 1968, four hundred thousand college age people came to Bethel, New York, to listen to a concert of then popular music. Calling themselves The Woodstock Nation after a small town in the vicinity of Bethel, they openly performed sex acts, smoked marijuana, used psychedelic drugs and walked about nude.

In 1969, an actor, Richard Schechner, performed *Dionysus 69*. This audience participation play consisted of nude actors running around the audience who were invited to also take their clothes off. This denuding was followed by a bacchanalian dance accompanied by hysterical screaming and blood letting from a cardboard device.[50]

In 1969, Philip Roth published *Portnoy's Complaint*. This book dealt with numerous sexual themes as told by a patient to his psychiatrist. It was indeed obscene from the view of the 1950s but expressed better than any other novel of the day the sexual revolution then in progress. Millions of readers, in the 1960s, also bought a softcover book called *Everything You Always Wanted to Know About Sex but Were Afraid to Ask*. Beatles star John Lennon and his wife, Yoko Ono, launched a "fuck for peace" campaign and participated in the production of a play called *Oh! Calcutta!*, which is public pornography and exhibitionism. In turn, homosexuals came out and introduced the public to such practices as fisting.

All of these activities were topped by even more exotic developments in the 1970s. Beginning in California, The Sexual Freedom League expanded nationwide in the interest of organized swinging parties. These parties introduced the participants to husband-wife swapping often organized on cruising ships. Swingers have developed their own subculture by publishing magazines, holding conventions and, like all subcultures, using a special language to describe their activities. Those who engage in this practice claim that this conduct avoids cheating, a term popularly used to designate extramarital sex. While all of these sexual activities are still in existence in the first part of the 21st century, they are mostly rejected by the American public.

An American Sex Survey conducted by ABC News in October of 2004 demonstrates that the extremes of the 1960s and 1970s no longer have much following in the United States. Indeed, there is no return to the repression of the 1950s. This is illustrated by the result of the survey to the effect that 84 percent of women and 64 percent of men said that there is too much sex on TV. The various activities which gained so much publicity in the 1960s and '70s are principally unpopular in 2008, although not as often condemned as was true in mid-century. In short, the sexual revolution is over but left behind a drive for female entitlement in the area of education, economics, politics, religion and government.[51]

Women's Sexual Liberation

Although men are undoubtedly the principal organizers of most of the American sex industry, there are also sex enterprises that cater mainly to women. A prominent example of a sex enterprise devoted to women is Eve's Garden, headquartered in Atlanta, Georgia, but also found in other cities and on the Internet. This supplier of sex related objects sells so-called sex toys, also sex furniture, books, videos and lingerie, i.e. women's underwear. The company advertises on the Internet with pictures of sexual activity, involving men and women or only a woman, sells various perfumes and lotions, and exhibits an entire library of books concerned with sexual behavior. These enterprises were started by women in the late 1970s and have grown considerably since then.

On June 9, 1973, the New York chapter of the National Organization for Women held a conference in New York City whose theme was "To Explore, Define and Celebrate Our Own Sexuality." This conference was then seen as a political rally based on the conclusion that violence directed against women was, and is, a political issue as depicted in *Sexual Politics* by Kate Millett.[52]

At that conference militant women demanded sexual freedom. They organized a number of workshops or discussion groups dealing with such topics as "Creating a New Sexual Identity," "Group Sex," "Religion and

Repression," "The Double Standard" and others. This conference also included a slide presentation of women's genitals presented as the catalyst for women's sexual liberation. That in turn led to an agreement that women had a right to buy vibrators, books and various objects leading to sexual gratification. These items were at that time seldom available to most women and were also a source of embarrassment for those who bought this type of equipment in a sex shop. Therefore Dell Williams resigned her position as an executive in an advertising agency and created Eve's Garden, a retail boutique and mail order house selling books and equipment to women.[53]

Another aspect of the sexual revolution has been the development of "naughty lady" parties where lingerie (French for linen) and sex paraphernalia are sold. An example of such parties is the Tickle Your Fancy Web site, which advertises that they will book parties in private homes in the Chicago area. At these parties the convener sells lingerie, massage oils, romance games and books, romantic gifts, tasty body toppings, and a full line of bedroom toys. Their motto is "enriching romance." Those willing to lend their home to such a party are rewarded with discounts on the items sold. The cost of these items vary from $14.00 for a belly button ring to bath salts for $35.00.[54]

Such parties follow the pattern of Tupperware parties or Mary Kay Cosmetics. However, these parties create a problem for potential customers of the products sold because the customers need to maintain their self-respect in an activity that was traditionally criticized as not ladylike. To overcome these scruples, the organizers call these events home sales parties or other neutralizing terms. Evidently, a sale of erotic items is far more comfortable if conducted in a home than in a public store. A home setting is far less threatening. This allows women to buy things they would not otherwise consider. The exclusion of men and the private nature of the setting in which the participants can avoid public scrutiny and the opinion of neighbors, family and friends concerning the possible violation of morality makes these parties successful.[55]

The Influence of the Sexual Revolution on Sexual Harassment

Sexual harassment is as old as the dependency of women on men for their subsistence. Therefore, the inclusion of this offensive behavior in Title VII of the Civil Rights Act of 1964 was indeed revolutionary in promoting the rights of women and can be credited to the consequences of the sexual revolution of the 1960s. The law, as amended since 1964, prohibits sex discrimination and hence sexual harassment in the workplace. According to the guidelines issued by the Civil Rights Commission, charged with enforcing this law, sexual harassment can occur in a variety of circumstances. These include, but are not limited to, these four situations. The harasser as well as the victim may be a man or a woman. The victim does not have to be of the opposite sex. The harasser can be the victim's supervisor, an agent of the employer, a supervisor in another area, a co-worker, or a non-employee. The victim does not have to be the one harassed but could be someone affected by the offensive conduct. Unlawful sexual harassment can occur without economic injury to the victim or discharge of the victim. Finally, the harasser's conduct must be unwelcome.

According to the statistics published by the commission, 84.6 percent of the 12,025 complaints received by the EEOC were filed by women in 2006 and 15.4 percent were filed by men. The EEOC received $48.8 million in benefits on behalf of the victims, some of whom also received monetary compensation through additional litigation.[56]

Two kinds of sexual harassment are described in the guidelines of the Equal Opportunity Commission. The first is called *quid pro quo* harassment, using a Latin term meaning something for something. This refers to demanding some kind of sexual action as a condition of employment. The second form of sexual harassment as defined by the commission is the promotion of a hostile work environment in which sexual conduct interferes unreasonably with work performance or creates an intimidating or offensive work environment. In 1993 these guidelines were further amended to include conduct not sexual in nature.[57]

Several difficulties arise at once whenever an effort is made to enforce these guidelines. First is the problem of establishing what is meant by sexually harassing behavior. Little doubt exists that touching another person without permission is unacceptable. But does that include a child of six who kissed a female classmate on the cheek? Evidently it does, as discovered by Jonathan Prevette, a first grader who was suspended from school in Lexington, North Carolina, for just that offense.[58]

In December 2006 a four-year-old child was suspended by the school administrators in Waco, Texas, because he hugged a teacher's aide. This hug was interpreted as inappropriately touching. A letter from the administration to the parents of the child accused the four-year-old of sexual conduct and sexual harassment.[59]

Likewise a first grader was suspended for sexual harassment in Brockton, Massachusetts, because he put two fingers into a classmate's waistband. The child said that a girl touched him. The school administrators refused to recognize that a 6 year old gains no sexual gratification from such an act and cannot understand the nature of the charges against him.[60]

The hysteria surrounding sexual harassment has now led to accusations based on a man opening a door for a woman, or having the photo of the wife on one's desk, as that may offend another worker, or hanging up a girly calendar in a garage, or boys and girls holding hands in grade school or, for that matter, any show of affection or friendship. In addition, jokes involving sex cannot be told and even unwanted looks are cause for sexual harassment lawsuits. These seemingly extreme interpretations of what constitutes sexual harassment were confirmed by Patricia A. Frazier and her colleagues after they administered a sexual experience questionnaire to faculty, civil service employees, graduate and undergraduate students at the University of Minnesota. It is indeed a grim world in which jokes cannot be told and looks are a crime.[61]

The Influence of the Sexual Revolution on Child Bearing and Abortion

According to the United Nations World Population Prospects report, American women had a fertility rate of 2.0 in 2007. This fertility rate has held steady for some years although it was interrupted in a few years with a fertility rate of 1.9.[62]

In the late 1950s American women were having children at the rate of 3.1 per woman but, by the mid 1970s and into the '80s, the number of births per woman declined to 1.8.

The evident decline in births per woman can certainly be attributed to the very lynchpin of female ascendancy in the late 20th and early 21st century, that is, birth control by means of the pill. The pill was invented by Dr. Gregory Pincus and Dr. John Rock in 1954 after they discovered a drug that could be taken in pill form. In addition to the low natural birth rate, abortion is also involved in the decline of live births in those years Indeed, during these same years, abortion among American women declined from 428 per 1,000 live births to 313 per 1,000 live births. That means nevertheless that 1,287,000 abortions take place in this country every year.[63]

Birth control has of course been attempted for at least 2,500 years of human civilization. Yet, it never really succeeded until the mid 1960s. Since then, the French have invented an abortion pill which has been used with great success in France but led to violent controversy in the United States, as has the entire issue of abortion. That controversy continues 35 years after the historic Supreme Court decision in *Roe v. Wade* in which the court held that it is the right of every women to have an abortion from a licensed physician during the first three months of her pregnancy.[64]

In 1989, the court revised this decision and supported the right of states to regulate abortions. This led to the prohibition of abortion in Guam and Louisiana. Political conservatives succeeded in again questioning the right of women to control their own bodies as these believers sought to bring about a constitutional amendment prohibiting abortion entirely. This has not succeeded as of 2008.

Underlying the argument or choice of prohibition of abortion is a fundamental difference of opinion concerning the emancipation of women. Conservatives claim that they are pro-life, which posture would make others anti-life. Such a position is of course untenable, since those who support abortion are surely not opposed to life on this earth. It is far more likely that pro-life supporters dislike the whole idea of liberating women from the drudgery of earlier years. Therefore the contenders in this dispute use rather inflammatory rhetoric such as "abortion epidemic" even when abortions have declined in this country. Of course that decline is mainly due to the decline in the birth rate as more and more educated women can afford to raise two children.

There is in this country a National Right to Life Committee. This committee, based in Washington, D.C., lobbies Congress on behalf of their cause, which is a constitutional amendment prohibiting all abortions.[65]

Essentially, the dispute between the pro-abortion faction and the anti-abortionists centers upon the question of women's right to express themselves sexually as they please. That right is also expressed in the number of children born to unmarried mothers in this country. The National Center for Health Statistics records that there are about 1.5 million births to unmarried mothers in this country every year. This constitutes 35.7 percent of all live births in the United States in 2005 to 2007. That this is an immense increase in such births may be seen by considering that in 1940 only 10 percent of children in the United States were born to an unmarried mother.[66]

Nothing illustrated more succinctly the liberation of women from the constraints of the past than the rate of births among unmarried mothers. This is not to say that the absence of fathers is a benefit to children. On the contrary. For many children the absence of a father not only guarantees poverty, but also deprives children of a male role model. This is as true for girls as boys.

In sum, it is evident from this review that numerous factors have conspired to bring about the liberation and ascendancy of American women in the 232nd year of our independence. Propelled by numerous catalysts for social change, American democracy is ever evolving as the rights of more and more Americans are included in the democratic institutions of the United States. These catalysts for social change may best be understood by investigating the nature of social change.

Summary

The United States has seen two sexual revolutions. The first occurred in the 1920s but failed for lack of birth control. The second occurred in the 1960s and succeeded in liberating homosexuals and women from the strictures of the 1950s. Adolescents also underwent a sexual revolution that was not always in their interest. Sex education entered the curriculum in schools and the Supreme Court invalidated laws aimed at suppressing sexual expression in the media. The sexual revolution did not finally succeed in promoting promiscuity, but became a catalyst for the emancipation of women labeled the gender revolution and is dependent on social change.

CHAPTER 10

The Sociology of Social Change

Social change is constant. This is not always apparent because sometimes social change is so slow that it is not noticed by those living with it. An excellent example of this is the period in European history sometimes called the Dark Ages. That term was originally used by Francesco Petrarcha (1304–1374) as criticism of the scant growth of literature and art during the early middle ages. Later the term became more popular and was used to describe the entire Middle Ages, i.e., the years between the fall of the Western Roman Empire in the 5th century to the fall of Constantinople to the Turks in 1453. The truth is, however, that many changes occurred in the lives of Europeans in those years. These were few and slow if compared to the rapidity with which American civilization has changed in just over 250 years and the ever greater speed with which change affects Americans in the 21st century.[1]

The manner in which women have achieved so much in the fifty years ending in 2008 is an example of rapid social change rooted in earlier social movements which contributed to the emancipation of women from household slave to professional and leadership positions in the United States.

Among these social movements are technology, science, universal public education, the civil rights movement and changes in norms or expected behavior.

Although the birth control pill is largely credited with the advances American women have made in the twentieth and twenty-first centuries, we cannot overlook labor saving devices and other technological inventions as major contributors to this social movement.

"The Queen of Inventions"

When the sewing machine was first introduced to the American home in the 1850s it was proclaimed a mechanical wonder that would transform the lives of women. *The New York Times* called the sewing machine "the best boon to woman in the nineteenth century."[2]

The great enthusiasm for the sewing machine was rooted in the fact that at that time sewing was a never ending, time consuming effort for all women, whether living on the farm or in the city, whether rich or whether poor. Fabric was expensive in the 19th century, so that women spent a great deal of time mending and remaking clothes. Women also made their own clothes and that of girls in the nineteenth century. Men's and boys clothing was already available ready to wear. In addition, women also made bed linens, curtains and other household items.[3]

Therefore, the investment American families had to make to buy a sewing machine seemed worthwhile despite the considerable cost of these machines in the mid 1800s. At that time sewing machines made by I.M. Singer cost $125.00 when the average family income was $500.00 a year. Therefore, Singer invented the installment plan, which allowed women to take home a sewing machine for $5.00 down. This led to greater and greater sales of these machines, so that by the mid–1870s there were half a million sewing machines in American homes.[4]

By the end of the nineteenth century women in all parts of America were using this mechanical invention and were sewing better and faster than ever before, so that by 1890, the sewing machine was no longer viewed as a marvel but as an ordinary part of domestic life. The erstwhile prestige which ownership of an expensive machine provided disappeared as cheaper machines were mass produced and many poor people owned them.

Furthermore, the ready-to-wear industry grew rapidly at the end of the nineteenth century, so that in the 20th century dressmaker was no longer a visible occupation in America. This is illustrated by the U.S. Census, which shows that in 1890 the ratio of dressmakers to the total female population of the United States was more than five times what it was in 1930.[5]

In the decade from 1910 to 1920, the treadmill sewing machine was abolished and electric sewing machines came into use. Homemade clothing continued to be produced for a while because it was cheaper and money was scarce, particularly during the Depression years in the early 1930s. Nevertheless, mass production became the norm in the clothing manufacturing industry and with it the sewing machine gradually disappeared from the American home.

As the production of clothes at home declined, the production of factory made garments took its place. The factories thereupon employed women to work the sewing machines in the sweatshops of the early twentieth century and beyond. Women became the majority of those working in these shops, where they held the poorest jobs within the industry.[6]

Women worked for less than men, so that in 1928 the International Ladies Garment Workers' Union reported that 70 percent of the members were women. Because of this, the sewing machines were manufactured to fit women. Manufacturers assigned women home work, which led to massive production of garments by women who were at the same time responsible for their housework. Young, unmarried women did not work at home but increasingly joined men in the factories until they outnumbered them.[7]

In 1860, women were 85 percent of New York garment workers. This declined to 66 percent in 1890 and to 54 percent in 1910. This decrease in women's share in the garment industry continued so that they became only 50 percent in 1920 and less than that as the century progressed.[8]

Three explanations for the decline in women's participation in the needle trades can be traced to immigration, the decline of home work and changing technology.

Immigrants were and still are the principal source of sweatshop labor in the garment and other industries. This was true in the last part of the 19th century when Russian Jews dominated the garment industry and continues to be true in 2008 when the worst jobs in that industry are held by Hispanic and Oriental immigrants. Because the immigration of Russian Jews coincided with the expansion of the garment industry in the late 19th century, those who came then became predominant in that type of work. However, in 1923, the United States adopted the quota system so that the Eastern European Jews could no longer enter the U.S. freely and therefore could no longer furnish the labor force needed. They were replaced by internal migrants from the south and, after the revision of American immigration laws, by Hispanic workers from Latin America.[9]

The New Office Technology

The invention of the typewriter has been attributed by historians to 52 different contributors. Although educated women view typing today as a form of drudgery assigned to women because of their lesser standing than that of men, it is nevertheless true that the introduction of the typewriter into American offices liberated many women from factory near-slavery.

The feminization of office work took place during the second half of the nineteenth century, when many corporations were expanding rapidly and there were not enough male office personnel to get all the work done. In addition, the Civil War (1861–1865) reduced the pool of male workers even more. Furthermore, managers recognized that women would work for less than men at a time when the typewriter first became accepted in the United States.[10]

Data on the number of female stenographer-typists from 1870 to 1930 show that in 1870 only 200 women were so employed. In 1850 the number had risen to 5,000 and then increased to 112,000 in 1900, 615,000 in 1920 and reached 811,000 in 1930.

Because office work required a high school education in the 19th and early 20th centuries, office work was viewed as an elite occupation. This was true because only the wealthy could send their children to high school. Some men who graduated from high school went on to college. Few women did. They became office workers and in Philadelphia earned $433.12 a year at a time when the average woman earned $301.48. Male office workers, of course, were paid a higher wage, earning $925.70 a year; the entire Philadelphia male labor force earned an average of $609.97.[11]

Likewise, men outnumbered women in business colleges directly after the Civil War, a number which declined rapidly in the 20th century. In 1868, 89 percent of students at the Peirce Business College in Philadelphia were men; in 1868, 90 percent of the students at the Dirigo Business College in Augusta, Maine, were men, and in 1871, 95 percent of students at all Chicago business colleges were men. Yet, by 1892 men's share of business college students had declined to 68 percent and by 1901 the Remington Typewriter Co. reported that in America's seven largest cities only 29 percent of the 16,247 stenographer-typists were men.[12]

These statistics plainly show that the invention of the typewriter and the introduction of stenography released numerous unmarried women from the drudgery of the factory on the path to eventual liberation.

The Invention of Household Appliances and the Decline in Domestic Labor

The invention of the washing machine and the invention of the refrigerator also promoted the liberation of women from household drudgery to a life of education and professional achievement. Prior to these and other labor saving devices women were constantly enslaved by the demands of their families. Poor women were of course far more subject to the immense strain which domesticity imposed on them than was true of wealthy women. The life of the numerous immigrant families who entered the United States between 1890 and 1924 was particularly burdensome, as illustrated by this account: "She had to look not only after the house and her husband and children, but also after the borders even during a period of advanced pregnancy. When the time for her parturition came, the worn-out woman in the throes of childbirth had to stifle her cries of pain in order not to wake up the borders. In the 1920s and 1930s ... women cooked, cleaned and washed throughout the day and deep into the night without the aid of modern labor saving devices."[13]

Child rearing occupied most of the time of these women. Since women then married at about age 23 they were in the mid-fifties, then and now, before their youngest child reached maturity and left home. In the 1920s and 1930s, and certainly earlier, the median size of an American household consisted of 5.7 persons. Therefore, one-half of all households included more people than 5.7 at a time when four or more children were not uncommon. Many families also took in borders so that the burden on housewives was increased beyond their family responsibilities. In time, the size of the American household declined, so that in 1965 it was down to 3.7 persons and in 1971 it had reached 3.1 persons.[14]

In 2008 the median American household contained 2.5 persons. This decline of over 20 percent reflects not only the ever increasing number of married couples without children, but also illustrates the tendency to remain single, which has grown steadily over the thirty years ending in 2008.[15]

Prior to the arrival of the post-industrial era in the United States in 1980, women had to adjust themselves to the cycle of work demanded of their husbands. Indeed, factory work declined in the United States before 1980. In the 1920s and 30s however, it was the most common work done by men. Since men worked shifts that could begin at any time around the clock, the work of women was also unending. Some men would start work at 2 or 3 or 4 A.M., others started at 6 or 7 A.M. In many families the oldest sons worked different shifts than their fathers or brothers. Furthermore, shifts often changed from morning to evening or vice versa. Women had to provide the working men with food at different times of the day, even as children started school at 8 A.M. and came home hungry at 3 P.M. Therefore, women would cook meals all of the time so as to give breakfast, lunch and supper to everyone.

Few women received any appreciation for all that work. Lacking all mechanical contrivances to help them, women labored ceaselessly. Their working husbands took all of this for granted, particularly because men were away from home and on the job most of the time.[16]

Electrical appliances in the home changed all that, as did effective birth control and the decline of immigration in the 1920s.

In 1919 the majority of American homes had less than three appliances, and frequently had no appliances at all. Ten years later, in 1929, over half of all American homes had as many as five appliances or more. Before 1920, the most common household appliance in use was the electric iron. Toasters and washing machines were also among the earlier appliances in use. The electric refrigerator became commonly in use in the early 1930s at a time when the washing machine and the sewing machine were also introduced into the American home in great numbers.[17]

The increase in appliances made it possible for women to work less at home and more outside as extra breadwinners. It also meant that some women could now go to school and learn skills enabling them to become more and more independent and leave their grandmothers' slavery behind.

Labor saving devices also impinged on the servant occupation. Many families no longer hired servants because they did not need them or they hired servants familiar with using such items as the electric iron, vacuum cleaner, washing and drying machines and the refrigerator.[18]

At the beginning of the 21st century the work once done at home even with labor saving devices is often done outside the home. Dry cleaning, shoe repair, ready to wear clothes for men, women and children, haircuts, beauty enhancements for women, sewing, baking and numerous other services are now bought in stores and other establishments as women earn more and more and birth control has limited the size of the family.

Immigration and the Impact of Artificial Birth Control on the Lives of American Women

Before 1840, marital fertility in the United States had not declined in many years. At that time the population of the United States stood at 5 million and the total fertility rate of the white population of the United States was 6.6 children per woman.[19]

By 1900, the population of the United States had reached 75 million and the fertility rate in the United States had dropped to 3.6 children per woman. The growth in population was largely due to highly fertile immigrants who came mainly from Europe. Alone in 1907, one and one-half million immigrants arrived in this country, thereby raising the population of the United States to 89 million, including immigrants of previous years and those born in the United States.[20]

Of the immigrants who came after 1900, 47.4 percent came from Eastern Europe. By contrast, during the thirty years from 1869 to 1900, only 23.5 percent came from Eastern Europe. This new immigration had major consequences for the composition of American cities and the birth rate among the immigrants. Since New York City was the main port of entry for these millions of immigrants, the population density of that city at that time is an indication of the misery which followed.

In 1890 the average number of persons per dwelling in the United States was 5.45. In New York City, that same year, it was 18.52. Even in smaller cities such as Hartford, Boston, Chicago and Cincinnati, eight persons lived in one room.

This overcrowding brought with it terrible sanitary conditions and city slums "with their sickening odor of disease, vice and crime."[21]

Because the conditions of immigrant life were so appalling, promoters of birth control tried to introduce the population of America's east coast to the limited knowledge then available concerning the limitation of childbirth. As early as the 1830s, before the flood of immigrants had come, Robert Dale Owen and Charles Knowlton had written books designed to help women prevent excessive births. These books told the readers that "the entrance of the sperm into the uterus must precede conception." While a present reader would view such information as no news and known to anyone, it suggests that at the time these books were written a good number of people were utterly ignorant of the facts of reproduction.[22]

In mid 19th century a number of books discussing reproduction and birth control were labeled obscene and became objects of scrutiny of censors who sought to have such books suppressed by the courts and the authors penalized. This was particularly the case when books of this kind included pictures or the human reproductive organs and their medical names such as vagina, uterus, clitoris, ovaries and fallopian tubes. In 1873, all of these instructions and descriptions were outlawed by Congress with the passage of the Comstock Act, named after a Christian crusader who viewed any material concerning sex or reproduction as obscene, lewd and lascivious. The law prohibited the distribution of birth control information or devices across state lines. In addition, 24 states also passed laws prohibiting such devices within states. Nevertheless, birth control was routinely made, sold, bought and used.

The devices used before the introduction of the pill were made of rubber and were sold illegally by poor immigrants and other disadvantaged folk who earned twice as much as they could at legitimate employment. A German immigrant, Julius Schmidt, made a fortune by selling Sheik and Ramses brands of condoms. Schmidt was able to do so because the courts were reluctant to enforce the Comstock laws. As a result, fifteen companies produced 1.44 million condoms a day in the early 1930s. Likewise, the so-called diaphragm for women was also produced illegally until, in 1936, a federal appeals court ruled that Congress could not interfere with doctors providing contraception to their patients.[23]

These rulings were the product of the work of Margaret Sanger, who made the use of diaphragms respectable when in the 1920s she argued that these devices be fitted only by doctors and not sold over the counter. Because women were embarrassed to submit to an internal examination, diaphragms were hardly used. Instead, 85 percent of birth control consisted of all kinds of jellies and douches all through the middle of the 20th century.

By 1940, several social trends in the birth control movement had become visible. These trends included a very considerable liberalization of public opinion, as shown by numerous polls, democratization of contraceptive knowledge, cooperation by physicians with the birth control movement, and public education in the area of birth control. This greater acceptance of birth control led to the founding of the Birth Control Federation of America in 1939. This had been preceded in November of 1935 by Margaret Sanger's founding of *The Journal of Contraception,* a name that was changed to *Human Fertility* in 1940. All this led to a rapid growth of clinics, legal decisions which negated the laws prohibiting birth control, and an effort to reconcile religious opinion with this important social movement.[24]

During all these years, many women were reluctant to discuss birth control with doctors because they were embarrassed at the internal examinations that needed to be performed. Then, when the birth control pill arrived in the 1960s, women were far more willing to consult doctors concerning birth control. The pill is of course responsible for many of the achievements of women during the forty-eight years ending in 2008. This is true of the United States and Europe, although it has made little if any difference in Third World countries.[25]

Birth control is today a well accepted activity in the United States. Nevertheless, Comstockery still exists in America in the early 21st century, as demonstrated by the anti-abortionists who succeeded in banning the French pregnancy prevention pill known as RU-486. Available in France, Britain and Sweden in the 1980s, the United States threatened to boycott any drug company that sold RU-486.

The sewing machine, the typewriter, electric household appliances and the pill are all technological or scientific inventions which promoted the social changes leading to the eventual achievements of American women. In addition, social movements also influenced the changes that benefited women in America. The first of these was education.

Social Change and the Influence of the School on the Liberation of American Women

When women first entered higher education at the beginning of the 20th century it was assumed by professors that women were to attain a college education so as to be better wives and mothers. It was implied and often said outright that women were of course unable to compete with men for college level occupations such as engineering, and that therefore women were to be confined to studying history and English and similar subject matter. Everyone knew that science and mathematics were outside the realm of female competence. Nevertheless, there were many educators at the time who feared that any higher education was masculinizing women. It was claimed that the low marriage rate and low fertility rate of educated women was evidence for this belief.

Even as women were viewed as becoming masculine, it was also claimed that colleges were being feminized by women's interest in liberal arts courses. The result of all these fears was that women were segregated into separate women's colleges, as it was also believed that women with a college education would not work in college level jobs but stay at home and deal with household chores. In short, the education of women in the early 20th century did not bring women emancipation because every effort was made by men to prevent that.[26]

In the early twentieth century, Americans were almost all of European descent, with a predominance of those whose ancestors had come from the British Isles or northern Europe. Protestants were in the distinct majority and the traditional family system was regarded as the only legitimate gender arrangement essential to the maintenance of American society.

Then a high school education was regarded as a considerable achievement, leading to employment in business establishments and in the growing corporations of the time. In fact, in 1900 only 7 percent of high school age adolescents were enrolled in a high school, of whom most were boys.[27]

High schools were at one time only private. But directly after the Civil War high schools across the country became public, leading to a debate as to whether girls should be admitted because it was thought that girls would exhaust their reproductive functions if they studied too much so as to keep up with boys. This debate turned out to be spurious in that taxpayers were unwilling to pay for separate high schools for boys and girls, so that 95 percent of high schools became co-educational by 1895. This in turn led to making girls the majority of high school students, so that girls constituted 60 percent of all high school students in 1900.

That great increase in female participation in high schools led some educators to believe that high schools were in danger of losing their coeducational character and becoming "female seminaries."[28]

The irony was that schools planned for boys had a majority of girl students. This led the educators of the day to conclude that there must be something wrong with the American high school program and that therefore the schools were not serving the public good. These beliefs were bolstered by the most prominent American psychologist of the time, G. Stanley Hall, who claimed in his then famous book *Adolescence* that "female nature is more generic and less specific than male nature," and that there is an ideal woman but that there is no ideal man. Hall meant that males were suited for energetic performance but that females were passive and mediocre. He also claimed that "girls could accept with more patience learning that is merely conventional." He further claimed that any subject studied by girls would become feminized and "hyper methodic." This led Hall to the conclusion that the educational process involving too many girls would prevent boys from putting forth their full intellectual energy. Surrounded by inferior females, males would not be stimulated to attain their highest achievements.[29]

These theories, based on popular prejudices, overlook that female socialization and job opportunities have a lot more to do with the numerical female dominance in the early 20th century. From an overall point of view it needs to be exhibited that a majority of both boys and girls left high school before graduation in the first two decades of the twentieth century but that boys were even more likely not to finish high school than girls because they had more job opportunities than girls. By 1850 all states had public education, but only Connecticut and Massachusetts had made it compulsory and free. The last state to establish free public and compulsory education was Mississippi, which did so in 1918. Before the advent of universal compulsory public education, school attendance declined precipitously after age fourteen. In 1890, 49 percent of boys and girls age 5 to 9 attended grammar schools. Seventy-nine percent of boys age 10 to 14 attended school and 80 percent of girls of that age group attended. Those fifteen years old or more were less inclined to attend school, as only 37 percent of boys and girls did so. By 1910 this had risen slightly to 37 percent and 39 percent respectively. Evidently the compulsory free public education was a social movement which led to the considerable achievements of American women in the 20th and 21st centuries.[30]

In the early days of public education, compulsory or not, girls stayed in school longer and dropped out less often than boys, not only because schools afforded them more freedom than they enjoyed at home, but also because of their limited job opportunities. While men were employed in business in numerous capacities, girls knew that they could be employed only as teachers, clerical workers or in social services. All of these occupations required at least a high school education while the many business opportunities available to men did not.[31]

In addition, a considerable preponderance of high school boys prepared for college as compared to girls, although normally only the children of wealthy parents did so. All these attitudes and expectations remained very much in force until the end of the Second World War in 1945. Thereafter, high schools and colleges became more and more elevators advancing the interests of both men and women until, in the 21st century, women are rising faster and in greater numbers by means of advanced education than anyone predicted only fifty years earlier.

Social Change and the Civil Rights Movement

The Vietnam War coincided with a major upheaval in American society when the black minority, with the help of many white Americans, demanded the right to vote even as both races sought to overthrow by the ballot box or by violence the establishment of political leaders and moral dictators.

It may well be useless to speculate whether the civil rights movement of the decades after 1954 or the war in Vietnam were the precipitating cause of the social revolution that has taken place in the United States since then. It is however evident that the great advances women have made in the years since 1975 are very much intertwined with the advances African Americans have achieved in these years, together with the effort to extend more civil rights to prisoners and to protect homosexuals from abuse. All of these expansions of democracy in America have worked together and each has become a catalyst for the others.

When the Supreme Court ruled in *Brown vs. Board of Education of Topeka, Kansas* in 1954 that segregated schools were not equal and therefore unconstitutional, the ruling had an impact on the professional progress of female teachers as well as on the children involved in that historic desegregation decision. Prior to *Brown* African American women had been teachers and principals of segregated schools for years since the Supreme Court had ruled in 1896 in *Plessy vs. Ferguson* that separate but equal education was constitutional. After *Brown,* black women faced various forms of gender discrimination with respect to their supervisory roles because the desegregated schools now included a good number of white parents who did not want black women to be principals in their schools.[32]

When in 1955 Rosa Parks refused to give up her seat on a segregated bus in Montgomery, Alabama, she not only entered the history books but also provided women everywhere with a role model for resistance to bigotry and resistance to the subservience of women. The result of Rosa Parks' courage in face of white male violence was a bus boycott which lasted for more than a year and resulted in the desegregation of buses on December 21, 1956.

Rosa Parks worked as a seamstress most of her life. She had little education, having been born in Tuskegee, Alabama, in 1913, and was therefore the victim of endless insults, repression and threats by the white majority. It is difficult to understand how Parks developed the courage to refuse the request of a bus driver, James Blake, to board a bus in the rear and not in the front. Blake then demanded that Parks surrender her seat to a white man in accordance with the laws of Montgomery, Alabama, at that time. Parks refused to move and the outcome became a great social revolution led by Martin Luther King, Jr. Yet, it was Rosa Parks who was a moral hero and who, with her extraordinary courage, inspired all Americans to resist oppression. This episode, led by a woman, contributed greatly to the women's liberation movement.[33]

The names of men associated with the civil rights movement are so well known that they have literally become household words. This overlooks that a number of women were most active in promoting that movement and did at least as much as men in finally winning those rights which a later generation is now taking for granted.

Ella Jo Baker (1903–1986) is no doubt the most outstanding example of a civil rights leader whose name is seldom mentioned and utterly unknown to most of those now benefiting from her efforts. She spent her entire adult life working for social change but was largely ignored because women were not taken seriously in the era of the great civil rights revolution. A native of North Carolina, her grandfather told her about his youth as a slave. Her family taught her that her relationship to people should be far more important than the possession of money.

In the 1940s, before the civil rights movement existed, Baker traveled for the National Association for the Advancement of Colored People, a position she was well prepared to occupy after she graduated from Shaw University. She refused to become a teacher because that was just about the only college level occupation available to black women at the time. Instead she joined the editorial staffs of two black newspapers, *American West Indian News* and *Negro National News*. She also joined several labor organizations in the hope of alleviating the exploitation of black domestic female employees. All that led to her appointment in 1963 to national director of branches by the NAACP, which led her to travel all over the South so as to gain more membership for the organization. The membership of the NAACP was about 400,000.

In 1946 she became president of the New York branch of the NAACP and thereafter also worked for the Urban League as a fund raiser. When, in the mid–1950s, Bayard Rustin and Stanley Levinson founded the Southern Christian Leadership Conference, she was asked to become an organizer with the aim of securing voter registration of blacks in the South. This led to her involvement in the founding of the Student Nonviolent Coordinating Committee. This organization recruited college students to go into southern rural areas in the summertime in order to register blacks to vote. The violence with which southern residents confronted these students is part of American history. It led to murder and bloodshed, but in the end succeeded. That success could not have occurred without the work of Ella Baker. Baker was so successful because she insisted on group-centered leadership instead of leader centered groups. This meant that she believed that people will do things for themselves and therefore should not be induced to rely on a few leaders. She also demanded that all who undertook to participate in the civil rights movement be nonviolent. Further she objected to media recognition, which she believed corrupted many leaders into playing to the white oppressors in order to gain attention to themselves. She thought that too many male civil rights leaders were more interested in becoming media stars than in promoting the interests of the poor and disenfranchised. To her the undramatic work of organizing was far more important than leading demonstrations or holding mass meetings and huge rallies. She deserves to be remembered as the mother of the civil rights movement which has benefited so many who have never heard her name.[34]

Fannie Lou Hamer (1917–1977) had a quality usually called charisma and labeled moral density by the French sociologist Emile Durkheim (1858–1917). When Hamer was 45 years old, civil rights workers came to her town in rural Mississippi and induced her to register to vote at great risk to herself and her family. She did so after hearing speeches by James Foreman and James Bevel of the Southern Christian Leadership Conference. Both men spoke in her hometown, Ruleville, Mississippi. She tried to register to vote but was first forced to take a most difficult literacy test. When her boss heard that she had attempted to register she was fired from her job. She was forced to leave her house on the plantation where she had worked and was subjected to 16 gunshots fired into the house she now occupied. She was also told she failed the literacy test. She then rode to Charleston, South Carolina, on a bus with other citizens seeking to participate in a workshop on voter registration when she was arrested with other female registration workers and viciously beaten by law enforcement officers, leaving her with a permanent kidney injury.

Hamer then traveled all through the South and spoke to audiences about her own experience but also about the truth about the state of race relations in America. She had an oratorical style which fascinated audiences despite her grammatical problems. She spoke as she understood her situation and that of the black population of the South and she made no apologies if her speeches offended whites or anyone. Particularly, she denounced men who wanted to lead but lacked the courage which she possessed. She captured the essence of the struggle for equality so that all could understand, and thereby drew more and more people into the movement.

In 1964, Hamer appeared at the Democratic National Convention. She was refused admission by the all white party, and therefore founded the Mississippi Freedom Democratic Party. That party challenged candidates for office in Mississippi until the voter registration drive succeeded and blacks were admitted as candidates and delegates to the party's convention. There can be little doubt that Hamer was the forerunner of a movement that made it possible for a black to be a serious candidate for the presidency in 2008.

In sum, Hamer had a fighting spirit which was more important in her short career than her lack of education, her butchered grammar and her failure to observe the niceties of middle class manners.[35]

Numerous other women were also responsible for the great changes that came to America because of the civil rights movement. They may not be as well known as the names of men associated with that great revolution. Yet, their legacy remains.

Both black and white women participated in the 1960s civil rights struggle in the South. Black women were more likely to work in high risk situations, as they had experienced the hatred and anger of the white majority in their home states. White women were more likely to work at low risk organizational jobs, except during Freedom Summer in 1963, when a large contingent of white students came to Mississippi to help blacks to vote and encountered bloodshed and even murder.[36]

The Student Nonviolent Co-ordinating Committee included a large number of women. Many worked only in offices and on organizational needs. However, a good number also risked direct confrontations with southern police and citizens who frequently resorted to violence to preserve their way of life. This meant that the subsequent effort by educated women to demand their own civil rights was largely induced by the civil rights struggle in the South.[37]

In October of 1967, eighteen men, including White Knights of the Ku Klux Klan wizard Sam Bowers, Neshoba County sheriff Lawrence Rainey, and Deputy Cecil Price, were tried in federal court under the Due Process Clause of the 14th Amendment and found guilty of the murders of James Earle Chaney, a black native of Mississippi, Michael Schwerner, a Jewish activist from New York, and his friend, Andrew Goodman, also from New York, as were one-half of all the white volunteers who went to Mississippi in the summer of 1964 so as to participate in the voter registration drive organized by the Student Non-violent Coordinating Committee.

That two of the three murder victims were Jewish was no accident because 50 percent of the civil rights lawyers and 50 percent of Northern whites who came to Mississippi to work for black equality were and are Jewish. Jewish leaders were arrested along with Martin Luther King, Jr., even as the theologian and prominent rabbi Abraham Joshua Heschel marched arm in arm with Dr. King in the 1965 March on Selma. The Jewish Brandeis University in Massachusetts admitted black men despite their lack of high school achievements as the American Jewish Committee, the American Jewish Congress and the Jewish Anti–Defamation league sponsored lawyers who vigorously defended the black organizers of the civil rights movement in the courts. It is therefore remarkable that anti–Jewish beliefs and hatred of Jews, while nearly extinct in the European American community, involves one-third of African Americans as late as 2007 and this bigotry is preached by black leaders as part of their political and religious messages.[38]

The civil rights movement had immense consequences for American women. Just as the anti-slavery moment of the nineteenth century induced women to organize in order to bring about women's right to vote, so did the 20th century civil rights movement influence women to demand economic, sexual and legal equality with men in the years from 1972 to the present. Each social movement influenced the other in a form of circular interaction so that democracy expands continuously with each generation.

Changes in Norms and Expected Behavior

Sociologists call norms expected behavior. Included are injunctive norms, which are viewed as being approved by the majority of other people. There are also descriptive norms, which describe how people really conduct themselves, whether or not such conduct is approved by anyone else. Explicit norms are written rules which, in some societies, are only an oral tradition. Implicit norms are not openly spoken and are never written, but come into view when someone violates these norms. Then there are subjective norms, which are expectations that significant others in our lives have as to our conduct and, finally, there are personal norms, which refer to our private opinion as to how we should conduct ourselves.

These norms are subject to change. In rather static societies these norms change very little over many years. In American society these norms also remained fairly intact for many years leading up to the First World War and beyond. At the end of the 20th century many norms changed and by 2008 almost all the norms governing male and female relationships have been altered dramatically in this country.

An excellent example of these changes are attitudes toward childlessness at the end of the twentieth century and later. Students of population, demographers, know that childlessness and the acceptance of it have increased since the 1970s. This may be seen by looking at women born in the 1950s, of whom 19 percent were still childless at age forty. These women did expect to be mothers at one time in their lives but postponed pregnancy so long that the delay cost them their fertility. Twenty-nine percent of women born in the 1960s have remained childless, a trend which has continued since then.[39]

Children continue to be valued because of the emotional bonds they provide together with the satisfaction parents gain from their growth and their accomplishments. Children also create continuity and immortality, as there are a conduit for the transmission of our genes and our values. Nevertheless, the increased divorce rate and the increase in women's employment have also increased the number of married couples who have remained childless. While parenthood was inevitable as late as the first part of the twentieth century, it became a matter of choice after the 1970s, as the cost of raising children through the age of twenty-two became greater and greater. Furthermore, nonmarital cohabitation, sexually active singles and the delay in fertility have contributed greatly to the decline in childbearing in the early 21st century.[40]

In earlier years motherhood and femininity were linked in public opinion to such an extent that childless married women were viewed as unnatural or at least peculiar. This kind of pressure to become mothers has declined considerably in 21st century America so that the expectation or norm for fulfilling female identity has shifted from motherhood to professional achievement among many women. Furthermore, the increasing number of childless married women has bolstered their status, since nothing so neutralizes any negative consequences than the support of others.[41]

Childlessness has been stigmatized over the centuries. Biblical literature abounds with stories of women who were rejected or felt deprived because they had no children. No better example of this expectation, this norm, is found than in Genesis 16. "Now Sarai, Abram's wife, bore him no children; ... and Sarai said to Abram: the Lord has prevented me from bearing." The story continues with the birth of Abram's son Ishmael by Sarai's maid, Hagar. Sarai then complains that "she had conceived and I became of little esteem in her eyes." It is only when Sarai herself bears a son, Isaac, that she felt that she was really worthwhile (Genesis 21). The norm, the expectation, was that women must have children to be worthy of being a wife.

As secularism has progressed considerably during the century ending in 2008, beliefs about childbearing have changed. In earlier years, when the lifespan was a good deal less than it is in the 21st century, few parents survived very long after their children left their home. In 21st century America the lifespan is so much longer than it has ever been that it is common for married couples to spend decades together after the last child has been emancipated. This is particularly true because few mothers have more than two children. In sum, greater acceptance of childlessness is one example of norm changes during the last decades of the 20th century.[42]

Changes in norms and expected behavior accompanied the changes in women's employment in the 1970s and have continued ever since. Prior to those years, few women worked full time, so that protection against illness, as well as higher education and retirement, were dependent on lifetime marriages. This means that social insurance came from men who worked full time until they and their spouses received old age benefits.

In the first decade of the 21st century these norms have changed considerably. Now women with small children are frequently working full time even as men are dealing with insecure employment and incomes. Even those who are earning substantially nevertheless look upon the work of women as partial insurance against economic and marital insecurity. This insecurity is derived from the high rate of divorce and desertion as well as the considerable increase in unmarried motherhood.[43]

In 1996 Congress passed, and President Clinton signed, the Personal Responsibility and Work Opportunity Act. This law eliminated welfare as previously known, as it abolished the Aid to Families with Dependent Children program, commonly known as welfare, as an entitlement program. Instead, the new law requires recipients to work or look for work, placed a lifetime limit on benefits paid by the federal government, and gave the states a block grant. The outcome has been that most states have seen a caseload reduction of 50 percent in welfare payments. All this was accomplished because the norms concerning mothers working had changed as the homemaker role was challenged and the employment of mothers was no longer unusual.[44]

Because American women have attained more and more education, it is to be expected that they will continue to be upwardly mobile and follow lifelong careers. This expectation alone guarantees that the role of homemaker, once the mainstay of American female occupation, has declined in numbers and also in expectations. Homemaker is not the norm anymore.

Heterosexual cohabitation was at one time roundly condemned by the vast majority of the American public. In the past, cohabitation was labeled shacking up, serial monogamy, or living in sin. Yet, in recent years the norms concerning cohabitation have changed, as can be seen by comparing the numbers of unmarried couples living together in 1960 and in 2000. In 1960 only 439,000 couples were cohabiting. This rose to 523,000 in 1970, to 1,589,000 in 1980, to 2,856,000 in 1990, and reached 5,500,000 in 2000. This means that in 1960 there were ninety married couples for every cohabiting couple. In 2007 there were twelve married couples for every cohabiting couple and by 2010 there will be seven married couples for every cohabiting couple.[45]

The motives for cohabitation reveal a profound change in norms in the first decade of the 21st century as compared to all previous stages in gender relations in the United States. While the past relationships between the genders may best be described as a patriarchy, the cohabitation movement seeks to remedy this and create an egalitarian relationship. This does not mean that there are not egalitarian marriages in the United States. This is not the view of the cohabiting couples, who believe that they are resisting conventional conduct and strictures associated with traditional marriages.[46]

The principal reason for cohabitation therefore is the need for the participants to distinguish themselves from married couples. The wish to escape the conventions of marriage by maintaining freedom to manage their own finances, independent of the other to have their own identity. All that defeats societal expectations and in addition, as cohabiting couples see it, allows them personal development without restraint. This view includes the belief that since marriage is sanctioned by the state, cohabitation escapes the bureaucracy of government, particularly because cohabitation is an insurance against divorce. Cohabitation prevents the possibility of failure, which is so common in view of the 40 percent divorce rate and all the additional breakups which are desertions without legal recourse.

All of these assumptions are of course limited if children are present. Those who cohabit and then become parents are of course obliged to deal with that obstacle to separation. Their freedom is therefore limited by offspring whom they must support for legal and moral reasons involving shared property and social pressures derived from the needs of children.

Of course, those cohabiting couples who have no children pride themselves that they hold together without legal recourse and only because they wish to do so, without being forced by marriage contracts or divorce proceedings. Cohabiting couples like to view themselves as partners in a voluntary enterprise unrestrained by middle class values. In view of the ever increasing popularity of cohabitation, this erstwhile revolutionary conduct is losing its appeal as it is now commonplace. Therefore we can look forward to future generations who will undoubtedly find yet other means of altering the norms for the sake of gaining self expression.

Summary

Change is universal, although it occurs at different speed in various civilizations. In the United States change has taken place rapidly during the past century and included various norm changes.

These changes made the liberation of women possible as women left the chores of housekeeping and paid employment in sweatshops or offices to become professionals.

Chapter Notes

Chapter 1

1. Census Bureau, 2005 American Community Survey (2006), p. 1.
2. *Ibid.*, pp. 4–6.
3. Census Bureau, Current Population Survey, Table 29-2 (November 2005).
4. Sandy Baum, Kathleen Payea, and Patricia Steele, "Education Pays," *Trends in Higher Education* (2006): 8.
5. Census Bureau, "Facts for Features" (February 22, 2006):1.
6. *Ibid.*, p. 2.
7. Claudia Buchman and Thomas I. DiPrete, "The Growing Female Advantage in College Completion: The Role of Family Background and Academic Achievement," *American Sociological Review* 71, no. 4 (August 2006): 515–541.
8. *Ibid.*, 518.
9. Federal Interagency Forum on Child and Family Statistics, "American Children in Brief: Key National Indicators of Well Being" (Washington, D.C.: Government Printing Office, 2004), p. 4.
10. Linda J. Pfiffner, Keith McBurnett, and Paul J. Rathouz, "Father Absence and Family Anti-Social Characteristics," *Journal of Abnormal Child Psychology* 29, no. 5 (October 2001): 357.
11. Franklin B. Krohn and Zoe Bogan, "The Effects Absent Fathers Have on Female Development and College Attendance," *College Student Journal* 35 no. 4 (December 2001): 598.
12. Larry V. Hedges and Amy Nowell, "Sex Differences in Mental Test Scores, etc." *Science* 269 (1995): 41–45.
13. Baum, Payea and Steele, *Trends in Higher Education*: 2.
14. U.S. Census Bureau, *U.S. Census of Population* 1 (2007), p. 20.
15. U.S. Department of Labor, Bureau of Labor Statistics, "Median Usual Weekly Earnings of Full Time Wage and Salary Workers by Detailed Occupation and Sex," Table 18 (2005).
16. "Professional Women: Vital Statistics," *Fact Sheet* (2007):1–5.
17. U.S. Department of Labor, Women's Bureau, "Quick Stats, 2006" (Washington, D.C.: Government Printing Office, May 22, 2007).
18. Audrey Williams June, "For All the Attention Paid to Diversity, Older White Men Still Lead Most Colleges, Presidential Survey Find," *The Chronicle of Higher Education* (February 12, 2007): 1.
19. U.S. Department of Education, National Center for Education Statistics, "Fall Staff 1999," Table 229. (2001).
20. "Harvard Names Drew G. Faust as Its 28th President," *The Harvard University Gazette* (February 15, 2007) 1.
21. "Susan L. Graham: Short Biography," http://www.eecs.berkeley.edu.
22. "Linda B. Buck," in *Encyclopedia Britannica Online,* article 9400258.
23. Maclyn McCarty, "The Double Helix and the Wronged Heroine," in *Nature* 421, no 6921 (2003).
24. John Gettings, David Johnson, Borgna Brunner, and Chris Frantz, "Wonder Women," *Infoplease,* infoplease.com.
25. Valerie Scher, "Despite Gains, Women Conductors Are Not Exactly Crowding the Podium," *The San Diego Union Tribune* (October 16, 2005).
26. Vivien Schweitzer "Boston Symphony Orchestra Appoints Two New Assistant Conductors" (February 13, 2007): 1.

27. B. Drummond Ayeres, Jr., "A Reputation for Excellence: Sandra Day O'Connor," *The New York Times* (July 8, 1981): A1.
28. Richard L. Berke, "Clinton Names Ruth Ginsburg, Advocate for Women, to Court," *The New York Times* (June 15, 1993): 1.
29. Pamela Stallsmith, "First Female Police Chief Announced," *Richmond Times* (December 30, 3006): 1.
30. Sean M. Wood, "Women in Aviation," *San Antonio Express News* (May 20, 2007): 1K.
31. "2003 National Salary Survey of Nurse Practitioner," *Advance for Nurse Practitioners* (March 4, 2007): 1.
32. I.S. Palmer, "Nightingale Revisited," *Nursing Outlook* 33 (1983): 229–233.
33. Eliot Freidson, *Profession of Medicine* (New York: Dodd, Mead, 1970), p. 369.
34. Anne Witz, *Professions and Patriarchy* (New York: Routledge, 1992).
35. Jane Spencer, "Getting Your Health Care at Wal-Mart," *The Wall Street Journal* (October 5, 2005): 5.
36. U.S. Department of Labor, Bureau of Labor Statistics, "Occupational Employment and Wages: Social Workers," Table 21-1029 (May 2006).
37. Michael C. Barth, "Social Work Labor Market: A First Look," *Social Work* 46, no.1 (January 2003): 9.
38. http:www.collegegrad.com/careers/proft41.shtml.
39. U.S. Department of Labor, Bureau of Labor Statistics, Table 18, "Median Usual Weekly Earnings of Full Time Wage and Salary Workers by Detailed Occupation and Sex," 2004.
40. General Accounting Office, "Women's Earnings," October 2003.
41. Bureau of Labor Statistics, *Highlights of Women's Earnings in 2005*, Table 12. "Median Usual Weekly Earnings of Full Time Wage and Salary Workers in Constant (2005) Dollars by Sex and Age 1979–2005."
42. Bureau of Labor Statistics, "Unemployment and Earnings for Workers Age 25 and Over by Educational Attainment," http://www.bls.gov/emp/emtab7.htm.
43. Bureau of Labor Statistics, Current Population Survey, "Wives Who Earn More Than Their Husbands 1987–2003."
44. U.S. Bureau of Labor Statistics, "Relative Labor Market Outcomes and Worker Characteristics," http://www.bls.gov./emp/htm.
45. Claudia Goldin, *Understanding the Gender Gap: An Economic History of American Women* (New York: Oxford University Press, 1990).
46. Melissa S. Kearney, "Intergenerational Mobility for Women and Minorities in the United States," *The Future of Children* 16, no. 2 (Autumn 2006): 37–53.
47. *Ibid.*, 41.
48. U.S. Bureau of Labor Statistics, "Women in the Labor Force: A Databook," www.bls.gov/cps/wlfdatabook2005htm.
49. Anne Maass, Mara Cadinu, Gaia Guanieri, and Annalisa Graselli, "Sexual Harassment Under Social Identity Threat," *Journal of Personality and Social Psychology* 85, no. 5 (2003): 854.
50. *Ibid.*, 855.
51. Deborah Prentice and Dale Miller, "The Emergence of Homegrown Stereotypes," *American Psychologist* 57, no. 5 (May 2002): 532–559.
52. K.R. Allen, "Feminist Visions for Transforming Families," *Journal of Family Issues* 22 (2001): 791.
53. Michelle Adams, "Women's Rights and Wedding Bells," *Journal of Family Issues* 28, no. 2, (April 2007): 3.
54. Gerhard Falk, *Man's Ascent to Reason* (Lewiston, NY: Edwin Mellen Press), p. 11.
55. U.S. Department of Health and Human Services, Centers for Disease Control and Prevention, National Center for Health Statistics, *Health, United States, 2006* (Washington, D.C.: Government Printing Office, 2006), p. 176.
56. U.S. Census Bureau, *Occupation by Sex: 2000*, Summary File 3.
57. Paul R. Amato, Alan Booth, David Johnson, and Stacy Rogers, *Alone Together: How Marriage in America Is Changing* (Cambridge, MA: Harvard University Press, 2007).
58. David Espo, "Pelosi Makes History as Speaker," *The Buffalo News,* January 5, 2007, A1.

Chapter 2

1. William I. Thomas, *The Child in America* (New York: Knopf, 1929), p. 572.
2. Caroll Smith Rosenberg and Charles Rosenberg, "Sexuality, Class and Role in 19th Century America," *American Quarterly* 25 (1973): 131–153.
3. Kevin Freking, "Committee Chairman Says U.S. Government Spending for

Sexual Abstinence Program Will Stop," The Associated Press (May 16, 2007).

4. John L. Rury, "Sexuality, Sex Equity and Education in Historical Perspective," *Peabody Journal of Education* 64, no. 4 (Summer 1987): 45.

5. Neil Larry Chumsky, "Tacit Acceptance: Respectable Americans and Segregated Prostitution, 1870–1910," *Journal of Social History* 19, no. 4 (Summer 1986): 665–679.

6. David Tyack and Elizabeth Hansot, "Silence and Policy Talk: Historical Puzzles About Gender and Education," *Educational Researcher* 17 (1988): 33–41.

7. Rosenberg and Rosenberg, "Sexuality, Class and Role," 131–153.

8. John L. Rury, "Vocationalism for Home and Work: Women's Education in the United States, 1880–1939," *History of Education Quarterly* 24 (1984): 21–44.

9. Leila J. Rupp, "Reflections on Twentieth-Century Women's History," *Reviews in American History* 9, no. 2 (June 1981): 275–278.

10. Michael B. Katz, Mark J. Stern, and James Fader, "Women and the Paradox of Economic Inequality in the Twentieth Century," *Journal of Social History* 39, no. 1 (Fall 2005): 65.

11. U.S. Department of Labor Statistics, U.S. Department of Labor, Report 996, "Women in the Labor Force: A Databook" (Washington, D.C.: Government Printing Office, (2006): 12.

12. "Study: Women's Wages Gains Exceed Men's, but Gap Remains," *Business Journal*, March 6, 2007: 1.

13. U.S. Department of Labor, Bureau of Labor Statistics, "Women in the Labor Force," 2006 edition: 10.

14. Elyce Rotella, *From Home to Office: U.S. Women at Work* (Ann Arbor, MI: University of Michigan Press, 1981).

15. Katz et al., "Women and the Paradox of Economic Inequality," 7.

16. Donald Tomaskovic-Devey, "Sex Composition and Gendered Earnings Inequality," in Jerry A. Jacobs, ed., *Gender Inequality at Work* (Thousand Oaks, CA: Sage, 1995).

17. Barbara F. Reskin and Patricia A. Roos, *Job Queues, Gender Queues: Explaining Women's Inroads into Male Occupations* (Philadelphia: Temple University Press, 2002).

18. Katz et al., "Women and the Paradox of Economic Inequality,"10.

19. John J. Macionis, *Sociology*, 8th ed. (Englewood Cliffs, NJ: Prentice Hall, 2001), p. 274.

20. U.S. Census Bureau, "Industry by Sex and Median Earnings in the Past 12 Months," S2404 (Washington, D.C.: Government Printing Office, 2005).

21. Elizabeth K. Nottingham, "Toward an Analysis of the Effects of Two World Wars on the Role and Status of Middle-Class Women in the English Speaking World," *American Sociological Review* 12, no. 6 (December 1947): 666–675.

22. Maureen Honey, *Creating Rosie the Riveter* (Amherst, MA: Amherst University Press, 1984), p. 26.

23. Sheila Tobias and Lisa Anderson, *What Really Happened to Rosie the Riveter?* (New York: MSS Modular Publications, 1974).

24. Ruth Milkman, "Rosie the Riveter Revisited: Management's Post War Purge of Women Automobile Workers," in Nelson Lichtenstein and Stephen Meyer, eds., *On the Line: Essays on the History of Auto Work* (Urbana, IL: University of Illinois Press, 1987), p. 135.

25. John L. Matthews, "The 'Roughneck' Oil Worker," *The International Engineer* 22 (March 1949): 1617.

26. Eleanor Perenyi, "Live Alone and Loathe It," *Harper's Bazaar* (August 1950): 113.

27. Marlene Dietrich, "How to Be Loved," *Ladies Home Journal*, January 1954, p. 37.

28. Bette Davis, "Is a Girl's Past Ever Her Own?" *Photoplay* 19 (October 1940): 74.

29. "U.S. Agencies Study Female Job Status," *The New York Times*, December 19, 1961, p. 31.

30. Marjorie Hunter, "U.S. Panel Urges Women to Sue for Equal Rights," *The New York Times*, October 12, 1963, p. 1.

31. Public Law 88-352, 88th Congress, H.R. 7152. July 2, 1974.

32. Abby Bar-Lev, "Equal Rights Amendment Overdue," *The Minnesota Daily*, November 12, 2005, p. 1.

33. Ashley Montagu, *The Natural Superiority of Women* (New York: Collier Books, 1952).

34. Betty Friedan, *The Feminine Mystique* (New York: Norton, 1997).

35. Alfred Kinsey, *Sexual Behavior in the Human Male* (Philadelphia Saunders, 1948).

36. Alfred Kinsey, *Sexual Behavior in the Human Female* (Philadelphia: Saunders, 1953).

37. Federal Interagency Forum on Child

and Family Statistics, "America's Children: Key National Indicators of Well Being 2005." http://www.Child Stats.gov., 4.

38. Norbert Elias, *The Civilizing Process* (Oxford: Basil Blackwell, 1978), pp.456–519.

39. Claudia Goldin and Lawrence F. Katz, "The Power of the Pill: Oral Contraceptives and Women's Career and Marriage Decisions," National Bureau of Economics Research, Working paper no. 2757 (2000).

40. Victor Sigusch and Gerald Schmidt, "Psychosexual Stimulation," in V. Sigusch, G. Schmidt and E. Schorsch, eds., *Tendencies in Sex Research (Tendenzen der Sexualforschung)* (Stuttgart, Germany: Anke Verlag, 1970), pp. 39–53.

41. Graham J. Spanier, "Sexualization and Premarital Sexual Behavior," *The Family Coordinator* 24, no. 1 (January 1975): 35.

42. Shusheela Singh and Jacqueline F. Darroch, "Trends in Sexual Activity Among Adolescent American Women," *Family Planning Perspectives* 31, 1999: 212.

43. Larry Copeland, "Title IX: Public Gets a Chance to Sound Off," *USA Today*, August 27, 2002: C1.

44. 18 USC Section 2261; 2261 A; 2262 and 922(g)(8).

45. Patricia Tjaden and Nancy Thoennes, "Prevalence and Incidence of Violence against Women," *The Criminologist* 24, no. 3 (May-June 1999):13–14.

46. James Placek, "Battered Women in the Courtroom," *Crime, Law and Social Change* 35, (2001): 363.

47. Patricia Frazier and Beth Haney, "Sexual Assault Cases in the Legal System: Police, Prosecutor and Victim Perspectives," *Law and Human Behavior* 20 (1996): 607.

48. Gilbert Geis, "Rape-in-Marriage: Law and Law Reform in England, the United States, and Sweden," *Adelaide Law Review* 6, (1978): 284.

49. "Ferguson, Miriam Amanda Wallace," *The Handbook of Texas* (Austin, TX: Texas Historical Association, June 6, 2001).

50. "Women Officeholders: Fact Sheets and Summaries," http://www.cawp.rutgers.edu/Facts.html.

51. U.S. Department of Commerce, Bureau of the Census, *Public Use Micro-data samples* (1960–2000).

52. David M. Blau, "The Effect of Income on Child Development," *Review of Economics and Statistics* 8, (1999): 261.

53. Steven P. Martin, "Women's Education and Family Timing," in Kathryn M. Neckerman, ed., *Social Inequality* (New York: Russell Sage Foundation, 2004), pp.79–118.

54. Gary A. Akerlof, J.L. Yellen, and M.L. Katz, "An Analysis of Out-of-Wedlock Childbearing in the United States," *Quarterly Journal of Economics* 15 (2000): 715.

55. Valerie K. Oppenheimer, "Men's Career Development and Marriage Timing During a Period of Rising Inequality," *Demography* 34, (1997): 311.

56. Kelly McClung, "Women's Studies Grow Diversity," *The Capital Times*, February 8, 2007: C1.

57. "University of Arizona Women's Studies Department to Offer Doctoral Degrees," *U.S. States News*, April 26, 2007.

58. U.S. Department of Justice, Federal Bureau of Investigation, *Uniform Crime Reports*, Table 33 (Washington, D.C.: Government Printing Office, 2006).

59. Freda Adler, *Sisters in Crime* (New York: McGraw-Hill, 1975), p. 6.

60. "Sex Teacher Beds Teen," *The Mirror* (October 9, 2006):14.

61. Dave Hughes, "Greenwood Student: Had Sex with Teacher Twice," *Arkansas Democrat Gazette*, September 20, 2006, p. 1.

62. Mark Cowan, "Pupil Tells of Sex with Teacher," *Birmingham Evening News* November 7, 2006, p. 1.

63. Stephen Hunt, "Teacher Jailed for Sex with Student," *The Salt Lake Tribune*,(January 11, 2007, p. 1.

64. Vance Packard, *The Sexual Wilderness* (New York: McKay, 1968).

Chapter 3

1. Dorothy R. Blitsten, *The World of the Family* (New York: Random House, 1963), p. 5.

2. Edith B. Gelles, "Abigail Adams: Domesticity and the American Revolution," *The New England Quarterly* 52, no. 4 (December 1979): 500.

3. 1 Corinthians, 7:9; 11:3 and 14:34.

4. Max Weber, *The Protestant Ethic and the Spirit of Capitalism* (New York: Scribner, 1976).

5. David McClelland, *The Achieving Society* (New York: Irvington, 1976).

6. Derek Freeman, *Margaret Mead and Samoa: The Making and Unmaking of an Anthropologist Myth* (Harmondsworth, Middlesex, England, and New York: Penguin Books,1983).

7. Tamara Orr, *Sally Ride: The First American Woman in Space* (New York: Rosen, 2004).

8. Elizabeth Armstrong, "Small Beginning, Big Impact," *The Christian Science Monitor*, September 15, 2004, p. 1.

9. Charlotte Baum, *The Jewish Woman in America* (New York: Dial Press, 1976) p. 17.

10. Norma Fain Pratt, "Transitions in Judaism: The Jewish American Woman through the 1930s," *American Quarterly* 30, no. 5 (Winter 1978): 682.

11. Helen F. Eckerson, "Immigration and National Origins," *Annals of the American Academy of Political and Social Sciences* 367, (1966): 6.

12. George Johnson, "Scholars Debate Roots of Yiddish, Migration of Jews," *The New York Times*, October 9, 1996, C1.

13. Mark Zborowkski and Elizabeth Herzog, *Life Is with People* (New York: Schocken Books, (1952), p. 29.

14. Pratt, *Transition in Judaism*, p. 685.

15. Solomon Ganzfried, *Shulchan Aruch, Code of Jewish Law* (New York: Hebrew Publishing, 1927).

16. S. Daniel Breslauer, "Intermarriage as Punishment and Folly," in *Meir Kahane: Ideologue, Hero, Thinker*, (Lewiston, NY: Edwin Mellen Press, 1986), p.114.

17. Charlotte Green Honigman-Smith, "Mazel: The Luck of the Irish," in Tobin Belzer and Julie Pelc, eds., *Joining the Sisterhood: Young Jewish Women Write Their Lives* (Albany, NY: SUNY Press, 2003), p. 72.

18. Eve Rosenbaum, "Bai Yaakov Girl," in *ibid.*, p. 13.

19. Lynne Meredith Schreiber, "Meeting in the Middle," in *ibid.*, p. 164.

20. Joseph C.G. Kennedy, *Population of the United States in 1860* (Washington, D.C.: Government Printing Office, 1864), p. 675.

21. Hasia R. Diner, *Erin's Daughters in America: Irish Immigrant Women in the Nineteenth Century* (Baltimore: Johns Hopkins University Press, 1983), p. 80.

22. *Ibid.*, p. 80.

23. Brendan A. Rapple, "Irish Americans," http://everyculture.com/multi/Ha/La/Irish-Americans.html

24. Robert F. Foerster, *The Italian Immigration of Our Times* (New York: Russell and Russell, 1919), p.4

25. U.S. Department of Commerce, Bureau of the Census, *1940 Census of Population; Differential Fertility 1940 and 1910 Women by Number of Children Ever Born*, tables 8, 9 and 10 (Washington, D.C.: Government Printing Office, 1945).

26. Cindy Hahamovitch, "Workshop to Office: Two Generations of Italian Women in New York City, 1900–1950," *Journal of Social History* 28, no. 1 (Fall 1994): 228.

27. Bernard Asbell, "Ella Grasso," *New York Times Magazine*, July 27, 1975.

28. Kay S. Hymowitz, "The Black Family: Forty Years of Lies," *City Journal* 15, no. 3 (Summer 2005): 12–23.

29. Virgil Thomson, "Notes on People," *The New York Times*, July 22, 1981, B20.

30. http://www.gale.com/free_resources/bhm/bio/rice_c.htm

31. Jeanine Defoe, "Helping Asian Women Find Their Voices," *The New York Times*, September 21, 1997.

32. Kate Stone Lombardi, "Defining Judaism: A Rabbi of Many Firsts," *The New York Times*, July 20, 2003.

33. "Maya Lin: Architect," Answers.com.

34. "Study: Suicide Up for Young Asian Women," *St. Petersburg Times*, April 4, 2004, p. 1.

35. Hendrik Mills, "American Indians and Welfare Liberalism: A Deadly Mix," *American Enterprise* 9, no. 6 (November-December 1998): 56.

36. Amber Rach, "Dr. Zoe Locklear Named Dean of the School of Education," University pf North Carolina Newswire, November 4, 2005, www.uncp.edu/news/2005/zoe_locklear_2.htm.

37. "Wilma Mankiller," *Native American Rhymes*, http:nativeamericanrhymes.com/women/wilamakiller.htm.

38. "Maria Tallchief," *Native American Rhymes*, http:nativeamericanrhymes.com/women/mariatallchief.htm.

39. Francis Galton, *Hereditary Genius* (New York: St. Martin's Press, 1978). See also: Catherine M. Cox, *The Early Mental Traits of Three Hundred Geniuses* (Palo Alto, CA: Stanford University Press, 1926).

40. Gerhard Falk and Vern Bullough, "Achievement Among German Jews Born Between 1785 and 1885," *Mankind Quarterly* 27, no. 3 (Spring 1987): 337–367.

41. *Ibid.*

Chapter 4

1. Marcia Triggs, "Female Soldiers Fight and Die for Their Country," *Army News Service*, March 26, 2004, p. 1.

2. Mady Wechsler Segal, "Women's Military Roles Cross-Nationally: Past, Present and Future," *Gender and Society* 9, no. 6 (December 1995): 757.

3. Bonnie Bullough, "Nurses in American History: The Lasting Impact of World War II on Nursing," *The American Journal of Nursing* 76, no. 1 (January 1976): 118.

4. Vern Bullough, *American Nursing* (New York: Garland, 1992), p. 3.

5. "Raising the Stakes for Female Troops," *The Philadelphia Inquirer*, May 15, 2006, p. 1.

6. Nona Brown, "The Army Finds Woman Has a Place," *The New York Times Magazine*, December 26, 1948.

7. Department of Defense, *Selected Manpower Statistics, Fiscal Year 1980* (Washington, D.C.: Directorate for Information, Department of Defense, 1981), p.78–79, 112–113.

8. Annie Schleicher, "More Women Soldiers Dying in Iraq," NewsHour Extra, August 7, 2005, http://www.pbs.org/newshour/extra/features/july-dec06/militarywomen_12-18.html.

9. "Army Women to get Combat Duty," *The New York Times*, December 23, 1977, p. 13.

10. No author, "A Woman in Uniform," *The New York Times*, January 2, 1990, p. E7.

11. Barbara A. Wilson, "Military Women 'Firsts,'" http://userpages.aug.com/captbarb/firsts.html

12. "Kathleen McGrath, the First Woman to Command a U.S. Warship," *The San Francisco Chronicle*, October 2, 2002: A19.

13. Holly Yaeger, "Soldiering Ahead: Since Women Began Advancing into Its Upper Ranks, the U.S. Military Has Become Both a More Humane Workplace and a More Lethal Fighting Force. What Role Has Female Leadership Played?" *The Wilson Quarterly* (Summer 2007): 54.

14. *Ibid.*, p. 56.

15. "Coed Citadel Still a Work in Progress," *USA Today*, August 12, 2006, p. 1.

16. Eric Schmitt, "Navy Official Widens Inquiry into Sexual Assaults by Pilots," *The New York Times*, June 4, 1992, p. B11.

17. "Excerpts from the Pentagon Report," *The New York Times*, April 24, 1993, p. 9.

18. "Woman Wins $5 Million for Tailhook," *The New York Times*, November 1, 1994, p. A24.

19. Neil L. Lewis, "Tailhook Affair Brings Censure of 3 Admirals," *The New York Times*, October 16, 1993, p. 1.

20. Eric Schmitt, "Study Says Sexual Harassment Persists at Military Academies," *The New York Times*, April 5, 1995.

21. Laura L. Miller, "Not Just Weapons of the Weak: Gender Harassment as a Form of Protest for Army Men," *Social Psychology Quarterly* 60, no. 1 (March 1997): 32.

22. *Ibid.*, p. 37.

23. Kari Koch, "Military Women Share Success Stories," *The Minnesota Daily*, April 11, 2005, p. 1.

24. "Female General Looks Back on Her Climb," Associated Press, August 14, 2006, p. 1.

25. http://www.cbsnews.com/stories/2000/03/31/national/main178537.shtml.

26. Maureen Magee, "City Schools Recruit Ex-Admiral," *Union Tribune*, August 8, 2001.

27. Marion F. Sturkey, *Warrior Culture of the U.S. Marines* (Plum Branch, SC: Heritage Press International, 2003), p. 189.

28. "Nontraditional Occupations for Women in 2006," U.S. Department of Labor, Bureau of Labor Statistics, March 2007.

29. U.S. Department of Justice, "Increase Seen in Number of Women in Nation's Law Enforcement Agencies," April 7, 1996.

30. Bureau of Justice Statistics, *Law Enforcement Management and Administrative Statistics*, (2003), p.1.

31. United States Department of Justice, Bureau of Justice Assistance Bulletin, "Recruiting & Retaining Women: A Self-Assessment Guide for Law Enforcement" (Washington, D.C.: Government Printing Office, 2001).

32. *Ibid.*, p. 4

33. *Ibid.*, p. 5.

34. Marie Richmond-Abbott, *Masculine and Feminine: Sex Roles Over the Life Cycle* (Reading, MA: Addison-Wesley, 1983), p. 89.

35. Peter B. Hoffman and Edward R. Hickey, "Use of Force by Female Police Officers," *Journal of Criminal Justice* 33, (2005): 145.

36. *Ibid.*, p. 149.

37. John R. Lott, Jr., "Does a Helping Hand Put Others at Risk? Affirmative Action, Police Departments and Crime," *Economic Inquiry* 38, no. 2 (April 2000): 239–283.

38. Inger Sagatun, "The Issue of Entrapment in Prostitution," *Journal of Contemporary Criminal Justice* 4, no. 3 (1988): 139–149.

39. Ronald Weitzer, "Deficiencies in the Sociology of Sex Work," *Sociology of Crime, Law and Deviance* 2, (2000): 259.

40. Mary Dodge, Donna Starr-Gimeno,

and Thomas Williams, "Puttin' on the Sting: Women Police Officers' Perspectives on Reverse Prostitution Assignments," *International Journal of Police Science & Management* 7, no. 2 (2005): 76–77.

41. Lois Higgins, "Historical Background of Policewomen's Service," *Journal of Criminal Law and Criminology* 46, no. 6 (1951): 824.

42. Bonnie Devore, "Past and Present, 1915–Today," International Association of Women Police, http://www.iawp.org.

43. *Ibid.*

44. Penny Harrington, *Triumph of Spirit: An Autobiography* (Chicago: Brittany, 1999).

45. Penny Harrington and Kimberly A. Lonsway, *Investigating Sexual Harassment in Law Enforcement and Nontraditional Fields for Women* (Upper Saddle River, NJ: Prentice Hall, 2007).

46. Lisa Belkin, "Woman Named Police Chief of Houston," *The New York Times*, January 20, 1990, p. A 10.

47. Suzanne Herel, "Chief Fong Picked as Permanent Head of Police," *San Francisco Chronicle*, April 13, 2004, p. 1.

48. Noel C. Paul, "The Woman Chosen to Lead Boston Police," *The Christian Science Monitor*, March 16, 2004, p. 1.

49. Jeff Lemberg, "Women Reach Top at Police Ranks, Growth Still Slow," *Women's News*, March 23, 2004, p. 1.

50. Michal Janofsky, "Pittsburgh Is Showcase for Women in Policing," *The New York Times*, June 21, 1998, p. 14.

51. Donna Leinwand, "Lawsuits of '70s Shape Current Police Leadership," *USA Today*, April 25, 2004, p. 1.

52. Terese M. Floren, "Women in the Fire Service," http://www.wfsi/org/index.php.

53. *Ibid.*

54. *Ibid.*

55. David Gottlieb, "Career Climb Slow for Female Firefighters," *Women's News*, March 25, 2004, p. 1.

56. *Ibid.*, p. 2.

Chapter 5

1. Paul Zakrzewski, "The Pioneering Rabbi Who Softly Made Her Way," *The New York Times*, May 20, 2006, p. A11.

2. "Female Rabbis," U.S. Department of Labor, *Occupational Outlook Handbook*, March 30, 2000, http://www.umsl.edu./services.govdocs.ooh20002001/247.htm.

3. *Ibid.*

4. "General Information," New York: Jewish Theological Seminary of America (2007): 6.

5. Rita J. Simon, Angela J. Scanlan and Pamela Nadel, "Rabbis and Ministers: Women of the Book and the Cloth," *Sociology of Religion* 54, no. 1 (Spring 1993): 18.

6. *Ibid.*, p. 121.

7. "Woman to Head Reform Rabbis," *The Washington Post*, March 28, 2005, p. A9.

8. Nelia Beth Scovill, "The Liberation of Women in Religious Sources," *The Religious Consultation*, pp. 2–3.

9. Blu Greenberg, "Will There be Orthodox Women Rabbis?" *Judaism* 33, no. 1 (2001): 23.

10. *Ibid.*, p. 28.

11. Justin Frumkin, "Disabilities of Women Under Jewish Law," *Journal of Comparative Legislation and International Law* 12, no. 4 (1930): 269–277.

12. Jonathan Sacks, ed., *The Standard Prayer Book* (New York: Harper Collins, 2007) p. 6.

13. Sheila Shulman, "The Impact of Women in the Rabbinate," *European Judaism* 34, no. 2 (Autumn 2001): 5.

14. David Zucker, "Women Rabbis: A Novel Idea," *Judaism* 55, nos.1–2 (Summer-Fall, 2006): 1.

15. Ann Rodgers, "Faiths Seeing Wider Spectrum of Female Clergy," *Pittsburgh Post-Gazette*, January 2, 2007.

16. Linda Kramer, "Christian Science — Making a Comeback," *The Midwest Christian Outreach Journal* (Spring 2001).

17. "Who 2 Biography: Antoinette Brown," http://www.answers.com/topic/antoinette-louisa-brown.

18. John W. Hazzard, "Marching on the Margin: An Analysis of the Salvation Army in the United States," *Review of Religious Research* 40, no. 2 (December 1988): 125.

19. *Ibid.*, p. 135.

20. Rodgers, "Faiths Seeing Wider Spectrum," p. 3.

21. Jean Caffey Lyles, "Dealing with Rebels," *The Christian Century* 17, no. 22 (August 2, 2000): 780.

22. Neela Banerjee, "A Woman Is Installed as Top Episcopal Bishop," *The New York Times*, November 5, 2006, p. A28.

23. Peter Steinfels, "Woman Episcopal Bishop Approved," *Albany Times Union*, January 25, 1989, p. A1.

24. Edward C. Lehman, "Research on Lay

istry," *Review of Religious Research* 26, no. 4 (1987): 319–339.
25. "Church of England Clergy Increasingly Female, Study Finds," *National Catholic Reporter*, December 8, 2006, p. 3.
26. Paul Perl, "Are Former Catholic Women Over Represented Among Protestant Clergy?" *Sociology of Religion* 66, no. 4 (2005): 359–379
27. Associated Press, "Woman Picked to Lead Upstate Lutheran Synod," *Albany Times Union*, June 5, 2002, p. B2.
28. "Evangelical Lutheran Church to Install Bishop Today," *The Buffalo News*, September 21, 2002, p. C2.
29. Pervaiz Shalwani, "Pastor Is First Woman to Lead Area Synod: Montco Reverend to Join 7 Other Females in U.S. to Hold Bishop Title," *Morning Call*, Allentown, PA, May 9, 2006, p. 1.
30. Mathew J. Price, *The State of the Clergy* (New York: Church Pension Group, 2006), p. 9.
31. Barbara Brown Zigmund, Adair T. Lummis, and Patricia M.Y. Chang, *Clergy Women: An Uphill Calling* (Louisville, KY: Westminster John Knox Press, 1998).
32. Laura R. Olson, *Women with a Mission* (Tuscaloosa, AL: University of Alabama Press, 2005), p. 8.
33. John Paul II, Ordinatio Sacerdotalis," Women for Faith and Family, http://www.wf-f.org/OrdSac.html, p. 3.
34. *Ibid.*, p. 4.
35. Janet I. Tu, "Female Bishop Challenges Catholic Church to Change," *Seattle Times*, November 11, 2006, p. 1.
36. Mary Ann Rossi, "Priesthood, Precedent and Prejudice: On Recovering the Women Priests of Early Christianity," *Journal of Feminist Studies in Religion* 7, no. 3 (Spring 1991): 71–94.
37. Mary Fainsod Katzenstein, "Feminism Within American Institutions: Unobtrusive Mobilization in the 1980s," *Signs* 16, no.1 (Autumn 1990): 37.
38. *Ibid.*, p. 46.
39. *Ibid.*
40. Tracy Schmidt and Lisa Takeuchi Cullen, "Today's Nun Has a Veil — and a Blog," *Time*, November 13, 2006.
41. Heidi Schlump, "The Other New Feminists," *The US Catholic*, January 2007.
42. Aminah B. McCloud, "American Muslim Women and U.S. Society," *Journal of Law and Religion* 12, no. 1 (1995): 51–59.
43. *Ibid.*, p.58.
44. Sharon Green, "Judge Made the Right Call," *The Buffalo News*, December 20, 1998, p. H3.
45. Dan Browning, "Ramsey Woman Fearing Genital Mutilation Wins Deportation Reprieve," *Star Tribune*, January 24, 2007, p. 1.
46. "Georgia Man Convicted in Daughter's Mutilation," *The New York Times*, November 2, 2006, p. 19.

Chapter 6

1. *New Formulas for America's Workforce: Girls in Science and Engineering* (Arlington, VA: National Science Foundation, 2003).
2. *Ibid.* p. 3.
3. *Ibid.*
4. "Trends in the Welfare of America's Youth: Mathematics Proficiency," National Center for Educational Statistics, (2005).
5. Sean Cavanaugh, "Educators Revisit Girls' Loss of Math, Science Interest," *Education Week* 24, no. 34 (September 25, 2007): 6.
6. Leonard Sax, *Why Gender Matters* (New York: Doubleday, 2005).
7. Cheryl Fields, "Summers on Women in Science," *Change*, May-June 2005: 8.
8. Natalie Angier and Kenneth Chang, "Gray Matter and Sexes: A Gray Area Scientifically," *The New York Times*, January 24, 2005.
9. "S&E Doctorates Hit All-time High in 2005," National Science Foundation, November 2006, p. 1.
10. "National Science Foundation Report: More Female Students Pursuing Science and Engineering Degrees," University of Massachusetts, September 25, 2007, http://www.massachusetts.edu/stem/nationalsciencefoundationreport.html.
11. Natalie Angier, "No Parity Yet, but Science Academy Gains More Women," *The New York Times*, May 6, 2003, p. F2.
12. Maureen O'Leary, "72 New Members Chosen by Academy," The National Academies News, May 1, 2007, p. 1.
13. "Helen Hobbs, M.D." *Scientists and Research*, October 2007.
14. "Laura Kiessling," *Women in Chemistry* (Philadelphia: Chemical Heritage Foundation, 2007).
15. Gina Kirchweger, "Salk Scientist Ursula Bellugi Elected to National Academy of

Sciences," Salk Institute for Biological Studies, May 1, 2007, http://www.salk.edu/news/news_press_details_20070502a.php.

16. Sue Nichols, "First MSU Woman Elected to National Academy of Science," *MSU Today*, October 8, 2007, p. 1.

17. Barbara McClintock Papers, Profiles in Science, the National Library of Medicine, http://profiles.nlm.nih.gov/LL/.

18. Tore Frangsmyr, "Gertrude B. Elion," *The Nobel Prizes, 1988* (Stockholm: The Nobel Foundation, 1989).

19. Catherine De Angelis, "Editorial Board," *Journal of the American Medical Association*, October 10, 2007: 1608.

20. Erin Prather, "Women Doctors: Increasing Numbers Have Changed Medicine," *Texas Medicine*, September 2005: 1.

21. "Women in Medicine — the Metrics," *Women's Calendar*, September 2006, p. 1.

22. Hedwa B. Levy, "Women in Pharmacy 2006: A Good Match," *The Annals of Pharmacotheraphy* 40 (May 2006): 952.

23. Karen Hassell and Martin Eden, "Workforce Update — Joiners, Leavers and Practicing Pharmacists," *The Pharmaceutical Journal* 276 (2006). http://www.pionline.com.

24. *Ibid*.

25. Surrey M. Walton and Judith A. Cooksey, "Differences Between Male and Female Pharmacists in Part-time Status and Employment Setting," *Journal of the American Pharmacists Association* 41, no. 5 (2001): 703.

26. David A. Mott, "Pharmacist Job Turnover," *American Journal of Health System Pharmacy* 57, no. 10 (2000): 975.

27. "2007 Pharmacy Compensation Survey," *Pharmacy Week*, Spring 2007: 1.

28. "2007-2008 APHA Board of Trustees," *American Pharmacists Association* 2007: 1.

29. U.S. Department of Education, "Average Scale Scores and Achievement-Level Results in Mathematics by Gender," *The Nation's Report Card* 2005: 9.

30. Jean E. Taylor and Sylvia M. Wiegand, "AWM in the 1990s," *AWM Newsletter* 38, no. 7 (September 1991): 738. See also: National Science Foundation, "Enrollment Status of S&E Graduate Students by Field and Sex 2004," *Women and Minorities in Science and Mathematics*, 2004: D-10.

31. David J. Lutzer, Stephen B. Rodi, Ellen E. Kirkman, and James W. Maxwell, *Statistical Abstract of Undergraduate Programs in the Mathematical Sciences in the United States* (Washington, D.C.: American Mathematical Society, 2007), pp. 102–103.

32. National Science Foundation, "Enrollment Status of S&E Graduate Students by Field and Sex 2004," *Women, Minorities, and Persons with Disabilities in Science and Engineering*, 2004: C-4.

33. *Ibid*., D-10.

34. Linda M. Abriola and Margery W. Davies, "Attracting and Retaining Women in Engineering," Paper presented at the Cornell Higher Education Research Institute Policy Research Conference on Doctoral Education and the Faculty of the Future, Ithaca, NY, October 8–9, 2006.

35. Chris Hedges, "Dancing to the Robotic Engineering Beat," *The New York Times*, November 9, 2004, p. B4.

36. Susan Lang, "Numbers Indicate Steady Growth for Women in Engineering at CU," *Cornell Chronicle*, September 4, 2003: 1.

37. Brian Neill, "Designing Women," *Bradenton Herald*, October 8, 2007, p. 7.

38. "SWE Organizational History," Society of Women Engineers, www.csulb.edu/org/swe/history.htm.

39. Peter Benesch, "Start-Up to Ring in the Disposable Cell Phone Era," *Inventor's Business Daily*, February 21, 2001: 1.

40. Hans Joachim Braun, "Advanced Weaponry and the Stars." *American Heritage of Invention and Technology*, Spring 1970): 10–16.

41. Biographies of women inventors found available at http://library.thinkquest.orgCR0210181.images/invertors.htm.

42. "Biographical Data,' National Aeronautics and Space Administration, http://www.jsc.nasa.Gov/Bios/htmlbios./Sullivan-kd.html.

43. John Schwartz, "Space Docking with Women at the Helm of Both Crafts," *The New York Times*, October 26, 2007, p. A21.

Chapter 7

1. The New Jersey Constitution of 1776.

2. McGoldrick, Neale and Margaret Crocco, *Reclaiming Lost Ground: The Struggle for Woman Suffrage in New Jersey* (New Brunswick: New Jersey Council for the Humanities, 1993), p. 5.

3. Wayne King, "The 1990 Elections: What Went Wrong? Bradley Says He Sensed Voter Fury," *The New York Times*, November 8, 1990, p. 1.

4. Sarah Baxter, "Hillary Runs for the White House as 'New Thatcher,'" *The Sunday Times*, January 21, 2007, p. 1.

5. Biographies of U.S. senators are available at http://www.corzine.senate.gov/reference/reference_index_subjects/Senators_vrd.htm.

6. Robert Pear, "Hillary Clinton Sees Hurdles in Forging Health Care Plan," *The New York Times*, February 12, 1992, p. A23.

7. Hubert S. Nelli, "The Hennessey Murder and the Mafia in New Orleans," *Italian Quarterly* 75 (1975): 77–95.

8. Richard Epstein, "Campaign 2006: Eighth Congressional District," *San Francisco Chronicle*, October 20, 2006, p. B1.

9. Zachary Coile, "Bay Lawmakers Among Wealthiest: Feinstein and Pelosi Continue to Top the List of the Richest Members of Congress," *The San Francisco Chronicle*, June 26, 2006, p. 1.

10. Joan Biskupic, "O'Connor Era Ends at Court, Continues in Law," *USA Today*, January 30, 2006, p. 4A.

11. William A. Galston, "Judge Not," *Blueprint Magazine*, May 31, 2005, p. 1.

12. David Madden, "Gavel Passing to Mark Changing of the Guard for Ninth Circuit Court of Appeals," News Release, United States Courts for the Ninth Circuit, November 23, 2007.

13. Daniel Fusfeld, "Frances Perkins," *Industrial and Labor Relations Review* 30, no. 4 (July 1977): 548.

14. Nadine Brozan, "Chronicle," *The New York Times*, February 9, 1993, p. 1.

15. Matthew A. Wald, "Bush Chooses Transportation Nominee," *The New York Times*, September 6, 2006, p. 1.

16. Sam Dillon, "For a Key Education Law, Reauthorization Stalls," *The New York Times*, November 6, 2007, p. A19.

17. Editorial, "Demanding vs. Doing," *The New York Times*, July 26, 2006, p. A16.

18. Sam Dillon, "Soccer Mom Education Chief Plays Hard Ball," *The New York Times*, April 28, 2005, p. A1.

19. Jo Freeman, "Ruth Bryan Owen: Florida's First Congresswoman," *F.A.W.L. Journal*, Spring 2000: 15.

20. Bess Furman, "Mrs. Mesta Named Luxembourg Envoy," *The New York Times*, June 22, 1949, p. 1.

21. John Fritze, "Dixon Sworn in as Mayor: Vows to Fight Crime, Help Neighborhoods," *The Baltimore Sun*, December 5, 2007, p. 1.

22. Dahleen Galton, "Atlanta's First Female Mayor Tackles Homelessness, Other City Problems Head On," *Chicago Tribune*, November 4, 2005, p. 1.

23. Michael G. Ditmore, "A Prophetess in Her Own Country: An Exegesis of Anne Hutchinson's 'Immediate Revelation,'" *William and Mary Quarterly* 57, no. 2 (2000): 349–392.

24. Katie Gill, "Dyer, Mary," *Oxford Dictionary of National Biography* (New York: Oxford University Press, 2004).

25. Gerda Lerner, *The Grimke Sisters from South Carolina* (Chapel Hill: University of North Carolina Press, 2004).

26. Margaret Hope Bacon, *Valiant Friend: The Life of Lucretia Mott* (New York: Walker, 1980).

27. Harriet Siegerman, *Elizabeth Cady Stanton: These Rights Are Ours* (New York: Oxford University Press, 2001).

28. "Susan Brownell Anthony," *Women in History: Living Vignettes of Women from the Past*, http://www.lkwdpl.org/wihohio/anth-sus.htm. Accessed March 21, 2006.

29. Richard Claude, "Constitutional Voting Rights and Early U.S. Supreme Court Doctrine," *The Journal of Negro History* 51, no. 2 (April 1966): 114.

30. Kendal Mobley, "Susan B. Anthony and Helen Barrett Montgomery," *Baptist History & Heritage* 40 (Summer 2005): 40–50.

31. Stacy Schiff, "Desperately Seeking Susan," *The New York Times*, October 13, 2006.

32. Elizabeth D. Leonard, *Yankee Women: Gender Battles in the Civil War* (New York: Norton, 1994).

33. *The New York Times* published stories about Alice Paul and the suffragettes almost every day from 1910 until the passage of the 19th Amendment.

34. "Alice Paul Sentenced," *The New York Times*, October 23, 1917, p. 12.

35. "Suffragists Plan to Continue Trouble," *The New York Times*, June 28, 1917, p. 7.

36. "Alice Paul," *Encyclopedia of World Biography* (New York: Thompson-Gale, 2006).

37. Kira Sanbumatsu, "Gender Related Political Knowledge and the Descriptive Representation of Women," *Political Behavior* 25, no. 4 (December 2003): 367.

Chapter 8

1. Edward Wyatt, "Katherine Anne Couric: Coming Back to Hard News," *The New York Times*, April 6, 2006, p. A1.

2. http://www.answers.com/topic/katie-couric.
3. Mike Allen, "Anchorwoman Wins $8.3 Million Over Sex Bias," *The New York Times*, January 29, 1999, p. B1.
4. Bill Carter, "CNN Cancels Her Program, and Chung Quits Network," *The New York Times*, March 26, 2003, p. C1.
5. Jim Rutenberg and William E. Carter, "Connie Chung Gets CNN Prime Time Spot," *The New York Times*, January 23, 2002, p. C9.
6. "Lou Walters, Nightclub Impresario and Founder of Latin Quarter, Dies." *The New York Times*, August 16, 1977, p. 36.
7. Elizabeth Bumiller, "TELEVISION: So Famous, Such Clout, She Could Interview Herself," *The New York Times*, April 21, 1996, p. H1.
8. Jerry Oppenheimer, *Barbara Walters: The Unauthorized Biography* (New York: St. Martin's Press, 1990).
9. Bumiller, "TELEVISION: So Famous," p. H1.
10. Jeremy Gerard, "Deciding Who Makes a Million in TV News," *The New York Times*, February 20, 1989, p. D1.
11. Jeremy Gerard, "Anchors in New Roles Are Gaining Wealth, but Not Much Prestige," *The New York Times*, February 19, 1990, p. C11.
12. Noreen Welle, "Minorities Gain on Local Television News Staff," *Radio/Television News Directors Association*, July 7, 2006.
13. Paul Farhi, "Men Signing Off," *Washington Post*, July 23, 2006, p. N1.
14. Ibid.
15. Shera Gross, "Network Poll: Women Get More Air Time but Men Dominate the News," *Albany Times Union*, May 24, 1990, p. C8.
16. David Bauder, "Are Female Anchors Taken Seriously?" *Albany Times Union*, June 5, 2007, p. E4.
17. "Robin Meade," Anchors and Reporters, CNN.com, http://www.cnn./CNN/anchors-reporters/meade.robin.html.
18. "Judy Woodruff Plans to Leave CNN in June," *The New York Times*, April 29, 2005.
19. Bob Papper, "Women and Minorities in the Newsroom," *Communicator*, July-August 2007: 22.
20. Ann Oldenburg, "Just Jane: Pauley Gets Personal," *USA Today*, August 18, 2004, p. 1.
21. "Lunden Closes the Door on Her TV Job," *New York Post*, June 16, 2003, p. 83.

22. Rick Maloney, "As Circulation Falls, News Seeks Solutions," *Business First*, November 19, 2005.
23. U.S. Department of Labor, Bureau of Labor Statistics, *Employment and Earnings*, Annual Averages, Table 11, 2007.
24. Heidi Benson, "Behind the Sweet Smile Is a Steely Eyed Writer: Maureen Dowd Is an 'Equal Opportunity' Skeptic," *San Francisco Chronicle*, September 9, 2004, p. E1.
25. "Ellen Goodman," The Washington Post Writer's Group, June 15, 2004, p. 1.
26. Neil Downing, "So Long, Mighty Quinn," *The Providence Journal*, October 2, 2001.
27. Howard Kurtz, "Criminal Contempt Could Lengthen Reporter's Jail Time," *Washington Post*, July 16, 2005, p. A06
28. "Press Freedom on the Precipice," *The New York Times*, October 16, 2004, p. A 16.
29. Michael Massing, "Now They Tell Us," *The New York Review of Books*, February 26, 2004.
30. Peter King, "Inside the NFL: Shame on the Patriots," *Sports Illustrated*, October 1,1990, p. 54.
31. Mark Fitzgerald, "Lisa Olson Redux," *Editor and Publisher*, January 25, 1997, p. 11.
32. Thomas George, "Patriots and 3 Players Fined in Olson Incident," *The New York Times*, November 28, 1990, p. 29.
33. http://premierspeakers.com/ann_Coulter.
34. Steven J. Hayes, "Erma Bombeck," Women Journalists and Editors, in Basic Famous People, http://www.basicfamouspeople.com/index.php?aid=38
35. Globe Staff, "Veteran Globe Reporter, Elizabeth Neuffer, Killed in Car Accident in Iraq," *The Boston Globe*, May 8, 2003, p. 1.
36. Diane J. Ducharme *Elizabeth Shepley Sergeant Papers*, Yale Collection of American Literature, Beinecke Rare Book and Manuscript Library (New Haven, Connecticut, Yale University, 1986). http://webtext.library.yale.edu/xml2html/beinecke.SERGEANT.com.html.
37. Sherry Richiardi, "The Women Who Paved the Way," *American Journalism Review*, March 1994, p. 1.
38. "Diversity Slips in U.S. Newsrooms," *American Society of Newspaper Editors*, March 26, 2007, p. 3.
39. Ibid.
40. Lindsey Wray, "Women Journalists Connect at the IWMF Network Breakfast in Boston," "Women Journalists Connect at the

IWMF Networking Breakfast in Boston." International Women's Media Foundation. Accessed April 23, 2007. http://www.iwmf.org/features/10003.

41. http://www.iwmf.org/about/.

42. Marilyn Berger, "Katharine Graham of Washington Post Dies at 84," *The New York Times*, July 18, 2001, p. A1.

43. Arlene Notoro Morgan, "Coming Home," *American Society of Newspaper Editors*, September-October 2002, p. 1.

44. Jaques Steinberg, "Panel Says Poor Standards Allowed Deception at USA Today," *The New York Times*, April 23, 2004, p. A16.

45. Sharon R. King, "Gannett's USA Today Names New Editor," *The New York Times*, March 10, 1999, p. C9.

46. U.S. Department of Labor, Bureau of Labor Statistics, Total Median Weekly Income, Table 18 (2006).

47. "Author and Editor Panelists," Avon FanLit (Harper Collins Publishers) 2008, http://avon.fanlit.com/Panelists.htm.

48. "The Female Persuasion," *American Demographics*, February 1, 2006, p. 1.

49. *O: The Oprah Magazine*, http://www.oprah.com/omagazine/200802/omag-_features.jhtml.

50. "Biography of Oprah," http://www/imbsd.com/name//nm0001856/bio.

51. Cathy Horyn, "Is This the Woman to Rescue Harper's Bazaar?" *The New York Times*, June 10, 2001, p. ST1.

52. Rebecca Seal, "News: Cosmo at 35," *The Observer*, February 4, 2007, p. 17; http://en.wikipedia.org/wki/Helen_Gurley_Brown.

Chapter 9

1. Christopher Hibbert, *Queen Victoria* (New York: Basic Books, 2000), pp.13–15.

2. Katherine Bement Davis, *Factors in the Sex Lives of Twenty Two Hundred Women* (New York: Harper & Bros. 1929), pp.53, 189.

3. John Levi Martin, "Structuring the Sexual Revolution," *Theory and Society* 25, no.1 (February 1996): 112.

4. Alice Reid, "The Long Sexual Revolution," *Medical History* 49, no. 3 (July 2005): 375–377.

5. Philip E. DeWitt, "Sex in America," *Time* Magazine, October 17,1994, p. 1.

6. Robert T. Michael, John H. Gagnon, Edward O. Laumann, and Gina Kolata, *Sex in America* (New York: Little, Brown, 1994).

7. Susan Jacoby, "Sex in America," *AARP Journal*, July and August, 2005, p. 1.

8. *Ibid.*, p. 2.

9. *Ibid.*, p. 3

10. "AIDS — acquired immune deficiency syndrome," http://www.britannica.com/ebs/artucke-9354784

11. David Lear, "AIDS in the African Press," *International Quarterly of Community Health Education* 10 (1990): 253.

12. "Homosexuals Admit AIDS Culpability," *World Net Daily*, December 6, 2003, p. 1.

13. J. Lever, D.B. Kanouse, W.H. Rogers, and R. Hertz, "Behavior Patterns and Sexual Identity of Bisexual Males," *Journal of Sex Research* 29 (1992): 141.

14. *Ibid.*, p. 142.

15. Sara M. Evans, "They Came Out Fighting," *The New York Times*, June 27, 1993, p. BR15.

16. Ben J. Harpaz, "Gay Parade Celebrate Pride, Stonewall Riots Anniversary," *The Buffalo News*, June 28, 1999, p. A5.

17. Editorial, "Caving In on Hate Crimes," *The New York Times*, December 10, 2007.

18. http:www.gallup.com/poll/1651/Homosexual-Relations.aspx.

19. Joseph J. Macionis, *Sociology*, 3rd ed. (Englewood Cliffs, NJ: Prentice Hall, 1991), p.115.

20. Graham B. Spanier, "Sexualization and Premarital Sexual Behavior," *The Family Coordinator* 24, no. 1 (January 1975): 35.

21. *Ibid.*, p. 32.

22. Elizabeth Cooksey, Frank L. Mott, and Stefanie A. Neubauer, "Friendship and Early Relationships: Links to Sexual Initiation Among American Adolescents Born to Young Mother," *Perspectives on Sexual Reproductive Health* 34, no. 3 (2002): 121.

23. Katherine K. Wallman, "America's Children: Key National Indicators of Well-Being, 2007" (Washington, D.C.: Office of Management and Budget), pp. 1–2.

24. D. Daly and V.C. Wong. *Between the Lines: States' Implementation of the Federal Government's Section 510(b) Abstinence Education Program in Fiscal Year 1998*. New York: SIECUS, 1999.

25. Anne Grunseit, "Sexuality Education and Young People Sexual Behaviors: A Review of Studies," *Journal of Adolescent Research* 12, no. 4 (October 1997): 421–453.

26. Rebekah Saul, "Whatever Happened to the Adolescent Family Life Act?" *The Guttmacher Report on Public Policy* 1, no. 2 (1998): 5.

27. Ibid.

28. Jacqueline Darroch Forrest and Jane Silverman, "What Public School Teachers Teach About Preventing Pregnancy, AIDS and Sexually Transmitted Diseases," *Family Planning Perspectives* 21, no. 2 (March-April, 1989): 65.

29. David Whitney, "Teen Pregnancy Rate Improvement at Risk," *Fresno Bee*, May 7, 2004, p. B8.

30. David B. Hart, "The Pornography Culture," *The New Atlantis*, no. 6 (Summer 2004): 82–89.

31. Grant Gross, "Court Rules Against Child Online Protection Act," IDG News Service, June 29, 2004.

32. Randy D. Fisher, Ida J. Cook, and Edwin C. Shirkey, "Correlates of Support for Censorship of Sexual, Sexually Violent and Violent Media," *The Journal of Sex Research*, vol. 31, no.3, (1994):229–240.

33. Albert C. Gunther, "Overrating the X-Rating: The Third Person Perception and the Support for Censorship of Pornography," *The Journal of Communications Research* 45 (1995): 27.

34. Larry Barron, "Pornography and Gender Equality: An Empirical Analysis," *The Journal of Sex Research* 27, no. 3 (August 1990): 363.

35. Kimberly A. Davies, "Voluntary Exposure to Pornography and Men's Attitude Towards Feminism and Rape," *The Journal of Sex Research* 34, no. 2 (May 1993): 161–170.

36. Gloria Cowan and Kerri F. Dunn, "What Themes in Pornography Lead to Perceptions of the Degradation of Women?" *The Journal of Sex Research* 31, no. 1 (1994): 11–21.

37. Hans Bern Brosius, James H. Weaver, and Jonathan Staab, "Exploring the Social and Sexual Reality of Contemporary Pornography," *The Journal of Sex Research* 30, no. 2 (May 1993): 161–170.

38. L. Monique Ward, "Talking About Sex: Common Threads About Sexuality in Prime Time Television Programs Children and Adolescents View Most," *Journal of Youth and Adolescence* 24, no. 5 (October 1995): 595–615.

39. "Review of the Supreme Courts Term," *The United States Law Week* 66, no. 4 (July 22, 1997): 1.

40. Linda Greenhouse, "High Court Voids Curb on 'Indecent' Internet Material," *The New York Times Cyber Times*, June 1997.

41. John M. Broder, "Clinton Readies New Approach on Internet Indecency," *The New York Times Cyber Times*, June 27, 1997.

42. Lyle Denniston, "Supreme Court Revisits Arguments in Online Pornography Case," *The Boston Globe*, March 3, 2004.

43. William Gibson, *Neuromancer* (New York: Ace Books, 1984).

44. Sylvia Kierkegaard, "Cybering, Online Grooming and Age Play," *Computer Law and Security Report* 24, no. 1 (2008): 41–55.

45. Erving Goffman, *The Presentation of Self in Everyday Life* (New York: Overlook Press, 1973).

46. John E. Bingham and Chris Piotrowski, "On-line Sexual Addiction: A Contemporary Enigma," *Psychological Reports* 79, no. 1 (August 1996): 257.

47. Keith F. Durkin and Clifton D. Bryant, "Log On to Sex: Some Notes on the Carnal Computer and Erotic Cyberspace as an Emerging Research Frontier," *Deviant Behavior: An Interdisciplinary Journal* 16, no. 3 (July–September 1995): 179.

48. Ibid., pp. 194–195.

49. John Heidenry, *What Ecstasy: The Rise and Fall of the Sexual Revolution* (New York: Simon and Schuster, 1997), Chapter 3.

50. Ibid.

51. Gary Langer, Cheryl Arnedt, and Dalia Sussman, "Poll: American Sex Survey" http://abcnews.go.com/Primetime/PollVault/story?id=156921&page=1.

52. Kate Millett, *Sexual Politics* (New York: Simon and Schuster, 1990).

53. Dell Williams, "The Roots of the Garden," *The Journal of Sex Research* 29, no. 3 (August 1990): 461–466.

54. http://www.tickleyourfancyparties.com.

55. Ellen E. Baumann, "Negotiating Respectability in Ambiguous Commerce: Sex Paraphernalia at Home Parties," *Canadian Review of Sociology and Antropology* 28, no. 3 (August 1991): 377–392.

56. U.S. Equal Employment Opportunity Commission, "Sexual Harassment," http://www.eeoc.gov/types/sexual_harassment.html.

57. Equal Opportunity Commission, *Guidelines on Discrimination Because of Sex* (Washington, D.C.: Federal Register, Vol. 45, Sec. 1604, 11, 1980 and No. 58, 1993), pp. 51266–51269.

58. "Worst First Grade Shocker," *Parade Magazine*, December 29, 1996, p. 13.

59. "Waco Boy, 4, Suspended for 'Sexual' Hug," *The Dallas News*, December 10, 2006, p. 1.

60. "First Grader Suspended for Sexual Harassment," *USA Today*, February 29, 2006, p. 1.
61. Patricia A. Frazier, Cariline C. Cochran, and Andrea M. Olson, "Social Science Research on Lay Definitions of Sexual Harassment," *Journal of Social Issues* 51, no. 1 (1995): 21.
62. UN World Population Prospects 1950–2050. The 2006 Revision Database. Department of Economic and Social Affairs, Population Division. New York.
63. U.S. National Center for Health Statistics, *Vital Statistics of the United States, Annual 1960–2006*.
64. N. Binkin, J. Gold, and W. Cates, "Illegal Abortion Deaths in the United States: Why Are They Still Occurring? *Family Planning Perspectives* 14, no. 3 (1990): 163–167.
65. Wanda Franz, "National Right to Life Committee," People for the American Way, http://www.org/pfaw/general/derfault.aspx?oid=4103.
66. National Center for Health Statistics, *National Vital Statistics Reports* 55, no. 1 (September 29, 2006), Table 84.

Chapter 10

1. John J. Norwich, *A Short History of Byzantium* (New York: Vintage Books, 1997), p. 304.
2. No author, "The Story of the Sewing Machine," *The New York Times*, January 7, 1860, p. 2.
3. Susan Strasser, *A History of American Housework* (New York: Pantheon Books, 1982), pp. 125–131.
4. Ruth Brandon, *Singer and the Sewing Machine* (London: Barrie and Jenkins, 1977), p. 116.
5. "Number of Dressmakers and Seamstresses and Ratio to U.S. Female Population," (Washington, D.C.: United States Census Reports, 1860–1930), Table 1.
6. Christine Stansell, "The Origins of the Sweatshop: Women and Early Industrialization in New York," in Michael Frish and Daniel J. Walkowitz, eds., *Working Class America: Essays on Labor, Community and American Society* (Urbana: University of Illinois Press, 1983): 78–103.
7. A.B. Baroff, "Our Union and Its Problems," *The Message*, April 17, 1914, pp. 4–5.
8. "Distribution of Male and Female Workers in Metropolitan Area, by Crafts, 1934" ILGWU Archives, Dress Joint Board 30, no. 7.
9. Mirjana Morokvasic, "Birds of Passage Are Also Women," *International Migration Review* 18, no. 4 (Winter 1984): 886–907.
10. Margery Davies, "Women's Place Is at the Typewriter," *Radical America* 8, no. 4 (July-August 1979).
11. Jerome P. Bjelopera, *City of Clerks: Office and Sales Workers in Philadelphia* (Urbana: University of Illinois Press, 1870–1920, 2005), p. 17.
12. *Ibid.*, p. 68.
13. Sofia Skoric and George Vid Tomashevich, *Serbs in Ontario: A Socio-cultural Description* (Toronto: Serbian Heritage Academy, 1974), p. 69.
14. Stuart A. Queen and Robert W. Habenstein, *The Family in Various Cultures* (Philadelphia: Lippincott, 1974), p. 332.
15. Jennifer Cheeseman Day, *Projections of the Number of Households and Families in the United States: 1995–2010*, U.S. Bureau of the Census, Current Population Reports (Washington, D.C.: Government Printing Office, 2008), p. 25-1129.
16. S. J. Kleinberg, *The Shadow of the Mills* (Pittsburgh: University of Pittsburgh Press, 1989), p. 231.
17. Amy Hewes, "Electrical Appliances in the Home," *Social Forces* 9, no. 2 (December 1930): 237.
18. *Ibid.*, p. 239.
19. J. David Hacker, "Rethinking the Early Decline of Marital Fertility in the United States," *Demography* 40 (2003): 605–620.
20. Ralph Tomlinson, *Population Dynamics* (New York: Random House, 1965), p. 41.
21. Carl Degler, *Out of Our Past* (New York: Harper and Row, 1959), p. 312.
22. Robert Dale Owen, *Moral Physiology, or a Brief and Plain Treatise on the Population Question* (New York: Arno Press Reprint, 1972; originally published in London in 1859), p. 20.
23. Daniel J. Kevles, "The Secret History of Birth Control," *The New York Times*, July 22, 2001, p. BR11.
24. Norman E. Himes, "A Decade of Progress in Birth Control," *Annals of the American Academy of Political and Social Sciences* 212 (November 1940): 88–96.
25. Kevles, "The Secret History," p. BR11.
26. Lynn D. Gordon, "Co-Education on Two Campuses: Berkeley and Chicago, 1890–1912," in May Kelley, ed., *Women's Being,*

Women's Place (Boston: G.K. Hall, 1979), pp.154–170, 171–194.

27. U.S. Department of Commerce, *Historical Statistics of the United States, from Colonial Times to the Present*, vol. 15 (Washington, D.C.: Government Printing Office, 1975), p. 369.

28. *U.S. Commission on Education Report, 1894–1895*, vol. 1, pp. 1115–18.

29. G. Stanley Hall, *Adolescence* (New York: Appleton, 1904), pp. 505, 567.

30. Stratton D. Brooks, "Causes of Withdrawal from School," *Educational Review* 26 (November 1903): 385.

31. Adelaide Wyckoff, "Children's Ideals," *Pedagogical Seminary* 8 (December 1901): 482–490.

32. John D. Anderson, "Crosses to Bear and Promises to Keep: The Jubilee Anniversary of *Brown v. Board of Education*," *Urban Education* 39 (2004): 359–373.

33. Michael Anderson, "No: A Life of Rosa Parks, Whose Quiet Demurral Sparked the Montgomery Bus Boycott," *The New York Times*, July 16, 2000, p. BR3.

34. Charles Payne, "Ella Baker and Models of Social Change," *Signs* 14, no. 4 (Summer 1989): 885–889.

35. Janice D. Hamlet, "Fannie Lou Hamer," *Journal of Black Studies* 20, no. 5 (May 1996): 560–576.

36. Jenny Irons, "The Shaping of Activist Recruitment and Participation: A Study of Women in the Civil Rights Movement," *Gender and Society* 12, no. 6 (December 1998): 692–709.

37. *United States vs. Price et al.*, 1965, *U.S. Reporter* 383, pp.787–820.

38. Lee Siegleman, "Blacks, Whites and Anti-Semitism," *The Sociological Quarterly* 36, no. 4 (Autumn 1995): 649–656.

39. National Center for Health Statistics, *Vital Statistics of the United States, 2000*, vol. 1 (Hyattsville, MD: National Center for Health Statistics, 2002).

40. S.P. Morgan and R.B. King, "Why Have Children in the 21st Century? Biological Predisposition, Social Coercion, and Rational Choice," *European Journal of Population* 17, no. 3 (2001): 20.

41. G. Letherby, "Challenging Dominant Discourses: Identity and Change and the Experience of Infertility and Involuntary Childlessness," *Journal of Gender Studies* 11 (2002): 277.

42. Morris G. Ory, "The Decision to Parent or Not: Normative and Structural Components," *Journal of Marriage and the Family* 40 (1978): 531–539.

43. Megan M. Sweeney, "Two Decades of Family Change: The Shifting Economic Foundations of Marriage," *American Sociological Review* 67 (2002): 132–147.

44. James Midgley, "The United States: Welfare, Work and Development," *International Journal of Social Welfare* 10, no. 7 (2000): 284.

45. Wendy D. Manning and Pamela J. Smock, "Measuring and Modeling Co-Habitation: New Perspectives from Qualitative Date," *Journal of Marriage and Family* 67, no. 4 (2005): 989–1002.

46. Jo Van Every, "Deconstructing Gender: Women in Anti-Sexist Living Arrangements," *Womens' Studies International Forum* 18 (1995): 259–269.

Bibliography

Books

Adler, Freda. *Sisters in Crime*. New York: McGraw-Hill, 1975.
Amato, Paul R., Alan Booth, David Johnson, and Stacy Rogers. *Alone Together: How Marriage in America is Changing*. Cambridge MA: Harvard University Press, 2007.
Bacon, Margaret Hope. *Valiant Friend: The Life of Lucretia Mott*. New York: Walker, 1980.
Baum, Charlotte. *The Jewish Woman in America*. New York: Dial Press, 1976.
Bement, Katherine Davis. *Factors in the Sex Lives of Twenty Two Hundred Women*. New York: Harper & Bros., 1929.
Bjelopera, Jerome P. *City of Clerks: Office and Sales Workers in Philadelphia*. Urbana: University of Illinois Press, 1870–1920, 2005.
Blau, David M. "The Effect of Income on Child Development." *Review of Economics and Statistics* 8, 1999: 261.
Blitsten, Dorothy R. *The World of the Family*. New York: Random House, 1963.
Brandon, Ruth. *Singer and the Sewing Machine*. London: Barrie and Jenkins, 1977.
Breslauer, S. Daniel. "Intermarriage as Punishment and Folly." In *Meir Kahane: Ideologue, Hero, Thinker*. Lewiston, NY: Edwin Mellen Press, 1986.
Bullough Vern. *American Nursing*. New York: Garland, 1992.
Cooksey, Elizabeth, Frank L. Mott, and Stefanie A. Neubauer. "Friendship and Early Relationships: Links to Sexual Initiation Among American Adolescents Born to Young Mothers." *Perspectives on Sexual Reproductive Health* 34, no. 3 (2002)
Cox, Catherine M. *The Early Mental Traits of Three Hundred Geniuses* Palo Alto, CA: Stanford University Press, 1926.
Davies, Margery. "Women's Place Is at the Typewriter." *Radical America* 8, no. 4 (July-August 1979).
Day, Jennifer Cheeseman. *Projections of the Number of Households and Families in the United States: 1995–2010*. U.S. Bureau of the Census, Current Population Reports. Washington, D.C.: Government Printing Office, 2008.
Degler, Carl. *Out of Our Past*. New York: Harper and Row, 1959.
Diner, Hasia R. *Erin's Daughters in America: Irish Immigrant Women in the Nineteenth Century*. Baltimore: Johns Hopkins University Press, 1983.
Elias, Norbert. *The Civilizing Process*. Oxford: Basil Blackwell, 1978.
Equal Opportunity Commission. *Guidelines on Discrimination Because of Sex*. Washington, D.C.: Federal Register 45, Sec. 1604, 11, 1980, and No. 58, 1993.
Falk, Gerhard. *Man's Ascent to Reason*. Lewiston, NY: Edwin Mellen Press, 2002.
Foerster, Robert F. *The Italian Immigration of Our Times*. New York: Russell and Russell, 1919.

Frangsmyr, Tore. "Gertrude B. Elion." *The Nobel Prizes, 1988*. Stockholm: The Nobel Foundation, 1989.
Freeman, Derek. *Margaret Mead and Samoa: The Making and Unmaking of an Anthropologist Myth*. Harmondsworth, Middlesex, England, and New York: Penguin Books, 1983.
Freidson, Eliot. *Profession of Medicine*. New York: Dodd, Mead, 1970.
Friedan, Betty. *The Feminine Mystique*. New York: Norton, 1997.
Galton, Francis. *Hereditary Genius*. New York: St. Martin's Press, 1978.
Ganzfried, Solomon. *Shulchan Aruch: Code of Jewish Law*. New York: Hebrew Publishing, 1927.
Gill, Katie. "Dyer, Mary." *Oxford Dictionary of National Biography*. New York: Oxford University Press, 2004.
Goffman, Erving. *The Presentation of Self in Everyday Life*. New York: Overlook Press, 1973.
Goldin, Claudia. *Understanding the Gender Gap: An Economic History of American Women*. New York: Oxford University Press, 1990.
Gordon, Lynn D. "Co-Education on Two Campuses: Berkeley and Chicago, 1890–1912." In May Kelley, ed., *Women's Being, Women's Place*. Boston: G.K. Hall, 1979.
Hall, G. Stanley. *Adolescence*. New York: Appleton, 1904.
Harrington, Penny. *Triumph of Spirit: An Autobiography*, Chicago: Brittany, 1999.
_____, and Kimberly A. Lonsway. *Investigating Sexual Harassment in Law Enforcement and Nontraditional Fields for Women*. Upper Saddle River, NJ: Prentice-Hall, 2007.
Heidenry, John. *What Ecstasy: The Rise and Fall of the Sexual Revolution*. New York: Simon and Schuster, 1997.
Hibbert, Christopher. *Queen Victoria*. New York: Basic Books, 2000.
Honey, Maureen. *Creating Rosie the Riveter*. Amherst, MA: Amherst University Press, 1984.
Honigman-Smith, Charlotte. "Mazel: The Luck of the Irish." In Tobin Belzer and Julie Pelc, editors, *Joining the Sisterhood: Young Jewish Women Write Their Lives*. Albany, NY: SUNY Press, 2003.
Kennedy, Joseph C.G. *Population of the United States in 1860*. Washington, D.C.: Government Printing Office, 1864.
Kinsey, Alfred. *Sexual Behavior in the Human Female*. Philadelphia: Saunders, 1953.
_____. *Sexual Behavior in the Human Male*. Philadelphia: Saunders, 1948.
Kleinberg, S.J. *The Shadow of the Mills*. Pittsburgh: University of Pittsburgh Press, 1989.
Leonard, Elizabeth D. *Yankee Women: Gender Battles in the Civil War*. New York: Norton, 1994.
Lerner, Gerda. *The Grimke Sisters from South Carolina*, Chapel Hill: University of North Carolina Press, 2004.
Lutzer, David J., Stephen B. Rodi, Ellen E. Kirkman, and James W. Maxwell. *Statistical Abstract of Undergraduate Programs in the Mathematical Sciences in the United States*. Washington, D.C.: American Mathematical Society, 2007.
Macionis, John J. *Sociology*, 8th ed. Englewood Cliffs, NJ: Prentice Hall, 2005.
_____. *Sociology*, 3rd ed. Englewood Cliffs, NJ: Prentice Hall, 1991.
Martin, Steven P. "Women's Education and Family Timing." In Kathryn M. Neckerman, editor, *Social Inequality*. New York: Russell Sage Foundation, 2004.
McClelland, David. *The Achieving Society*. New York: Irvington, 1976.
McGoldrick, Neale, and Margaret Crocco. *Reclaiming Lost Ground: The Struggle for Woman Suffrage in New Jersey*. New Brunswick: New Jersey Council for the Humanities, 1993.
Michael, Robert T., John H. Gagnon, Edward O. Laumann, and Gina Kolata. *Sex in America*. New York: Little, Brown, 1994.
Milkman, Ruth. "Rosie the Riveter Revisited: Management's Post-War Purge of Women Automobile Workers." In Nelson Lichtenstein and Stephen Meyer, eds., *On the Line: Essays on the History of Auto Work*. Urbana: University of Illinois Press, 1987.

Millett, Kate. *Sexual Politics*. New York: Simon and Schuster, 1990.
Montagu, Ashley. *The Natural Superiority of Women*. New York: Collier Books, 1952.
New Formulas for America's Workforce: Girls in Science and Engineering. Arlington, VA: National Science Foundation, 2003.
Norwich, John J. *A Short History of Byzantium*. New York: Vintage Books, 1997.
Olson, Laura R. *Women with a Mission*. Tuscaloosa: University of Alabama Press, 2005.
Oppenheimer, Jerry. *Barbara Walters: The Unauthorized Biography*. New York: St. Martin's Press, 1990.
Orr, Tamara. *Sally Ride: The First American Woman in Space*. New York: Rosen, 2004.
Owen, Robert Dale. *Moral Physiology, or a Brief and Plain Treatise on the Population Question*. New York: Arno Press, 1972. First published in London in 1859.
Packard, Vance. *The Sexual Wilderness*, New York: McKay, 1968.
Price, Mathew J. *The State of the Clergy*. New York: Church Pension Group, 2006.
Queen, Stuart A., and Robert W. Habenstein. *The Family in Various Cultures*. Philadelphia: Lippincott, 1974.
Reskin, Barbara F., and Patricia A. Roos. *Job Queues, Gender Queues: Explaining Women's Inroads into Male Occupations*. Philadelphia: Temple University Press, 2002.
Richmond-Abbott, Marie. *Masculine and Feminine: Sex Roles Over the Life Cycle*. Reading, MA: Addison-Wesley, 1983.
Rotella, Elyce. *From Home to Office: U.S. Women at Work*. Ann Arbor, MI University of Michigan Press, 1981.
Sacks, Jonathan. *The Standard Prayer Book*. New York: Harper Collins, 2007.
Sax, Leonard. *Why Gender Matters*. New York: Doubleday, 2005.
Siegerman, Harriet. *Elizabeth Cady Stanton: These Rights Are Ours*. New York: Oxford University Press, 2001.
Sigusch, Victor, and Gerald Schmidt. "Psychosexual Stimulation." In V. Sigusch, G. Schmidt and E. Schorsch, eds., *Tendenzen der Sexualforschung (Tendencies in Sex Research)*. Stuttgart, Germany: Anke Verlag, 1970.
Skoric, Sofia, and George Vid Tomashevich. *Serbs in Ontario: A Socio-Cultural Description*. Toronto: Serbian Heritage Academy 1974.
Stansell, Christine. "The Origins of the Sweatshop: Women and Early Industrialization in New York." In Michael Frish and Daniel J. Walkowitz, eds., *Working Class America: Essays on Labor, Community and American Society*. Urbana: University of Illinois Press, 1983.
Strasser, Susan. *A History of American Housework*. New York: Pantheon Books, 1982.
Sturkey, Marion F. *Warrior Culture of the U S. Marines*. Plum Branch, SC: Heritage Press International, 2003.
Thomas, William I. *The Child in America*. New York: Knopf, 1929.
Tobias, Sheila, and Lisa Anderson. *What Really Happened to Rosie the Riveter?* New York: MSS Modular Publications, 1974.
Tomaskovic-Devey, Donald. "Sex Composition and Gendered Earnings Inequality.'" In Jerry A. Jacobs, ed., *Gender Inequality at Work*. Thousand Oaks, CA: Sage, 1995.
Tomlinson, Ralph. *Population Dynamics*. New York: Random House, 1965.
U.S. Department of Commerce, Bureau of the Census. *Public Use Micro-Data Samples*, 1960–2000.
Weber, Max. *The Protestant Ethic and the Spirit of Capitalism*. New York Scribner, 1976.
Witz, Anne. *Professions and Patriarchy*. New York: Routledge, 1992.
Zborowski, Mark, and Elizabeth Herzog. *Life Is with People*. New York: Schocken Books, 1952.
Zigmund, Barbara Brown, Adair T. Lummis, and Patricia M.Y. Chang. *Clergy Women: An Uphill Calling*. Louisville, KY: Westminster John Knox Press, 1998.

Papers Presented

Abriola, Linda M., and Margery W. Davies. "Attracting and Retaining Women in Engineering." Paper presented at the Cornell Higher Education Research Institute Policy Research Conference on Doctoral Education and the Faculty of the Future, Ithaca, NY, October 8–9, 2006.

Journal and Magazine Articles

Adams, Michelle. "Women's Rights and Wedding Bells." *Journal of Family Issues* 28, no. 2 (April 2007).
Akerlof, Gary A., J.L. Yellen, and M.L. Katz. "An Analysis of Out-of-Wedlock Childbearing in the United States." *Quarterly Journal of Economics* 15, 2000.
Allen, K.R. "Feminist Visions for Transforming Families." *Journal of Family Issues* 22, 2001.
Anderson, John D. "Crosses to Bear and Promises to Keep: The Jubilee Anniversary of Brown v. Board of Education." *Urban Education* 39, 2004.
Armstrong, Elizabeth. "Small Beginning, Big Impact." *The Christian Science Monitor*, September 15, 2004.
Baroff, A.B. "Our Union and Its Problems." *The Message*, April 17, 1914.
Barron, Larry. "Pornography and Gender Equality: An Empirical Analysis." *The Journal of Sex Research* 27, no. 3 (August 1990).
Barth, Michael C. "Social Work Labor Market: A First Look." *Social Work* 46, no. 1 (January 2003).
Baum, Sandy, Kathleen Payea, and Patricia Steele. "Education Pays." *Trends in Higher Education*, 2006.
Baumann, Ellen E. "Negotiating Respectability in Ambiguous Commerce: Sex Paraphernalia at Home Parties." *Canadian Review of Sociology and Anthropology* 28, no. 3 (August 1991).
Benesch, Peter. "Start-Up to Ring in the Disposable Cell Phone Era." *Inventor's Business Daily*, February 21, 2001.
Bingham, John E., and Chris Piotrowski. "On-Line Sexual Addiction: A Contemporary Enigma." *Psychological Reports* 79, no.1 (August 1996): 257.
Binkin, N., J. Gold, and W. Cates. "Illegal Abortion Deaths in the United States: Why Are They Still Occurring? *Family Planning Perspectives* 14, no. 3 (1990).
Braun, Hans Joachim. "Advanced Weaponry and the Stars." *American Heritage of Invention and Technology*, Spring 1970.
Brooks, Stratton D. "Causes of Withdrawal from School." *Educational Review* 26, November 1903.
Brosius, Hans Bern, James H. Weaver, and Jonathan Staab. "Exploring the Social and Sexual Reality of Contemporary Pornography." *The Journal of Sex Research* 30, no. 2, May 1993.
Buchman, Claudia, and Thomas I. DiPrete. "The Growing Female Advantage in College Completion: The Role of Family Background and Academic Achievement." *American Sociological Review* 71, no. 4 (August 2006).
Bullough, Bonnie. "Nurses in American History: The Lasting Impact of World War II on Nursing." *The American Journal of Nursing* 76, no. 1 (January 1976).
Cavanaugh, Sean. "Educators Revisit Girls' Loss of Math, Science Interest." *Education Week* 24, no. 34 (September 25, 2007).
Chumsky, Neil Larry. "Tacit Acceptance: Respectable Americans and Segregated Prostitution, 1870–1910." *Journal of Social History* 19, no. 4 (Summer 1986).

Claude, Richard. "Constitutional Voting Rights and Early U.S. Supreme Court Doctrine." *The Journal of Negro History* 51, no. 2 (April 1966).
Cowan, Gloria, and Kerri F. Dunn. "What Themes in Pornography Lead to Perceptions of the Degradation of Women?" *The Journal of Sex Research* 31, no. 1 (1994).
Darroch, Jacqueline Forrest, and Jane Silverman. "What Public School Teachers Teach About Preventing Pregnancy, AIDS and Sexually Transmitted Diseases." *Family Planning Perspectives* 21, no. 2 (March-April 1989).
Davies, Kimberly A. "Voluntary Exposure to Pornography and Men's Attitude Towards Feminism and Rape." *The Journal of Sex Research* 34, no. 2 (May 1993).
Davis, Bette. "Is a Girl's Past Ever Her Own?" *Photoplay* 19, October 1940
De Angelis, Catherine. "Editorial Board." *Journal of the American Medical Association*, October 10, 2007:1608.
DeWitt, Philip E. "Sex in America." *Time Magazine* 144, no. 16 (October 17,1994).
Dietrich, Marlene. "How to Be Loved." *Ladies Home Journal*, January 1954.
Ditmore, Michael G. "A Prophetess in Her Own Country: An Exegesis of Anne Hutchinson's 'Immediate Revelation.'" *William and Mary Quarterly* 57, no. 2 (2000).
Dodge, Mary, Donna Starr-Gimeno, and Thomas Williams. "Puttin' on the Sting: Women Police Officers' Perspectives on Reverse Prostitution Assignments." *International Journal of Police Science & Management* 7, no. 2 (2005): 76–77.
Durkin, Keith F., and Clifton D. Bryant. "Log On to Sex: Some Notes on the Carnal Computer and Erotic Cyberspace as an Emerging Research Frontier." *Deviant Behavior: An Interdisciplinary Journal* 16, no. 3 (July–September 1995).
Eckerson, Helen F. "Immigration and National Origins." *Annals of the American Academy of Political and Social Sciences* 367, 1966.
Falk, Gerhard, and Vern Bullough. "Achievement Among German Jews Born Between 1785 and 1885." *Mankind Quarterly* 27, no .3 (Spring 1987).
Fields, Cheryl. "Summers on Women in Science." *Change*, May-June 2005.
Fisher, Randy D., Ida J. Cook, and Edwin C. Shirkey. "Correlates of Support for Censorship of Sexual, Sexually Violent and Violent Media." *The Journal of Sex Research* 31, no. 3 (1994).
Fitzgerald, Mark. "Lisa Olson Redux." *Editor and Publisher*, January 25, 1997.
Frazier, Patricia, and Beth Haney. "Sexual Assault Cases in the Legal System: Police, Prosecutor and Victim Perspectives." *Law and Human Behavior* 20, 1996.
Frazier, Patricia A., Caroline C. Cochran, and Andrea M. Olson. "Social Science Research on Lay Definitions of Sexual Harassment." *Journal of Social Issues* 51, no. 1 (1995).
Freeman, Jo. "Ruth Bryan Owen: Florida's First Congresswoman." *F.A.W.L. Journal*, Spring 2000.
Frumkin, Justin. "Disabilities of Women under Jewish Law." *Journal of Comparative Legislation and International Law* 12, no. 4 (1930).
Fusfeld, Daniel. "Frances Perkins." *Industrial and Labor Relations Review* 30, no. 4 (July 1977).
Galston, William A. "Judge Not." *Blueprint Magazine*, May 31, 2005.
Geis, Gilbert. "Rape-in-Marriage: Law and Law Reform in England, the United States, and Sweden." *Adelaide Law Review* 6, 1978.
Gelles, Edith B. "Abigail Adams: Domesticity and the American Revolution." *The New England Quarterly* 52, no. 4 (December 1979).
Goldin, Claudia, and Lawrence F. Katz. "The Power of the Pill: Oral Contraceptives and Women's Career and Marriage Decisions." National Bureau of Economics Research, Working Paper no. 2757, 2000.
Greenberg, Blu. "Will There Be Orthodox Women Rabbis?" *Judaism* 33, no. 1 (2001).
Grunseit, Anne. "Sexuality Education and Young People Sexual Behaviors: A Review of Studies." *Journal of Adolescent Research* 12, no. 4 (October 1997).

Gunther, Albert C. "Overrating the X Rating: The Third Person Perception and the Support for Censorship of Pornography." *The Journal of Communications Research* 45, 1995.

Hacker, J. David. "Rethinking the Early Decline of Marital Fertility in the United States." *Demography* 40, 2003.

Hahamovitch, Cindy. "Workshop to Office: Two Generations of Italian Women in New York City, 1900–1950." *Journal of Social History* 28, no.1 (Fall 1994).

Hamlet, Janice D. "Fannie Lou Hamer." *Journal of Black Studies* 20, no. 5 (May 1996).

Hart, David B. "The Pornography Culture." *The New Atlantis* 6, Summer 2004.

Hassell, Karen, and Martin Eden. "Workforce Update — Joiners, Leavers and Practicing Pharmacists." *The Pharmaceutical Journal* 276, 2006.

Hazzard, John W. "Marching on the Margin: An Analysis of the Salvation Army in the United States." *Review of Religious Research* 40, no. 2 (December 1988).

Hedges, Larry V., and Amy Nowell. "Sex Differences in Mental Test Scores, etc." *Science* 269, 1995.

Hewes, Amy. "Electrical Appliances in the Home." *Social Forces* 9, no. 2 (December 1930).

Higgins, Lois. "Historical Background of Policewoman's Service." *Journal of Criminal Law and Criminology* 46, no. 6 (1951).

Himes, Norman E. "A Decade of Progress in Birth Control." *Annals of the American Academy of Political and Social Sciences* 212, November 1940.

Hoffman, Peter B., and Edward R. Hickey. "Use of Force by Female Police Officers." *Journal of Criminal Justice* 33, 2005.

Hughes, Dave. "Greenwood Student: Had Sex with Teacher Twice." *Arkansas Democrat Gazette*, September 20, 2006:1.

Hunt, Stephen. "Teacher Jailed for Sex with Student." *The Salt Lake Tribune*, January 11, 2007.

Hymowitz, Kay S. "The Black Family: Forty Years of Lies." *City Journal* 5, no. 3, (Summer 2005).

Irons, Jenny. "The Shaping of Activist Recruitment and Participation: A Study of Women in the Civil Rights Movement." *Gender and Society* 12, no. 6 (December 1998): 692–709.

Jacoby, Susan. "Sex in America." *AARP Journal*, July-August, 2005.

June, Audrey Williams. "For All the Attention Paid to Diversity, Older White Men Still Lead Most Colleges, Presidential Survey Finds." *The Chronicle of Higher Education*, February 12, 2007.

Katz, Michael B., Mark J. Stern, and James Fader, "Women and the Paradox of Economic Inequality in the Twentieth Century." *Journal of Social History* 39, no. 1 (Fall 2005).

Katzenstein, Mary Fainsod. "Feminism Within American Institutions: Unobtrusive Mobilization in the 1980s." *Signs* 16, no. 1 (Autumn 1990).

Kearney, Melissa S. "Intergenerational Mobility for Women and Minorities in the United States." *The Future of Children* 16, no. 2 (Autumn 2006).

Kierkegaard, Sylvia. "Cybering, online grooming and age play." *Computer Law and Security Report* 24, no. 1, 2008.

King, Peter. "Inside the NFL: Shame on the Patriots." *Sports Illustrated*, October 1, 1990.

Kramer, Linda. "Christian Science — Making a Comeback." *The Midwest Christian Outreach Journal*, Spring 2001.

Krohn, Franklin B., and Zoe Bogan. "The Effects Absent Fathers Have on Female Development and College Attendance." *College Student Journal* 35, no. 4 (December 2001).

Lang, Susan. "Numbers Indicate Steady Growth for Women in Engineering at CU." *Cornell Chronicle*, September 4, 2003.

Lear, David. "AIDS in the African Press." *International Quarterly of Community Health Education* 10, 1990.

Lehman, Edward C. "Research on Lay Members' Attitudes Toward Women in Ministry." *Review of Religious Research* 26, no. 4 (1987).

Letherby, G. "Challenging Dominant Discourses: Identity and Change and the Experience of Infertility and Involuntary Childlessness." *Journal of Gender Studies* 11, 2002: 277.

Lever, J., D.E. Kanouse, W.H. Rogers, S. Carson, and R. Hertz. "Behavior Patterns and Sexual Identity of Bisexual Males." *Journal of Sex Research* 29, 1992.

Levy, Hedwa B. "Women in Pharmacy 2006: A Good Match." *The Annals of Pharmacotheraphy* 40, May 2006.

Lott, John R. Jr. "Does a Helping Hand Put Others at Risk? Affirmative Action, Police Departments and Crime." *Economic Inquiry* 38, no. 2 (April 2000).

Lyles, Jean Caffey. "Dealing with Rebels." *The Christian Century* 17, no. 22 (August 2, 2000).

Maass, Anne, Mara Cadinu, Gaia Guanieri, and Annalisa Graselli. "Sexual Harassment Under Social Identity Threat." *Journal of Personality and Social Psychology* 85, no. 5 (2003).

Manning, Wendy D., and Pamela J. Smock. "Measuring and Modeling Cohabitation: New Perspectives from Qualitative Data." *Journal of Marriage and Family* 67, no. 4 (2005).

Martin, John Levi. "Structuring the Sexual Revolution." *Theory and Society* 25, no. 1 (February 1996).

Massing, Michael. "Now They Tell Us." *The New York Review of Books*, February 26, 2004.

Matthews, John L. "The 'Roughneck' Oil Worker." *The International Engineer* 22, March 1949.

McCarty, Maclyn. "The Double Helix and the Wronged Heroine." In *Nature* 421, no. 6921 (23 January 2003).

McCloud, Aminah B. "American Muslim Women and U.S. Society," *Journal of Law and Religion* 12, no. 1 (1995).

Midgley, James. "The United States: Welfare, Work and Development." *International Journal of Social Welfare* 10, no. 7 (2000).

Miller, Laura L. "Not Just Weapons of the Weak: Gender Harassment as a Form of Protest for Army Men." *Social Psychology Quarterly* 60, no. 1 (March 1997): 32.

Mills, Hendrik. "American Indians and Welfare Liberalism: A Deadly Mix." *American Enterprise* 9, no. 6 (November-December 1998).

Mobley, Kendal. "Susan B. Anthony and Helen Barrett Montgomery." *Baptist History & Heritage* 40, Summer 2005.

Morgan, Arlene Notoro. "Coming Home." *American Society of Newspaper Editors*, September-October 2002.

Morgan, S.P., and R.B. King. "Why Have Children in the 21st Century? Biological Predisposition, Social Coercion, and Rational Choice." *European Journal of Population* 17, no. 3 (2001).

Morokvasic, Mirjana. "Birds of Passage Are Also Women." *International Migration Review* 18, no. 4 (Winter 1984).

Mott, David A. "Pharmacist Job Turnover." *American Journal of Health System Pharmacy* 57, no. 10 (2000).

Nelli, Hubert S. "The Hennessey Murder and the Mafia in New Orleans." *Italian Quarterly* 75, 1975.

Nichols, Sue. "First MSU Woman Elected to National Academy of Science." *MSU Today*, October 8, 2007.

Nottingham, Elizabeth K. "Toward an Analysis of the Effects of Two World Wars on the

Role and Status of Middle-Class Women in the English Speaking World." *American Sociological Review* 12, no. 6 (December 1947).

Oppenheimer, Valerie K. "Men's Career Development and Marriage Timing During a Period of Rising Inequality." *Demography* 34, 1997.

Ory, Morris G. "The Decision to Parent or Not: Normative and Structural Components." *Journal of Marriage and the Family* 40, 1978.

Palmer, I.S. "Nightingale Revisited." *Nursing Outlook* 33, 1983.

Papper, Bob. "Women and Minorities in the Newsroom." *Communicator*, July-August 2007.

Payne, Charles. "Ella Baker and Models of Social Change." *Signs* 14, no. 4 (Summer 1989).

Perenyi, Eleanor. "Live Alone and Loathe It." *Harper's Bazaar*, August 1950.

Perl, Paul. "Are Former Catholic Women Over Represented Among Protestant Clergy?" *Sociology of Religion* 66, no. 4, (2005).

Pfiffner, Linda J., Keith McBurnett, and Paul J. Rathouz. "Father Absence and Familial Antisocial Characteristics." *Journal of Abnormal Child Psychology* 29, no. 5 (October 2001).

Placek, James. "Battered Women in the Courtroom." *Crime, Law and Social Change* 35, 2001.

Prather, Erin. "Women Doctors: Increasing Numbers Have Changed Medicine." *Texas Medicine*, September 2005.

Pratt, Norma Fain. "Transitions in Judaism: The Jewish American Woman Through the 1930s." *American Quarterly* 30, no. 5 (Winter 1978).

Prentice, Deborah, and Dale Miller. "The Emergence of Home-Grown Stereotypes." *American Psychologist* 57, no. 5 (May 2002).

Reid, Alice. "The Long Sexual Revolution." *Medical History* 49, no. 3 (July 2005).

Richiardi, Sherry. "The Women Who Paved the Way." *American Journalism Review*, March 1994.

Rosenberg, Caroll Smith, and Charles Rosenberg. "Sexuality, Class and Role in 19th Century America." *American Quarterly* 25, 1973.

Rossi, Ann Mary. "Priesthood, Precedent and Prejudice: On Recovering the Women Priests of Early Christianity." *Journal of Feminist Studies in Religion* 7, no. 3 (Spring 1991).

Rupp, Leila J. "Reflections on Twentieth-Century Women's History." *Reviews in American History* 9, no. 2 (June 1981).

Rury, John L. "Sexuality, Sex Equity and Education in Historical Perspective." *Peabody Journal of Education* 64, no. 4 (Summer 1987).

_____. "Vocationalism for Home and Work: Women's Education in the United States, 1880–1939." *History of Education Quarterly* 24, 1984.

Sagatun, Inger. "The Issue of Entrapment in Prostitution." *Journal of Contemporary Criminal Justice* 4, no. 3 (1988).

Sanbumatsu, Kira. "Gender Related Political Knowledge and the Descriptive Representation of Women." *Political Behavior* 25, no. 4 (December 2003).

Saul, Rebekah. "Whatever Happened to the Adolescent Family Life Act?" *The Guttmacher Report on Public Policy* 1, no.2 (1998).

Schlump, Heidi. "The Other New Feminists." *The US Catholic*, January 2007.

Schmidt, Tracy, and Lisa Takeuchi Cullen. "Today's Nun Has a Veil — and a Blog." *Time* 156, no. 20 (November 13, 2006).

Seal, Rebecca. "News: Cosmo at 35." *The Observer*, February 4 2007.

"Sex Teacher Beds Teen." *The Mirror*, October 9, 2006.

Shulman, Sheila. "The Impact of Women in the Rabbinate." *European Judaism* 34, no. 2 (Autumn 2001).

Shusheela, Singh, and Jacqueline F. Darroch. "Trends in Sexual Activity Among Adolescent American Women." *Family Planning Perspectives* 31, 1999.

Siegleman, Lee. "Blacks, Whites and Anti-Semitism." *The Sociological Quarterly* 36, no 4 (Autumn 1995): 649–656.
Simon, Rita J., Angela J. Scanlan, and Pamela Nadel, "Rabbis and Ministers: Women of the Book and the Cloth." *Sociology of Religion* 54, no. 1 (Spring 1993).
Spanier, Graham J. "Sexualization and Premarital Sexual Behavior." *The Family Coordinator* 24, no. 1 (January 1975).
Sweeney, Megan M. "Two Decades of Family Change: The Shifting Economic Foundations of Marriage." *American Sociological Review* 67, 2002.
Taylor, Jean E., and Sylvia M. Wiegand. "AWM in the 1990s." *AWM Newsletter* 38, no. 7 (September 1991).
Tjaden, Patricia, and Nancy Thoennes. "Prevalence and Incidence of Violence against Women." *The Criminologist* 24, no. 3 (May-June 1999).
Tyack, David, and Elizabeth Hansot. "Silence and Policy Talk: Historical Puzzles About Gender and Education." *Educational Researcher* 17, 1988.
Van Every, Jo. "Deconstructing Gender: Women in Anti-Sexist Living Arrangements " *Womens' Studies International Forum* 18, 1995.
Walton, Surrey M., and Judith A. Cooksey. "Differences Between Male and Female Pharmacists in Part-Time Status and Employment Setting." *Journal of the American Pharmacists Association* 41, no. 5 (2001).
Ward, L. Monique. "Talking About Sex: Common Threads About Sexuality in Prime Time Television Programs Children and Adolescents View Most." *Journal of Youth and Adolescence* 24, no. 5 (October 1995).
Wechsler Segal, Mady. "Women's Military Roles Cross-Nationally; Past, Present and Future." *Gender and Society* 9, no. 6 (December 1995).
Weitzer, Ronald. "Deficiencies in the Sociology of Sex Work." *Sociology of Crime, Law and Deviance* 2, 2000.
Williams, Dell. "The Roots of the Garden.' *The Journal of Sex Research* 29, no.3 (August 1990).
Wyckoff, Adelaide. "Children's Ideals." *Pedagogical Seminary* 8, December 1901.
Yaeger, Holly. "Soldiering Ahead: Since Women Began Advancing Into Its Upper Ranks, the U.S. Military Has Become Both a More Humane Workplace and a More Lethal Fighting Force. What Role Has Female Leadership Played?" *The Wilson Quarterly*, Summer 2007.
Zucker, David. "Women Rabbis: A Novel Idea." *Judaism* 55, no.1–2 (Summer-Fall, 2006).

Newspaper Articles

Allen, Mike. "Anchorwoman Wins $8.3 Million Over Sex Bias." *The New York Times*, January 29, 1999.
Anderson, Michael. "No: A Life of Rosa Parks, Whose Quiet Demurral Sparked the Montgomery Bus Boycott." *The New York Times*, July 16, 2000.
Angier, Natalie. "No Parity Yet, But Science Academy Gains More Women." *The New York Times*, May 6, 2003.
_____, and Kenneth Chang. "Gray Matter and Sexes: A Gray Area Scientifically." *The New York Times*, January 24, 2005.
Asbell, Bernard. "Ella Grasso." *New York Times Magazine*, July 27, 1975.
Associated Press. "Woman Picked to Lead Upstate Lutheran Synod." *Albany Times Union*, June 5, 2002.
Ayeres, B. Drummond, Jr. "A Reputation for Excellence: Sandra Day O'Connor." *The New York Times*, July 8, 1981.

Banerjee, Neela. "A Woman Is Installed as Top Episcopal Bishop." *The New York Times*, November 5, 2006.
Bar-Lev, Abby. "Equal Rights Amendment Overdue." *The Minnesota Daily*, November 12, 2005.
Bauder, David. "Are Female Anchors Taken Seriously?" *Albany Times Union*, June 5, 2007.
Baxter, Sarah. "Hillary Runs for the White House as 'New Thatcher.'" *The Sunday Times*, January 21, 2007.
Belkin, Lisa. "Woman Named Police Chief of Houston." *The New York Times*, January 20, 1990.
Benson, Heidi. "Behind the Sweet Smile Is a Steely Eyed Writer: Maureen Dowd Is an 'Equal Opportunity' Skeptic." *San Francisco Chronicle*, September 9, 2004.
Berger, Marilyn. "Katharine Graham of Washington Post Dies at 84." *The New York Times*, July 18, 2001.
Berke, Richard L. "Clinton Names Ruth Ginsburg, Advocate for Women, to Court." *The New York Times*, June 15, 1993.
Biskupic, Joan. "O'Connor Era Ends at Court, Continues in Law." *USA Today*, January 30, 2006.
Broder, John M. "Clinton Readies New Approach on Internet Indecency." *The New York Times Cyber Times*, June 27, 1997.
Brown, Nona. "The Army Finds Woman Has a Place." *The New York Times Magazine*, December 26, 1948.
Browning, Dan. "Ramsey Woman Fearing Genital Mutilation Wins Deportation Reprieve." *Star Tribune*, January 24, 2007.
Brozan, Nadine. "Chronicle." *The New York Times*, February 9, 1993.
Bumiller, Elizabeth. "TELEVISION: So Famous, Such Clout, She Could Interview Herself." *The New York Times*, April 21, 1996.
Carter, Bill. "CNN Cancels Her Program, and Chung Quits Network." *The New York Times*, March 26, 2003.
"Caving In on Hate Crimes." *The New York Times*, December 10, 2007.
Coile, Zachary. "Bay Lawmakers Among Wealthiest: Feinstein and Pelosi Continue to Top the List of the Richest Members of Congress." *San Francisco Chronicle*, June 26, 2006.
Copeland, Larry. "Title IX: Public Gets a Chance to Sound Off," *USA Today*, August 27, 2002: C1.
Cowan, Mark. "Pupil Tells of Sex with Teacher." *Birmingham Evening News*, November 7, 2006.
Defoe, Jeanine. "Helping Asian Women Find Their Voices." *The New York Times*, September 21, 1997.
"Demanding vs. Doing." *The New York Times*, July 26, 2006.
Denniston, Lyle. "Supreme Court Revisits Arguments in Online Pornography Case." *The Boston Globe*, March 3, 2004.
Dillon, Sam. "For a Key Education Law, Re-Authorization Stalls." *The New York Times*, November 6, 2007.
_____. "Soccer Mom Education Chief Plays Hard Ball." *The New York Times*, April 28, 2005.
Downing, Neil. "So Long, Mighty Quinn." *The Providence Journal*, October 2, 2001.
Epstein, Richard. "Campaign 2006: Eighth Congressional District." *San Francisco Chronicle*, October 20, 2006.
Espo, David. "Pelosi Makes History as Speaker." *The Buffalo News*, January 5, 2007.
Evans, Sara M. "They Came Out Fighting." *The New York Times*, June 27, 1993.
Farhi, Paul. "Men Signing Off." *Washington Post*, July 23, 2006.

Freking, Kevin. "Committee Chairman Says U.S. Government Spending for Sexual Abstinence Program Will Stop." Associated Press, May 16, 2007.
Fritze, John. "Dixon Sworn in as Mayor: Vows to Fight Crime, Help Neighborhoods." *The Baltimore Sun*, December 5, 2007.
Furman, Bess. "Mrs. Mesta Named Luxembourg Envoy." *The New York Times*, June 22, 1949.
George, Thomas. "Patriots and 3 Players Fined in Olson Incident." *The New York Times*, November 28, 1990.
Gerard, Jeremy. "Anchors in New Roles Are Gaining Wealth. But Not Much Prestige." *The New York Times*, February 19, 1990.
_____. "Deciding Who Makes a Million in TV News." *The New York Times*, February 20, 1989.
Glanton, Dahleen. "Atlanta's First Female Mayor Tackles Homelessness, Other City Problems Head On." *Chicago Tribune*, November 4, 2005.
Gottlieb, David. "Career Climb Slow for Female Firefighters." *Women's News*, March 25, 2004.
Green, Sharon. "Judge Made the Right Call." *The Buffalo News*, December 20, 1998.
Greenhouse, Linda. "High Court Voids Curb on 'Indecent' Internet Material." *The New York Times Cyber Times*, June 10, 1997.
Gross, Grant. "Court Rules Against Child Online Protection Act." IDG News Service, June 29, 2004.
Gross, Shera. "Network Poll: Women Get More Air Time But Men Dominate the News." *Albany Times Union*, May 24, 1990.
Harpaz, Ben J. "Gay Parade Celebrate Pride: Stone Wall Riots Anniversary." *The Buffalo News*, June 28, 1999.
Hedges, Chris. "Dancing to the Robotic Engineering Beat." *The New York Times*, November 9, 2004.
Herel, Suzanne. "Chief Fong Picked as Permanent Head of Police." *San Francisco Chronicle*, April 13, 2004.
Horyn, Cathy. "Is This the Woman to Rescue Harper's Bazaar?" *The New York Times*, June 10, 2001.
Hunter, Marjorie. "U.S. Panel Urges Women to Sue for Equal Rights." *The New York Times*, October 12, 1963.
Janofsky, Michael. "Pittsburgh Is Showcase for Women in Policing." *The New York Times*, June 21, 1998.
Johnson, George. "Scholars Debate Roots of Yiddish, Migration of Jews." *The New York Times*, October 9, 1996.
Kevles, Daniel J. "The Secret History of Birth Control." *The New York Times*, July 22, 2001.
King, Sharon R. "Gannett's *USA Today* Names New Editor." *The New York Times*, March 10, 1999.
King, Wayne. "The 1990 Elections: What Went Wrong? Bradley Says He Sensed Voter Fury." *The New York Times*, November 8, 1990.
Koch, Kari. "Military Women Share Success Stories." *The Minnesota Daily*, April 11, 2005.
Kurtz, Howard. "Criminal Contempt Could Lengthen Reporter's Jail Time." *Washington Post*, July 16, 2005: A06.
Leinwand, Donna. "Lawsuits of '70s Shape Current Police Leadership." *USA Today*, April 25, 2004.
Lemberg, Jeff. "Women Reach Top at Police Ranks, Growth Still Slow." *Women's News*, March 23, 2004.
Lewis, Neil L. "Tailhook Affair Brings Censure of 3 Admirals." *The New York Times*, October 16, 1993.

Magee, Maureen. "City Schools Recruit Ex-Admiral." *Union Tribune*, August 8, 2001.
Maloney, Rick. "As Circulation Falls, *News* Seeks Solutions." *Business First*, November 19, 2005.
McClung, Kelly. "Women's Studies Grow Diversity." *The Capital Times*, February 8, 2007.
Neill, Brian. "Designing Women." *Bradenton Herald*, October 8, 2007.
Oldenburg, Ann. "Just Jane: Pauley Gets Personal." *USA Today*, August 18, 2004.
Paul, Noel C. "The Woman Chosen to Lead Boston Police." *The Christian Science Monitor*, March 16, 2004.
Pear, Robert. "Hillary Clinton Sees Hurdles in Forging Health Care Plan." *The New York Times*, February 12, 1992.
Rodgers, Ann. "Faiths Seeing Wider Spectrum of Female Clergy." *Pittsburgh Post-Gazette*, January 2, 2007.
Rutenberg, Jim, and William E. Carter. "Connie Chung Gets CNN Prime Time Spot." *The New York Times*, January 23, 2002.
Scher, Valerie. "Despite Gains, Women Conductors Are Not Exactly Crowding the Podium." *The San Diego Union Tribune*, October 16, 2005.
Schiff, Stacy. "Desperately Seeking Susan." *The New York Times*, October 13, 2006.
Schmitt, Eric. "Navy Official Widens Inquiry Into Sexual Assaults by Pilots." *The New York Times*, June 4, 1992.
_____. "Study Says Sexual Harassment Persists at Military Academies." *The New York Times*, April 5, 1995.
Schwartz, John. "Space Docking with Women at the Helm of Both Crafts." *The New York Times*, October 26, 2007.
Shallwani, Pervaiz. "Pastor Is First Woman to Lead Area Synod: Montco Reverend to Join 7 Other Females in U.S. to Hold Bishop Title." Allentown, Pa., *Morning Call*, May 9, 2006.
Spencer, Jane. "Getting Your Health Care at Wal-Mart." *The Wall Street Journal*, October 5, 2005.
Stallsmith, Pamela. "First Female Police Chief Announced." *Richmond Times*, December 30, 3006.
Steinberg, Jaques. "Panel Says Poor Standards Allowed Deception at USA Today." *The New York Times*, April 23, 2004.
Steinfels, Peter. "Woman Episcopal Bishop Approved." *Albany Times Union*, January 25, 1989.
Stone-Lombardi, Kate. "Defining Judaism, a Rabbi of Many Firsts." *The New York Times*, July 20, 2003.
Thomson, Virgil. "Notes on People." *The New York Times*, July 22, 1981.
Triggs, Marcia. "Female Soldiers Fight and Die for Their Country." *Army News Service*, March 26, 2004.
Tu, Janet I. "Female Bishop Challenges Catholic Church to Change." *Seattle Times*, November 11, 2006.
"Veteran Globe Reporter, Elizabeth Neuffer, Killed in Car Accident in Iraq." *The Boston Globe*, May 8, 2003.
Wald, Matthew A. "Bush Chooses Transportation Nominee." *The New York Times*, September 6, 2006.
Whitney, David. "Teen Pregnancy Rate Improvement at Risk." *Fresno Bee*, May 7, 2004.
Wood, Sean M. "Women in Aviation." *San Antonio Express News*, May 20, 2007.
Wyatt, Edward. "Katherine Anne Couric: Coming Back to Hard News." *The New York Times*, April 6, 2006.
Zakrzewski, Paul. "The Pioneering Rabbi Who Softly Made Her Way." *The New York Times*, May 20, 2006.

Government Documents

Bureau of Justice Statistics. *Law Enforcement Management and Administrative Statistics*, 2003.
Daly, D., and V.C. Wong. *Between the Lines: States' Implementation of the Federal Government's Section 510(b) Abstinence Education Program in Fiscal Year 1998*. New York: SIECUS, 1999.
18 USC Section 2261; 2261 A; 2262 and 922g8.
Federal Interagency Forum on Child and Family Statistics. "American Children in Brief: Key National Indicators of Well Being." Washington, D.C.: Government Printing Office, 2004.
_____. "America's Children: Key National Indicators of Well Being 2005." http://www.ChildStats.gov.
Madden, David. "Gavel Passing to Mark Changing of the Guard for Ninth Circuit Court of Appeals." News release, United States Courts for the Ninth Circuit, November 23, 2007.
National Center for Health Statistics. *Vital Statistics of the United States, 2000*, vol. 1. Hyattsville, MD: National Center for Health Statistics, 2002.
_____. *National Vital Statistics Reports* 55, no. 1 (September 29, 2006).
New Jersey Constitution of 1776.
Public Law 88–352, 88th Congress, H.R. 7152. July 2, 1974.
United Nations World Population Prospects 1950–2050. The 2006 Revision Database. Department of Economic and Social Affairs, Population Division: New York.
U.S. Bureau of Labor Statistics. "Relative Labor Market Outcomes and Worker Characteristics." http://www.bls.gov./emp/htm.
_____. "Unemployment and Earnings for Workers Age 25 and Over by Educational Attainment." http://www.bls.gov/emp/emtab7.htm.
_____. "Women in the Labor Force: A Databook." May 2005, www.bls.gov/cps/wlfdatabook2005htm.
_____. Current Population Survey. "Wives Who Earn More Than Their Husbands 1987–2003."
_____. *Highlights of Women's Earnings in 2005*. Table 12: Median Usual Weekly Earnings of Full Time Wage and Salary Workers in Constant 2005 Dollars by Sex and Age 1979–2005."
_____. Report 996. "Women in the Labor Force: A Databook." Washington, D.C.: Government Printing Office, 2006.
_____. "Female Rabbis." *Occupational Outlook Handbook*, March 30, 2000. http://www/umsl.edu./services.govdocs.ooh200020C1/247.htm.
_____. "Nontraditional Occupations for Women in 2006." March 2007.
_____. "Median Usual Weekly Earnings of Full Time Wage and Salary Workers by Detailed Occupation and Sex." Table 18. 2005.
_____. "Occupational Employment and Wages: Social Workers." Table 21–1029. May 2006.
_____. "Women in the Labor Force." 2006 edition.
_____. *Employment and Earnings*. Annual Averages, Table 11. 2007.
_____. Table 18, "Median Usual Weekly Earnings of Full Time Wage and Salary Workers by Detailed Occupation and Sex." 2004.
_____. "Total Median Weekly Income." Table 18. 2006.
U.S. Census Bureau. "Industry by Sex and Median Earnings in the Past 12 Months." S2404. Washington, D.C.: Government Printing Office, 2005.
_____. "Occupation by Sex: 2000," Summary File 3.
_____. *U.S. Census of Population*, vol. 1, 2007.

_____. *1940 Census of Population; Differential Fertility 1940 and 1910; Women by number of children ever born*. Tables 8, 9 and 10. Washington, D.C.: Government Printing Office, 1945.
_____. 2005 American Community Survey, 2006.
_____. "Fact for Features." February 22, 2006.
_____. Current Population Survey, November 2005, Table 29.
U.S. Commission on Education Report, 1894–1895, vol. 1.
U.S. Department of Commerce. *Historical Statistics of the United States, from Colonial Times to the Present*, vol. 15. Washington, D.C.: Government Printing Office 1975.
U.S. Department of Defense, *Selected Manpower Statistics, Fiscal Year 1980*. Washington, D.C.: Directorate for Information, Department of Defense, 1981.
U.S. Department of Education. "Average Scale Scores and Achievement-Level Results in Mathematics by Gender." *The Nation's Report Card*, 2005.
_____. "Enrollment Status of S&E Graduate Students by Field and Sex, 2004," Washington, D.C.: Women in Science and Engineering.
_____. National Center for Education Statistics. "Fall Staff 1999," Table 229.
U.S. Department of Health and Human Services, Centers for Disease Control and Prevention, National Center for Health Statistics. *Health, United States, 2006*. Washington, D.C., United States Government Printing Office, 2006
U.S. Department of Justice. Bureau of Justice Assistance Bulletin. "Recruiting & Retaining Women: A Self-Assessment Guide for Law Enforcement." Washington, D.C.: Government Printing Office, 2001.
_____. "Increase Seen in Number of Women in Nation's Law Enforcement Agencies," April 7, 1996.
_____. Federal Bureau of Investigation, *Uniform Crime Reports*, Table 33. Washington, D.C.: Government Printing Office, 2006.
U.S. Department of Labor, Women's Bureau, "Quick Stats, 2006." Washington, D.C.: Government Printing Office.
U.S. General Accounting Office. "Women's Earnings." October 2003.
U.S. Government Printing Office, May 22, 2007.
U.S. National Center for Health Statistics, *Vital Statistics of the United States, Annual* 1960–2006.
United States vs. Price et al., 1965. U.S. Reporter, vol. 383.
Wallman, Katherine K. "America's Children: Key National Indicators of Well-Being, 2007." Washington, D.C.: Office of Management and Budget.

Web sites

Barbara McClintock Papers. National Library of Medicine. http://profiles.nlm.nih.gov/LL/.
"Linda B. Buck." *Encyclopedia Britannica Online*. 2007.
Devore, Bonnie, "Past and Present, 1915–Today." International Association of Women Police. http://www.iawp.org.
Ducharme, Diane J. *Elizabeth Shepley Sergeant Papers*. Yale Collection of American Literature, Beinecke Rare Book and Manuscript Library. (New Haven, Connecticut, Yale University, 1986). http://webtext.library.yale.edu/xml2html/beinecke.SERGEANT.con.html.
Gettings, John, David Johnson, Borgna Brunner, and Chris Frantz. "Wonder Women." Infoplease. *http://www.infoplease.com/spot/womenceo1.html*.
Hayes, Steven J. "Erma Bombeck." Basic Famous People. http://www.basicfamouspeople.com/index.php?aid=38.

John Paul II, "Ordinatio Sacerdotalis," Women for Faith and Family, http://www.wff.org/OrdSac.html.

Kirchweger, Gina. "Salk Scientist Ursula Bellug Elected to National Academy of Sciences." Salk Institute for Biological Studies, May 1, 2007. http://www.salk.edu/news/news_press_details_20070502a.php.

National Science Foundation. "Enrollment status of S&E graduate students by field and sex 2004," *Women, Minorities, and Persons with Disabilities in Science and Engineering*, 2004. http://www.nsf.gov/statistics/wmpd/archgradenroll.htm.

O'Leary, Maureen. "72 New Members Chosen by Academy." The National Academies News, May 1, 2007. http://www8.nationalacademies.org/onpinews/newsitem.aspx?RecordID=05012007.

Rach, Amber. "Dr. Zoe Locklear Named Dean of the School of Education." University of North Carolina Newswire, November 4, 2005. www.uncp.edu/news/2005/zoe_locklear_2.htm.

Schleicher, Annie. "More Women Soldiers Dying in Iraq." NewsHour Extra, August 7, 2005. http://www.pbs.org/newshour/extra/features/july-dec06/militarywomen_12-18.html.

Scovill, Nelia Beth. "The Liberation of Women in Religious Sources." The Religious Consultation on Population, Reproductive Health and Ethics. http://www.religiousconsultation.org/liberation.htm.

Welle, Noreen. "Minorities Gain on Local Television News Staffs." Radio/Television News Directors Association, July 7, 2006. http://www.aaja.org/news/releases/2006_07_07_02/.

Women in History. Susan B. Anthony biography. http://www.lkwdpl.org/wihohio/anth-sus.htm. Accessed March 21, 2006.

"Women Officeholders: Fact Sheets and Summaries." http://www.cawp.rutgers.edu/Facts.html.

Wray, Lindsey. "Women Journalists Connect at the IWMF Networking Breakfast in Boston." International Women's Media Foundation. Accessed April 23, 2007. http://www.iwmf.org/features/10003.

Index

abortion 130, 165, 181
Abraham, Spencer 155
Abriola, Linda 114
Academy of Television Arts and Sciences 144
Acquired Immune Deficiency Syndrome 166
Adams, Abigail Smith 136
Adler, Freda 45
Adolescent Family Life Act 170
Advance for Nurse Practioners 14
Air Force Academy 71
Air Force Reserve Officer Training Program 123
Alexander II 52
Altschul, Randi 116
American Anti-slavery Society 138
American Junior Miss Pageant 147
American Pharmaceutical Association 112
Anglican Church 92
annual salaries 97
Anthony, Susan B. 130
anti-discrimination 30
Apostles 99
Army nurse corps 68
Associated Press 144
Association of Electronic Journalists 147
Association of Women in Mathematics 112
average family income 185

Baez, Joan 51
Bailey, Glenda 162
Baker, Ella Jo 195
Ball, Lucille 171
Bat-Or, Rachel 88
Bellugi, Ursula 109
Benedict, Ruth 49
Benedict XVI 98
Bernstein, Bonny 149
Bible study 87
birth control 171, 184
Birth Control Federation of America 191
birth rate 59
Blodgett, Kathleen B. 116

Boaz, Franz 49
Bombeck, Erma 156
Booth, William 96
Border Patrol 84
Boston College 82
Boston Globe 155
Boxer, Barbara 57
Bray, Linda A. 70
Brown, Helen Gurley 162
Brown v. Board of Education 194
Bryn Mawr College 157
Buchdahl, Angela Warnick 62
Buffalo Symphony Orchestra 12
Bullough, Vern 37
Bureau of Labor Management 83
Bureau of Labor Statistics 160
Burkat, Cynthia 97
Bush, George W. 13
business college 187

Cable Act 133
Cabrillo, Juan 50
California 51
Carbonell, Josephina 51
Cather, Willa 157
Catholic school system 101
Central Conference of American Rabbis 88
Chapelle, Dickey 157
Chasan, Augusta 83
chat rooms 175
Cherokee Nation 64
Chicago Police Department 80
Child Online Protection Act of 1998 172
Christian Science 93
Chronicle of Higher Education 9
Chung, Connie 145
citizens band radio 176
Civil Rights Act of 1964 39
Civil Rights Commission 180
civil rights movement 197
clerical work 29
Clinton, Hillary R. 127

Cloud, Rosemary 84
Cochrane, Josephine G. 116
Code of Jewish Law 54
co-habitation 200
college dropout rate 6
college enrollment 4
College of William and Mary 130
Collings, Eileen 122
Communications Decency Act 174
compulsory free public education 193
computer age 174
computer sex 175
Comstock Act 190
Conference Board for Mathematical Sciences 113
Congregation for the Doctrines of the Faith 98
Cornell University 115
Coughlin, Paula A. 73
Coulter, Ann 155
Couric, Katie 144
Cox, Catherine 65
Cronkite, Walter 144
culture lag 105
cyberspace 175

Dark Ages 21
Dartmouth College 155
Daughters of Temperance 140
De Angeles, Catherine 60
Declaration of Sentiments 139
De Leon, Ponce 50
demographers 198
desegregated schools 194
Diner, Hasia 58
District of Columbia 40
divorce 20, 22, 43, 199, 201
Dixon, Sheila 134
Donaldson, Sam 147
Donovan, Helen 158
Donovan, Marion O. 117
The Double Helix 11
Dowd, Maureen 152
Due Process Clause 197
Dyer, Mary 136

Earhart, Amelia 13
earnings by age 17
Eastern European Jews 53, 186
Edwards Air Force base 123
electrical appliances 188
epidemics 167
Episcopal church 96
Equal Opportunity Commission 180
Equal Rights Amendment 141
Equity in Athletics Disclosure Act of 1994 39
Erbe, Bonnie 150
Evangelical Lutheran church 96
Eve's Garden 178

Family Research Council 37
fathers 6
Federal Gun Control Act of 1996 40
Feinstein, Dianne 57
The Feminine Mystique 36
feminization of office work 186
Ferguson, Miriam Amanda 42
Ferraro, Geraldine Anne 60
Ferron, Carrie 160
fertility rate 189
financial gender gap 17
firefighters 83
Five Pillars of Islam 103
Food and Drug Administration 38
Ford Motor Co. 33
Fox, Sally 117
Fox News channel 148
Fraker, Pamela 109
Franklin, Rosalind 10
Franklin, Shirley 134
Frazier, Margo 82
Frazier, Patricia A. 181
Freson, Patricia 99
Friedan, Betty 36, 137
friends with benefits 169
Froman, Veronica 76

Galton, Francis 65
Gelhorn, Martha 157
gender discrimination 77
gender gap 18
gender identity 169
General Staff College 76
Gephart, Richard 129
Ginsburg, Ruth Bader 12, 130
Glenn, John 128
Goodman, Ellen 152
Graham, Betty 118
Graham, Katherine Meyer 158
Graham, Susan L. 10
Grasso, Ella Tambussi 60
Grimke, Sarah Moore 138
Guttman, Amy 10

Hall, G. Stanley 192
Halstead, Rebecca 75
Hamer, Fannie Lour 196
Handler, Ruth 118
Harriman, Pamela 134
Harrington, Penny 81
Hartford Institute of Religious Research 97
Hebrew Union College 87
Herodotus 67
Heschel, Abraham J. 197
high school education 192
Hobbs, Helen 108
Hollywood Walk of Fame 146
homosexuality 165
Hopper, Grace Murray 49
House of Jacob 55

Hubble space telescope 122
Huerta, Dolores 50
Hunter's Hunks 176
Hutchinson, Anne 135
Hymowitz, Kay S. 61

immigration 22
inequitable social positions 173
informal sex education 169
International Women's Media Foundation 158, 163

Jerge, Marie C. 96
Jewish Theological Seminary 87
John Paul II 98
Joining the Sisterhood 56
Jonas, Regina 86
Jones, Amanda T. 118
Journal of Neurophysiology 109
Judaism 86
Jurgensen, Karen 159
juvenile death penalty 130

Kearney, Melissa S. 18
Kiesler, Hedwig Eva Marie 119
Kinsey, Alfred 37
Korean War 69
Kwolek, Stephanie 119

labor market 27, 29
labor saving devices 189
Ladies' Garment Workers Union 186
Ladies' Home Journal 34
Lamarr, Hedy 119
law enforcement 76
Laws of Moses and Israel 90
Leonard, Naomi 114
Lexis-Nexis 45
liberation of women 201
life expectancy 21
Lin, Maya 62
Lingle, Linda 42
Locklear, Zoe 63
Logan, Lara 156
Lonecki, Elizabeth 67
Lunden, Joan 151

MacArthur Foundation 110
Macro, Lucia 160
Magazine Publishers Hall of Fame Award 163
managerial jobs 30
Manhattan Institute for Policy Research 154
Mankiller, Wilma 64
Marder, Eve 109
marriage 22
Martonosi, Margaret 114
masculinity 19
mass production 185
Massachusetts Bay Colony 48, 136
Masters, Sybilla 120

maternity leave plan 96
mathematics 112
Matthew Shepard Act 168
McAuliffe, Christa Corrigan 122
McCabe, Allison 160
McClaney, Eula 61
McGrath, Kathleen 70
Mead, Margaret 49
Meade, Robin 148
Mendelssohn, Felix 65
Mesta, Perle 133
Michigan State University 115
Miller, Judith 153
Moorman, Charlotte 177
Mott, Lucretia 138
Muslim organization 102

National Academy of Sciences 108
National Aeronatic and Space Administration 122
National Assessment of Educational Process 106
National Association for the Advancement of Colored People 195
National Association of Police Women 81
National Association of Social Workers 15
National Center for Health Statistics 182
National Council of Catholic Women 35
National Guard 75
National Institute of Health 167
National Opinion Research Council 31
National Organization for Women 35, 36
National Public Radio 154
National Right to Life Committee 182
National Science Foundation 105
National Women's Christian Temperance Union 140
National Women's Hall of Fame 161
native Americans 63
The Natural Superiority of Women 36
Naval Academy 71
Navy nurse corps 68
Network Correspondence Visibility Study 148
Neuffner, Elizabeth 156
New Amsterdam 52
New Jersey 125
New York 53
New York Bureau of Social Hygiene 164
New York City 59
Niagara Falls, N.Y. 153
nuns 101
nursing 8, 14

Oberlin College 93
Ochoa, Ellen 120
O'Connor, Sandra D. 129
Office of Economic Opportunity 126
Olsen, Lisa 154
Olson, Theodore 174
Ono, Yoko 177

ordination of women 95
Otranto, Georgia 100
Owen, Ruth Bryan 133
Owens, Marie 80

Packard, Vance 46
parenthood 199
Parks, Rosa 194
patriarchy 137
Paul, Alice 142
Pauley, Jane 145, 151
Peace Corps 132
Pearl Harbor 32
Peckinpaugh, Janet 145
Pelosi, Nanci 23, 128
Perez, Emily J. 67
Perkins, Frances 131
Personal Responsibility and Work Opportunity Act 200
Petrarcha, Francesco 184
pharmacies 111
physical labor 26
physicians 17
Pincus, Gregory 181
Pittsburgh 82
population density 189
Population of the United States 3
pornography 172
predestination 136
pregnancy 78, 191
presidential election 4
Presidential Succession Act 128
Priesand, Sally 86
Program for International Student Assessment 106
prostitution 79
protestant ethic 48
Pulitzer Prize 152
Puritan Church 135
Purple Heart 70

Queen Victoria 25
Quimby, Phinneas 93
Quinn, Jane Bryant 153

race relations 196
Rankin, Janet 141
rape shield laws 40
Reed, Tatjana 67
Remington Typewriter Co. 187
Republican National Committee 126
Revolutionary war 92
rheumatoid arthritis 109
Rhode Island 135
Rice, Condoleezza 61
Ride, Sally 50
Rock, John 181
Roe v. Wade 181
Roosevelt, Franklin D. 131
Rosenbaum, Eve 55

Roth, Kathleen 111
Russo, Patricia 11
Rustin, Bayard 195

sacred orders 100
Salem, Adrianna A. 67
Salvation Army 93
Sanbumatsu, Kira 142
Sanger, Margaret 190
Saudi Arabia 69
Sawyer, Diane 146
Schmidt, Julius 190
Scholastic Aptitude Test 107
Schori, Katherine Jeffers 95
Schreiber, Lynn 56
Sex and the City 38
sex crimes 173
sex education 25
sexual abuse 25, 165
sexual harassment 19, 180
sexual revolution 179
Sexuality Information and Education Council 170
Shaking Quakers 92
Sherman, Patty 120
Siebert, Muriel 11
Simmons, Ruth 10
Sisters of Mercy 100
Smith, Charlotte Green Honigman 54
social workers 15
Society of Women Engineers 115
sociology 23
Soeteber, Ellen 159
Southern Christian Leadership Conference 196
Spelling, Margaret 132
Stanton, Elizabeth Cady 138
Stewart, Martha 45
Sullivan, Margaret 159
Supreme Court of the United States 129
swinging parties 178
synagogues 89

Tailhook Association 73
Tailhook scandal 72
Tallchief, Maria 64
teaching methods 106
teen pregnancy 171
temperance convention 93
Texas Association of School Boards 133
Texas State College for Women 163
Thomas, Valeri 121
Title VII of the Civil Rights Act 179
Torah 56
Towle, Katherine A. 76
Truman, Harry 131
Tupperware parties 179

Uniform Crime Reports 44
Unitarian Church 94

United Methodist Church 94
United Nations Environmental Award 117
U.S. Armed Forces 33
U.S. Bureau of Labor Statistics 12
U.S. Census Bureau 7
U.S. Congress 41
U.S. Constitution 35, 139, 142, 197
U.S. Department of Labor 9
United States Senate 41
U.S. Statistical Abstracts 169
U.S. Supreme Court 72
Universal Declaration of Human Rights 168
University of Arizona 44
University of Phoenix 132
University of Wisconsin 44

Vallino, Lisa 121
van Ogtrop, Kristin 162
Vatican II 100
Vietnam War 69, 194
Virgin Mary 99
Virginia Military Institute 71
Voting Rights Act of 1965 139

Walters, Barbara 146
war production plants 33
Ward, Monique 173
washing machine 187
Weber, Max 48
Wells, Alice 60

Wessel, Rita 84
West Point Academy 71
Whitman, Christine Todd 126
Winfrey, Oprah 161
Winslow, Linda 150
Wittenmyer, Annie 140
women: book editors 160; cadets 74; circumcision 103; clergy 95; competence 192; criminality 45; emancipation 43; employment 43; high school graduates 18; medical students 28; in the military 69, 74; in the newsroom 149; occupation 16 officers 71; police officers 77; in print journalism 151; rabbis 87, 91; in space exploration 121; working 3, 7
Women's Bureau 81
Women's Haggada 88
Women's Ordination Conference 102
women's rights convention 138
Women's Trade Union League 141
Woodruff, Judy 149
Woodstock Nation 177
World War I 27, 32
World War II 28
Wright, Frances 137

Yalow, Rosalyn 57
Young Feminist Network 102

Zeff, Lisa 150

www.ingramcontent.com/pod-product-compliance
Ingram Content Group UK Ltd.
Pitfield, Milton Keynes, MK11 3LW, UK
UKHW041941140426
5217IPUK00014B/609